STAFF TRAINING AND ASSESSMENT

Staff Training and Assessment

David Osborne

CASSELL

To Carol, Laurie and Alex

Cassell
Wellington House, 125 Strand, London WC2R 0BB
127 West 24th Street, New York, NY 10011

© David Osborne 1996

First published 1996

British Library Cataloguing-in-Publication Data
A catalogue record for this book is available from the British Library.

ISBN 0-304-33119-8 (hardback)
       0-304-33124-4 (paperback)

Designed and typeset by Kenneth Burnley at Irby, Wirral, Cheshire.
Printed and bound in Great Britain by Redwood Books, Trowbridge, Wiltshire.

Contents

Introduction

This book should be useful to anyone who is involved with training and developing people within an organizational context. The book should appeal to the line manager, the in-house trainer and the external provider. A 'how to' approach is adopted making use of a number of useful techniques, and is supported by a number of examples. The book is broadly structured in terms of:

Training issues
Chapter 1: Setting the scene
Chapter 2: Performance problems and training
Chapter 3: The training cycle and trainer role
Chapter 4: Training using the open system approach
Chapter 5: Design and evaluation of training

Learning strategies
Chapter 6: Effective learning strategies

Implementation
Chapter 7: Matching training interventions to organizational culture, management style and motivation

Techniques
Chapter 8: Investigative, problem-solving or training needs location methods
Chapter 9: Training Needs Analysis techniques
Chapter 10: Training methods and learning situations

In the Appendices, the author provides up-to-date reports on competence, changes in organizational values and trends, government initiatives and achievement of national targets, and provides a list of useful addresses and abbreviations.

As a response to the effects of the recession, organizations big and small have reacted differently. While some have put a hold on nearly all training activity, others have refocused their training effort on key areas of the business. One thing that has dramatically changed in most commercial and non-commercial organizations has been people's thinking. As witnessed by the changes in local and central government services, the question that is asked time and time again is, 'How do we get more from less?' Many organizations, when confronted with this proposition, have taken drastic action. Tall organizational pyramidic structures have been flattened by removing, in some cases, whole layers of middle managers. Coincidentally, more reliable computer technology has enabled greater efficiencies to be achieved. Wider use of teamwork and self-regulated work groups, and extensive delegating of responsibilities have also contributed to shaping leaner organizations. In addition, organizations have implemented proven cost-saving techniques and sought a variety of efficiencies via such systems as Total Quality Management, British Standard programmes and the Investors in People initiative.

As the nation hopefully enters an economic recovery, a number of questions will need to be asked as businesses start thinking of expansion. Does it follow that if organizations have become leaner, they have become fitter? Will we discover hidden skill shortages? Are we already seeing the signs of a lack of traditional apprentice training, for example? How will the new Standard Youth Credit Package and the Modern Apprenticeship Scheme contribute to the training of future technicians and craftsmen? Will we discover that through the drive to stay competitive, we have stored up a variety of training needs at all levels? How well are we coping with the demand for higher and broader skill needs? These are just some of the questions.

1
Setting the scene

INTRODUCTION

In this chapter we shall: provide descriptions of terms used in training; look briefly at what training can and cannot do; identify some changes that have occurred in training and management practices; identify British government initiatives over the last twenty years; see how organizations have responded to a changed economic climate and government initiatives; and identify the future role of the trainer.

Of particular importance in the coming years will be how the organizational trainer can better assist people to develop and organizations to prosper. Perhaps, as we shall see, the 'building blocks' are nearly in place; and perhaps, when we look back at the 1990s, we shall recognize the important change in ideas, practices and new ways of working together, that has taken place.

WHAT TO CALL IT – TRAINING, EDUCATION, LEARNING, EMPOWERING OR COMPETENCE?

If we learn within an organization we call it training and if we learn at school, college or university we call it education. No matter what we call it, however, we are learning. What, when and how we learn has long been the subject of training and education. To distinguish between training, education and learning let us examine some training terms as defined in the *Glossary of Training Terms* (1981).

Training

A 'planned process' to modify attitude, knowledge or skill behaviour through learning experience to achieve effective performance in an activity or range of activities.

The emphasis here is on the 'planned process' and 'effective performance'.

Education

Activities which aim at developing the knowledge, skills, moral values and understanding required in all aspects of life rather than knowledge and skill relating to only a limited field of activity.

Emphasis here is on 'moral values and understanding . . . of life'. Some trainers, however, would agree that moral values, ethics and understanding are also part of training.

Learning

> Learning is often regarded as a more or less permanent change in behaviour as a result of experience.

Learning is a general term that can embrace all experiences. Whereas training and education tend to focus on planned events, outside these formal boundaries we can learn accidentally, intuitively and we can learn through our own self-development. The term 'learning' is useful because it is free of 'edges': in other words, it reminds the facilitator that learners bring with them all their experiences and expectations to any learning situation. It also reminds the facilitator not to ignore what has shaped and what is shaping the learner's value system, emotions, behaviour and process of learning.

Empowering

> This is a strategic technique that gives power to another, and also authorizes another to perform effectively in the real world.

The implications of empowering others are far wider than any of the other activities. Although the term is used by some as a substitute for learning, training and education, the core meaning is far bigger. It means assisting learners to:

- acquire 'knowledge';
- gain 'understanding';
- 'apply' their understanding; and
- 'transfer' their knowledge and skill to unique situations.

It also means providing the resources to manage the whole process.

One assumption that underpins empowering in its full form, is that it enables managers to better exploit opportunities and strengths, because the individuals concerned are accountable. To empower someone to learn could also mean providing them with resources to decide their learning needs, select their learning 'providers' or 'suppliers', and transfer their knowledge and skills to new work situations. To empower is to provide the means to achieve the ends, and the resources to evaluate the cost-effectiveness of the decision. The facilitator therefore cannot take lightly that the learner is being held fully accountable.

Competence

For some, competence means Knowledge + Skills. For the Management Charter Initiative (MCI), it means Knowledge + Skills + Experience + Personal Qualities. For the National Vocational Qualifications (NVQ) scheme it takes the form of five levels of competence, as listed in Appendix 1. The word 'competence' can be problematic because the term itself (like leadership) is a process in the fullest sense, rather than an act. Added to this, competence when linked to effectiveness is a function of who defines it (Pye 1988). The competence formula has been examined in Appendix 2 and the following description is offered.

$$\text{Competence} = (K) + (S) + (E) + (PQ) = \text{Knowledge (K)} + \text{Skills (S)}$$
(which everyone agrees are the basic building blocks of performance)
$$+ \text{ Experience (E)}$$
(which enables repeated application of the Knowledge + Skills to be achieved)
$$+ \text{ Personal Qualities (PQ)}$$
(which provides the function for integrating personality and the factors above).

TRAINING NEEDS ANALYSIS

If business needs are identified, training can be planned and carried out to satisfy those needs. In order to identify needs and prepare a Training Plan, a Training Needs Analysis (TNA) must be undertaken. In Chapters 3 and 9, the TNA is examined more fully. The Training Needs Analysis is defined as:

An examination of the organization's present and expected operations and the manpower necessary to carry them out, in order to identify the numbers and categories of staff needing to be trained or retrained . . . to reach the required standard of performance in his/her current or future job.

We observe here how a global TNA approach need not just be a static audit, but will take account of planned and anticipated changes.

TRAINING NEEDS

From experience it could be said that:

A training need exists when the gap between actual and required performance is most economically met by a training intervention.

As all organizations work within economic constraints, the above definition seems reasonable. While some organizations may be prepared to spend more on training than others for a similar activity, the monetary criteria may act as a regulator regardless of the situation. If it is more effective to recruit people with the necessary skills rather than train them, this may be justified on economic grounds. If, however, team performance is likely to suffer as a result of 'buying-in', the decision to train may be taken.

WHAT TRAINING CAN DO

When people are trained well, there is little that cannot be done. If, however, training is imposed it may be resisted, and training effort will be wasted. When the learning climate is supportive, training can achieve the following:

- help secure repeat business;
- increase profits;
- increase productivity;
- enhance group work at all levels;
- create greater employee versatility;
- improve communications;
- improve morale;
- improve co-operation;
- increase employee job satisfaction;
- lower costs;
- lower personal injury rate.

WHAT TRAINING CANNOT DO

If the organizational culture is not supportive or if there are serious structural defects, training, however well meaning, will not remedy incompetent management decision-making. In short, training cannot:

- solve problems of faulty organization;
- remedy unsound initial selection;
- materially increase learning potential;

- guarantee increased performance;
- overcome the fact that forgetting is easier and quicker than learning;
- teach anyone anything, if a person doesn't wish to learn.

WHAT TRAINING SHOULD DO

Although writing about time management training, Claus Møller's (1987) Ten-Point Training Philosophy is very apt concerning the function of training. The Philosophy states that training:

1 should bring about change;
2 is a process;
3 is an integral part of the company's strategy;
4 requires management commitment;
5 must be inspirational;
6 is for everyone in the company;
7 should be easily understood;
8 should include tools and written material;
9 should be geared to the target group;
10 should be holistic.

CHANGE AND WHAT IS VALUED TODAY

During the late 1980s and the 1990s the effects of the worldwide recession forced industry to answer a question that it was not in the habit of asking: 'How do you get more from less?' Up until this point, the question was usually about 'How do you get more from more?' In her book, Kanter (1989) explains how American industry faced the same dilemma. As managers tried to become more efficient, they also found that manipulation of data using computers could be used in nearly every field of the business. It meant, in short, that tall pyramidal structures could actually be flattened, aided by the effective data-handling technology. As a result, whole levels of middle managers were no longer needed to manipulate information between top and bottom of the organization. To maintain market share and profits, competition intensified and restructuring became the norm for many organizations.

The comparison between yesterday's and tomorrow's values can be seen in Appendix 3. The comparisons are compiled from such observers of organizational life as Handy (1989), Naisbitt (1984), Drucker (1968, 1977, 1989), Harrison (1990), Bartlett (1989) and Kanter (1990). For the trainer, the comparisons are useful in that they all strike a particular attitude towards participation, choice, flexibility and self-help, thus moving away from autocracy, limited choice, rigidity and prescriptive solutions.

To examine the impact of change on people's behaviour, attitudes and work practices, trainers might like to use Exercises 1 and 2 at the end of this chapter.

BRITISH GOVERNMENT INITIATIVES

With the introduction of the Industrial Training Act in 1964, the British government took the view that economic prosperity results from an appropriately trained and educated workforce. Since 1964, the government has set up a wide range of schemes, subsidies and programmes to provide training, raise the employability of certain disadvantaged groups and help alleviate unemployment. As an example of the scale of what employers and educationalists have been dealing with since 1964, Appendix 4 provides an historical summary of government initiatives and actions. More than of historical interest, the list of interventions must be seen as an investment for the future. In one sense, these interventions have provided us with the results of a huge experiment in matching a variety of training, employment and vocational education needs. In effect the government's policy-makers have been on one of the longest learning curves in modern administrative history. Have they got it right now? The author believes that, at last, it does begin to feel right, and the idea of 'partnership' also feels right. The fact that such 'building blocks' as National Vocational Qualifications are more or less in place, seems right. Although Erridge (1993) says '. . . there is no conclusive evidence for the link between a country's economic performance and its commitment, or lack of it, to general and vocational education and training', my view is 'If people are able to focus and integrate their efforts around a co-operative approach, this should give us the right impetus to better satisfy the nation's education, training and development needs.'

In the Employment Department paper (1993) entitled 'Prosperity Through Skills', the goal and priorities for the nation's future are stated. The goal is:

> to increase individual and national prosperity by stimulating enterprise and developing excellence in skills.

The four priorities (summarized here) include:

1 Investing effectively in the skills needed for business creation and growth, and for individual success.
2 Equipping able-bodied and disadvantaged people for employment.
3 Maximizing young people's potential, and in particular to progress to NVQ/SVQ level 3 and beyond.
4 Making the market for vocational education and training respond better to the changing needs of employers and individuals quickly and cost-effectively.

To achieve this goal and the supporting priorities, a 'partnership' is in place to realize these requirements.

The UK Partnership

The five levels of the UK Partnership which support the government's goal are:

1 At the national level, the government itself.
2 At the sector level, the Industry Training Organizations.
3 At the local level,
   – the TECs/LECs;
   – the providers (including further education colleges);
   – the careers service.
4 At the organizational level.
5 At the individual level.

1 *At the national level*, the Employment Department and other government departments are:

• developing and promoting a strategy for Great Britain;
• maintaining an effective network of 82 TECs/LECs and over 120 ITOs;
• promoting best practices to improve performance and achieve value for money;
• ensuring national bodies and standards are in place;

- intervening actively to frame policies, where necessary, in areas of market failure;
- negotiating EU training policies and funding.

2 *At the sector level*, the Industry Training Organizations will support their sectors by:
- acting as a focal point for training matters in their sectors;
- monitoring future skill requirements;
- working with TECs/LECs to meet national targets;
- developing occupational standards and promoting them, NVQs and Investors in People;
- highlighting best practices;
- representing the interests of employers.

3 *At the local level*, the TECs/LECs will:
- establish local labour market needs and develop plans;
- reaffirm the culture of enterprise and participation, particularly among young people;
- create and sustain effective partnerships at the local, sectoral and regional levels;
- make the local market for training and education work better.

The providers (including further education colleges) will supply flexible vocational education and training of a high quality that respond cost-effectively to the changing needs of employers and individuals.

The Careers Service will assist young people to reach informed decisions about their future careers, education, training and employment routes. Appendix 5 identifies the post-16 education opportunities and Appendix 6 describes Youth Credits.

4 *At the organizational level*, employers will ensure their individual businesses are dynamic, developing and increasingly competitive by:
- having a clear vision;
- investing cost-effectively in the skills their business needs;
- training and motivating all staff;
- developing appropriate management and staff development approaches;
- influencing the provision of vocational education and training.

5 *At the individual level*, individuals will be encouraged to take responsibility for their own training and development throughout their working life.

By anyone's assessment this partnership represents a very powerful structure of co-operation. Let us hope, as good partners do, that we all continue to share the common goal that is before us. Let us hope, even if there is an upturn in the economy, the partners will not lose interest in training and developing their key resource, people. And if the economy worsens, let us hope we will not start all over again re-inventing another wheel.

HOW ORGANIZATIONS HAVE ADAPTED

The effect of recessions over the past twenty years on people at all levels in organizations has been both exhausting and challenging. In particular, change has become a way of life, and finding ways to get more from less has become normal. Economic forces have challenged both public and private sector organizations to seriously address their use of resources, and this has led everyone in turn to look hard at how business and public service priorities are justified.

The fact that the core ideas embedded in the government's initiatives have largely been 'accepted' by organizations in the 1990s is fairly incredible. When we consider that commerce has tended to play shy in these areas, and when we consider the heartbreaking adjustments that have occurred within industry, it is all short of a minor industrial revolution. Why, however, did it take economic pressure to force us to look seriously at our organizational structures, management practices, assumptions and values? This is a question that surely deserves answering much more frequently than has been the case. In brief, organizational change over the past twenty years has included:

- Flattening tall pyramidal organizational structures to reduce the salary bill of middle management functions, and increase overall efficiencies through improved work practices.
- Restructuring operations to reduce costs, improve decision-making and improve economies of scale.
- Introducing automation sooner rather than later to reduce the operational wage bill.
- Introducing new cost-saving techniques such as:
  – just-in-time methods to reduce stock-holding levels;
  – total quality assurance practices (right first time);
  – bar coding to obtain highly accurate stock control levels.
- Implementing proven cost-saving techniques such as:
  – controlling finished stock, work-in-progress levels;
  – reducing product ranges;
  – improving manufacturing margins;
  – reducing wastage;
  – changing purchasing practices;
  – introducing realistic costing systems;
  – refocusing marketing policy and effort;
  – changing employment and salary practices in favour of a smaller employed group supported by part-time and self-employed groups;
  – investing surplus funds more wisely.
- Delegating more deeply, and finding that people can cope with it.
- A realization that a partnership is required between government and industry sectors to:
  – better shape vocational work experience and qualification requirements;
  – better equip people with more sophisticated knowledge and skills to replace the traditional (Third-World level) manual craft skills;
  – better handle demographic workforce changes as they occur, i.e. training young people and supporting women returners;
  – better handle the much-needed hike in management competences;
  – better develop our global market networking and exporting skills;
  – better handle the introduction of new laws which focus on employee rights (equal opportunities) and the environment (health and safety);
  – better support for learners following open learning, self-development programmes, and computer-based learning materials.

THE FUTURE ROLE OF THE TRAINER

As a result of all this change which has penetrated nearly every part of life, the role of the trainer has become both wider and more focused. One move has been to balance the best of centralized training with the best of local training. Some types of skills training have been passed back to line managers and supervisors, for example.

With computer technology assisting more and more at every level in organizations, some trainers have made more use of computer-based learning. Likewise, with open and distance learning, trainers have found themselves increasingly supporting this activity as well. With National Targets for education and training, trainers find themselves helping to achieve national standards, as shown in Appendix 9. As if to emphasise the trainers' specialist information and networking role, examples of training, education and employment bodies are listed along with their many abbreviations in Appendix 10.

With fewer middle managers to manage similar numbers of operational staff, trainers have found themselves involved in assisting groups to find more effective ways to communicate, delegate, co-ordinate and manage boundaries. At an operational level, the changing role of the trainer has resulted in trainers:

- adopting a more business-like and strategic view;
- adopting an internal adviser and consultant role to support line management;
- assisting managers to find ways to communicate, co-ordinate and delegate more effectively;
- assisting staff to better manage internal and external boundaries;
- better identifying and managing their own and other people's roles (as well as jobs);
- becoming more involved in supporting technological systems;
- supporting a wider number of people engaged in self-development programmes.

With regard to the influence of the TECs/LECs, it is felt that trainers in large and small organizations are taking a greater interest in training and information providers. The author expects that many more smaller firms will seek assistance in some form than in the past.

With so much information available, and perhaps a greater willingness to share in a more prosperous future, trainers will find themselves becoming 'information specialists' in their own right, by acting as a 'signpost' to all sorts of sources of information, and by developing and linking in to a wider variety of networks than has been the case previously. Perhaps, more than before, there will also be a greater sharing of resources and expertise between organizations, as we all realize that we need not undermine organizational competitiveness by working together on common issues.

The change in management style that must allow such change to occur will take some time to achieve. Management, in general, do not give up things that work. Thus, only repeated demonstration and evidence of successful application will shift centuries of grounded practice and attitude. All said, this should prove a challenging and exciting future for the trainer.

SUMMARY

The term 'learning' can be applied in any context where knowledge and skill is being acquired. The term 'training' has tended to be used in a vocational or practical context, and the term 'education' is usually reserved for academic or theoretical study. 'Empowerment' in its full sense means providing learners with the means to achieve the ends, and to have the resources to evaluate the cost-effectiveness of those decisions. In a narrow sense, competence can be viewed as knowledge (K) + skills (S), but in a wider sense competence may be better understood in terms of K + S + experience + personal qualities. Regarding NVQs, competence can be defined within the five-level framework shown in Appendix 1.

As a precursor to other chapters, we looked at the idea of: the training need; the Training Needs Analysis and what training can do; what training cannot do and what training should do. Training should never be used as a 'cure all', an 'entertainment' or as a 'sticking plaster' to solve problems of a faulty organization.

When we looked at what is valued today (Appendix 3) in terms of values, ideas and practices, it seems, as others have observed, all to be pointing in a similar, demanding and exciting direction. The fact that 'autocracy' seems to be giving way to 'democracy' means, however, a very significant change in management and attitudinal style. In this respect, 'change' will need to be demonstrated and proven to work, perhaps many times over, before the 'change' in management attitude and practice takes on a more permanent look.

It was remarked that the sheer scale of government initiatives over the past thirty years has been considerable. The government's paper 'Prosperity Through Skills' (1993) is impressive for the fact that its goal and priorities are grounded in a partnership that involves all the nation's interested parties. Though this does not by itself mean it will work, surely it would work less well if the reverse were true.

While organizations have adapted themselves to better handle market and economic changes, the question that does not go away is 'Why did it have to take a recession to prompt some very basic questions about how to manage effectively?'

While the emphasis of the trainer's role will vary from organization to organization, it is likely that, in many cases, it will become both more strategic and focused. And if this is the case, trainers may well find themselves sitting alongside business leaders far more frequently than they have done in the past.

EXERCISES

Exercise 1: Change and your organization

Examine the changes that have occurred and are occurring within your organization, and *either* use Appendix 3 as a guide and tick which is closest, *and/or* describe below.

Previously valued and still valued	Valued today and tomorrow

Exercise 2: Impact on people and systems

Using the information from Exercise 1, what impact have these changes had, and what impact are these changes having, on:

- individuals;
- operating groups;
- supervisor and management groups;
- management styles;
- the role of the trainer;
- technical systems;
- payment systems;
- employment systems;
- the design of organizational structures;
- how customer/client is viewed;
- how competitors are viewed;
- how suppliers are viewed;
- how marketing intermediaries are viewed (wholesalers/retailers/advertisers/public relations)?

What is changing?	What effect is this having on people/systems?

Exercise 3: Skill trends

According to the Employment Department's 'Labour Market and Skill Trends 1995/96' report, unemployment has been reducing since early 1993, and the recovery in the labour market now seems well established. The following headline findings, from the report cited above, not only make interesting reading, but can also prompt the trainer to ask how such changes are impacting or are likely to impact on his/her organization. The current national labour market and skill trends indicate:

- steady growth in jobs likely to 2000;
- the current trend of growth in services and decline in primary and manufacturing industry is likely to continue;
- working full-time for an employer will continue to give way to more flexible forms of work;
- female employment and part-time working are expected to grow strongly;
- many women are still less able to get work which uses their abilities to the full;
- self-employment is expected to grow by almost one-fifth;
- small firms are expected to grow (those with fewer than twenty people already account for 96 per cent of all firms and 35 per cent of non-government employment);
- the labour force is ageing;
- ethnic minorities will be a growing component in the labour force;
- the quality of the labour force, as measured by qualifications, is increasing;
- there is no clear evidence of major current skill shortages, but businesses settling for 'second-best' can hide skill shortages;
- future success will demand higher, broader and more flexible skills;
- there is some evidence that employees are being under-utilized;
- the occupational mix is changing with a trend to higher-level jobs;
- young people are increasingly better qualified at 13;
- over 70 per cent of young people now stay on in education after 16;
- the majority of those who leave at 16 get training;
- the impact of GNVQs is beginning to be felt;
- higher education has an increasing role in providing knowledge and skills for young entrants to the labour market;
- 80 per cent of employees receiving training said the training was intended to improve their skills to do the work they were doing (20 per cent of training was to give them skills for a completely different type of work);
- 57 per cent of training was away from the job, 30 per cent was on-job and 13 per cent was a mixture of both;
- 43 per cent of training lasted less than a week, 15 per cent had no time limit and 42 per cent(including those on courses) lasted more than one week;
- training was most common for employees in public administration, education and health;
- establishments with twenty-five or more employees were more likely to have received training;
- employees in professional and technical occupations were most likely to train;
- training was more common among those with managerial responsibilities;
- newer employees, those who already have qualifications and young employees were most likely to get training;
- training was less common for the self-employed.

Questions

1 What do members think of these findings?
2 What trends do they perceive occurring?

(Note: Crown copyright is reproduced with the permission of the Controller of HMSO.)

Exercise 4: National targets

The current National Targets for education and training 1995 to 2000 and the progress to date since 1991 are shown in Appendix 9. These National Targets focus on achievement of GCSEs, GNVQs, NVQs, core skills, GCE A-levels and Investors in People. For example, 38 per cent of the workforce possess either two A-levels, an NVQ/SVQ 3, its vocational equivalent, or higher-level qualification, and by 2000 the target is 50 per cent.

Questions

1 Are such targets useful as a contribution to a more highly qualified workforce?
2 Have these targets been communicated well enough to managers to be sufficiently supportive of them?
3 How can such targets be achieved?

REFERENCES AND FURTHER READING

Bartlett, C. A. and Ghoshal, S. (1989) *Managing Across Borders*. London: Hutchinson Business Books.

Constable, J. and McCormick, R. (1987) *The Making of British Managers*. BIM/CBI.

Drucker, P. F. (1968) *Managing for Results*. London: Heinemann.

Drucker, P. F. (1977) *Management*. London: Pan Business Management.

Drucker, P. F. (1989) *The New Realities*. Oxford: Heinemann Professional Publishing Ltd.

Erridge, A. and Perry, S. (1993) 'Closing the Skills Gap: The National Standards Development Programme and Purchasing Competence'. *Management Education and Development 24, 4,* 369–87.

Glossary of Training Terms (1981). London: HMSO.

Handy, C. (1987) *The Making of Managers*. Joint publication with MSC/NEDC/BIM. London: HMSO.

Handy, C. (1989) *The Age of Unreason*. London: Hutchinson Ltd.

Harrison, R. (1990) *Empowerment*. Paper presented at AMED meeting.

Kanter, R. M. (1990) *When Giants Learn to Dance*. London: Unwin.

Manpower Services Commission (1981) *A New Training Initiative*. London: Manpower Services Commission.

Møller, C. (1987) *Personal Quality*. Denmark: Arnold Thomsen, Esbjerg.

Naisbitt, J. (1984) *Megatrends*. London: Futura Publications.

Prosperity Through Skills (1993). Sheffield: Department of Employment.

Pye, A. (1988) 'Management Competences in the Public Sector', *Public Money and Management*, 8, 4, Winter, 62–64.

Stewart, A. M. (1994) *Empowering People*. London: Pitman Publishing.

2

Performance problems and training

INTRODUCTION

In this chapter we will explore the training need in terms of a 'performance or training gap' which is defined by the comparison between 'actual' and 'required' performance. The trainer should find the visual description of the training need useful when defining training needs with managers and learners. The diagram (Figure 2.1), as a matter of interest, can also be used to examine shortfalls in strategies and policies, by examining differences in actual and required operational performance.

This chapter considers whether all performance discrepancies can be resolved through training, when undertaking a Training Needs Analysis (TNA) or when assisting line managers to solve operational problems. This in turn suggests that the trainer needs to have a very good grasp of who else inside and outside the organization can help remedy performance shortfalls. This chapter also deals with the process of managing change.

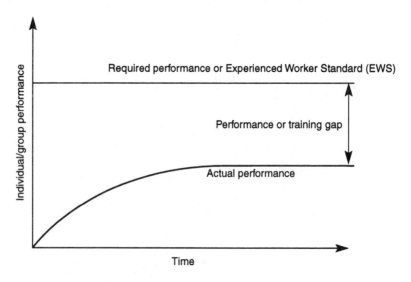

FIGURE 2.1 The Performance Gap Curve

THE PERFORMANCE GAP CURVE

To say someone needs training is to say there is a difference between the person's *actual* and *required* performance. As shown in Figure 2.1 it means there is a *gap* in performance.

To describe the gap is to be able to describe the performance discrepancy. One technique to identify a training need is to ask the parties involved to describe what is meant by actual and required performance. This is useful because it highlights whether 'like' descriptions are being compared. In other words, this approach soon spotlights if the discussion is about discrepancies in knowledge and skills, or whether it is about differences due to personality clashes. While in both cases a training intervention may be appropriate, the deployment of the wrong intervention would be a waste of resources and would be unprofessional.

THE PERFORMANCE GAP WINDOW

When dealing with performance problems it is essential to ask: 'Is training the only way to close the gap?' In practice there may be at least four different causes of a performance discrepancy.

As shown in Figure 2.2, possible solutions of poor performance can be determined from analysis of attitudes and levels of skill. In essence, poor or inadequate performance (of individual or group) may be due to:

1 Poor motivation: so *motivate*.
2 Inadequate resources to carry out task: so *provide resources*.
3 Wrong person for job, or wrong job for person (because the gap between task and the person's innate ability is simply too great): so *redesign job, transfer or dismiss person*.
4 Lack of training and development opportunities: so *train and develop*.

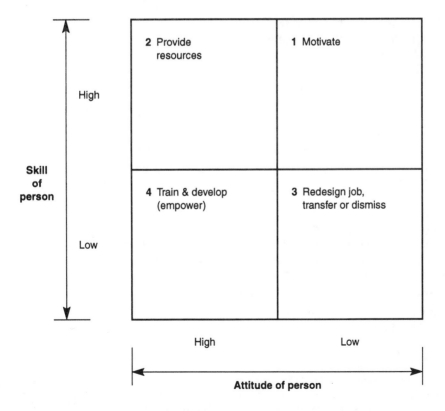

FIGURE 2.2 The Performance Gap Window

Exercise

- Show and discuss the Performance Gap Window with trainees.
- Ask the questions below (and list the team's answers).
- Explore team's answers in more detail, as this will lead to insights about how people view:
  - the organization, its culture(s) and its values, systems and procedures;
  - job constraints and demands, and more importantly job choices;
  - the supportiveness of the organization;
  - formal and informal relationships/communications;
  - their work (routines/challenging aspects);
  - promotional prospects;
  - the need for training and development.

When dealing with improving or changing performance, the need for training is but one of the four options that must be examined. To avoid selecting favourite solutions to performance problems, carefully consider all four options as a matter of routine. Let us briefly explore the solutions to poor performance.

1 Motivate

To improve performance when attitude is low and skill is high.
In general the need for motivation exists when the gap between the *actual* and *required* level of performance can be most economically met by a motivational solution.

What demotivates people? (Examples)

- Working within a non-supportive company culture.
- Negative management.
- Negative colleagues.
- Overwhelming job constraints and demands.
- Uncertainty about future.

What motivates people? (Examples)

- Working within a company culture that supports people to learn and take risks.
- Management that can train people:
  - to deal with change;
  - to lead;
  - to make decisions.
- Being part of a supportive team, and feeling the team spirit.
- Being able to make real choices within the constraints and demands of the job.
- Being, knowing or feeling part of something that wants to create a better future, even if there are uncertainties.
- Being rewarded in some way for work well done.

Also see Chapter 7 for more discussion on motivation, and see Chapter 10, item 58, 'Behaviour Modification'.

2 Provide resources

To improve performance when attitude and skills are high.
In general the need for resources exists when the gap between *actual* and *required* performance is most economically met by a resource allocation solution.

While managers are expected to both maintain systems and create change, all too often the budget and necessary resources do not match the task in hand. The reasons for this can range from sudden switch of task priority and lack of proper planning, to the sheer novelty of the situation.

The subject of resource allocation has always been a fragile one, simply because it is an easy excuse to make. From experience, it is when things change that resource problems occur. Examples can include:

- when key people leave and/or new people join;
- when the company gets bigger or smaller;
- when different tasks are taken on;
- when new equipment is used.

All too frequently, it is not just that new or better resources are required, it is also that the resources that are available are simply not being used effectively. The effects of the recession have led a great many businesses to rethink the use of their existing resources. In one example, a large organization having trimmed its hierarchy from seven to four effective levels, then re-distributed responsibilities. One result was for the maintenance foreman to show all visitors and potential clients around the factory, whereas this had previously been the task of a senior manager.

Examples of poor performance (due to lack of resources)

- Low output.
- High error rate.
- High accident frequency.
- Excessive maintenance cost.
- Poor quality.

Why did lack of resources occur?

Possible answers may include:

- Objectives and plans were not properly prepared, so the need for new systems was not triggered.
- New team structures were not put in place to meet the new demands.
- Someone made assumptions rather than:
  - think through what effect some change would have;
  - run a pilot to study likely problems.
- The need for resources was not properly communicated.

How can this outcome be avoided in future?

Review situation and ensure that the link between performance and resource allocation is analysed, monitored and action is taken. Also see 'Feeding forward' in Chapter 4.

Helping learner use resources

In addition to the lack of resources as the cause of poor performance, another often overlooked cause can be how best to use resources. 'How to get more from less' is today stretching managers to make better use of their human and physical resources. In summary, the cause of poor performance may be due to:

- a genuine lack of resources;
- a lack of imagination in how to use resources more effectively, be they human or physical.

3 Redesign job/transfer or discharge person

To improve performance when attitude and skills are low.

In general: 'The need to *redesign a job* to suit a person exists when the gap between *required* and *actual* performance can be closed, through a redistribution of job tasks.'

'The need to *transfer/discharge* a person exists when the gap between *required* and *actual* performance cannot be closed, and the decision to act is based on sound ethical considerations.'

Redesign of job

In the case where the job can be redesigned to accommodate a person, this option should be examined. Perhaps too frequently, managers see job tasks cast in stone, when in fact there is room for flexibility. Managers also have a tendency to focus on a person's weaknesses and therefore only see the limitations, rather than focus on a person's strengths and explore the opportunities that may exist.

Transferring

If transferring someone internally (because the person can no longer perform at that level or because selection procedures are at fault), managers should be trained to make the transfer as smooth as possible. In a case where guilt and humiliation are felt, counsellors can be engaged to reduce unnecessary damage to the person's ego.

Dismissal

If dismissing someone, the same positive attitude toward helping the person should exist. Managers should be trained to help with the transition, and respect for the individual should never be lost. Where possible, the individual should be helped to find alternative employment. Of all the causes of poor performance this situation must be handled with care. Unlike broken bones, shattered confidence may never be rebuilt.

What might be the cause for redesigning jobs, and transferring or dismissing a person?

- Poor job analysis linked to poor selection.
- Little thought given to matching and adjusting job to person, or person to job.
- Poor health, trauma or excessive stress levels.

How can such situations be avoided?

- Undertake thorough job analysis.
- Review and improve selection procedures.
- Consider what allowable adjustments can be made between the person and the job.
- Monitor physical and psychological well-being of staff and take necessary action to alleviate foreseeable dangers.

4 Train and develop

To improve performance when attitude is high and skill is low.
In general 'A training need exists when the gap between *actual* and *required* performance can be most economically met by a training intervention.'

Where/how are potential training needs found?

Training needs can be identified:

*   By undertaking a Training Needs Analysis (TNA). (See Chapter 1 for initial description of a TNA. See Chapter 3 for types of TNA, e.g. Organizational, Performance, Priority, Self-Help and Functional. See Chapter 9 for description of TNA techniques, e.g. interviewing, diary analysis, critical incidents.)
*   Through the interpretation of business plans, records and via examination of operational problems. (See Chapter 8.)
*   Through the understanding of how to match training interventions to the organizational culture. (See Chapter 7.)

In terms of who might need to be trained and developed, this can be applicable to individuals, groups and even applied to the organization as a whole. As a reminder of what training can be undertaken, the following represents examples of training activities that can be carried out both within and outside the organization.

EXAMPLES OF TRAINING ACTIVITY
Within the job

*   Receives a period of coaching.
*   Carries out tasks which have been delegated.
*   Undertakes projects.
*   Becomes project leader.
*   Replaces superior temporarily.
*   Takes part in job rotation.
*   Follows training programme.
*   Runs briefing session.
*   Prepares report.

Outside the job

*   Attends course/meeting/lecture.
*   Becomes member of working committee.
*   Performs observational/note-taking activities.
*   Learner gives lectures/participates in group discussions.
*   Tackles programme learning text.
*   Undertakes project work.
*   Follows reading list.
*   Attends professional association activities.
*   Performs community activities.
*   Carries out public speaking.
*   Takes part in secondment.

MANAGING CHANGE

As a change agent, the trainer must always consider the degree and impact that training will have on people, situations and systems. Guidelines for managing change, as a result of training, may include:

- Only change situations which you can control.
- Obtain agreement from your colleagues to seek change.
- Define the boundary for the change and consult widely within it.
- Involve people in the whole process and help them to take ownership.
- Plan how the change will be made.
- Don't feel you need to rush at making changes (the reality often is, that present attitudes have been fixed for some time), so be prepared, where appropriate, to introduce change gradually.
- Monitor and evaluate the results and repeat the process again, as required.

When involving others in the investigation and implementation of training activities, three questions that trainers find useful are:

- Who cares?
- Who knows?
- Who can?

Who cares?

Who has the emotional investment to change things? Who is involved in and committed to the outcome? Very often, for example, these are people who are directly involved.

Who knows?

Who has information about the problem? Who has the hard facts, not opinions, about the problem or performance shortfall?

Who can?

Who has the power to secure resources so that changes can occur? Who, when faced with facts, has the power to confront the problem?

SUMMARY

To define a training need in terms of the 'actual' and 'required' performance, as we saw in the Performance Gap Curve, is a useful technique for focusing the mind on the nature of the 'performance or training gap'. As comparisons between 'actual' and 'required' performance are sought from all the parties involved, any differences will help contribute to a full account of the training need.

When examining the Performance Gap Window, we were reminded of traps in thinking about problems and solutions. For the manager, there can be a tendency to see solutions in terms of manipulating resources and systems. For the trainer, on the other hand, there can be a tendency to see solutions only in terms of training solutions. As we saw, training may be one of four solutions which will help close performance gaps, namely:

1. Motivate staff.
2. Provide resources or make better use of resources.
3. Redesign the job or replace the individual with a better performer.
4. Train and develop individuals/groups.

When examining how to handle change as a result of training, useful guidelines were given, for example 'Only change situations which you can control.' This reminds us that when training either off-job or on-job, we must be clear about what can and can't be done. Thus, we must strive not to put learners in situations where they can be humiliated or physically injured. And although learning involves risks, we must be careful not to damage a person's confidence.

When involving others in the management of training and therefore change processes, we note that a useful guide to who can help, can include three questions: Who cares? Who knows? Who can?

REFERENCES AND FURTHER READING

Training needs

Boydell, T. H. (1983) *A Guide to the Identification of Training Needs*. London: British Association for Commercial and Industrial Education.

Fairbairns, J. (1991) 'Plugging the Gap in Training Needs Analysis'. *Personnel Management*. February.

Jennings, S. and Undy, R. (1984) 'Auditing Managers IR Training Needs'. *Personnel Management*. February.

Pettigrew, A. M., Sparrow, P. and Hendry, C. (1988) 'The Forces that Trigger Training'. *Personnel Management*. December.

Turrell, M. (1980) *Training Analysis: A Guide to Recognising Training Needs*. Plymouth: Macdonald and Evans.

Task analysis

Annett, J., Duncan, K. D., Stammers, R. B. and Gray, M. J. (1979) *Task Analysis: Training Information Paper*. London: Manpower Services Commission.

Boydell, T. H. (1977) *A Guide to Job Analysis*. London: British Association for Commercial and Industrial Education.

Duncan, K. D. and Kelly, C. J. (1983) *Task Analysis, Learning and the Nature of Transfer*. Sheffield: Manpower Services Commission.

Pern, M. and Kandola, R. (1988) *Job Analysis: A Practical Guide For Managers*. London: Institute of Personnel Management.

Seymour, W. D. (1968) *Skills Analysis Training*. London: Pitman.

Training strategies/function

Holden, L. and Livian, Y. (1992) 'Does Strategic Training Policy Exist?: Some Evidence from Ten European Countries'. *Personnel Review 21, 1*, 12–33.

Otto, C. P. and Glaser, R. O. (1970) *The Management of Training*. London: Addison-Wesley.

Pepper, A. D. (1984) *Managing the Training Development Function*. Aldershot: Gower.

Reid, M. A. and Kenny, J. (1987) 'Selecting and Evaluating Training Strategies'. *Personnel Management Handbook*. Aldershot: Gower.

3

The training cycle and trainer role

INTRODUCTION

Basic to the preparation of training budgets and training activity is the rationale that training exists to support the business plan. It is the business plan which dictates training activity in the widest sense, and it is the business plan which explains the connection between business objectives and investment in people. As many trainers and managers will testify, whenever training is correctly linked to improving performance in the workplace, the training function will always get executive support. And whenever training is not so linked, support will be lukewarm or absent.

Although some observers would argue that not all trainers have access to or are briefed about business plans, the trainer should, at least, seek interpretation of plans from functional heads. From the direction indicated by the business plan (which may embrace manpower and succession plans), the trainer should seek to locate areas where training is likely to be required. Examples of such areas may be indicated as a result of:

- intended restructuring of departments;
- acquisition of new machinery;
- changes in systems and procedures;
- quality improvement programmes to enhance products and services;
- the intention to break into new markets.

For a closer examination of the business/strategic planning process, see Gluck (1980), Rue (1989) and see Note 3.1 on page 33.

THE TRAINING CYCLE

Other names for the Training Cycle are Training Process, Training Function and Systematic Training Model. Like other disciplines such as marketing, training has a 'function': it is a 'process', there is a cycle of activity, it can be approached systematically and it follows a problem-solving pattern.

This chapter alerts the reader to the idea that within the total process of training, the trainer needs to recognize that certain roles and skills are appropriate at each stage. Within some large organizations and within some trainer provider setups, some roles are carried out by different trainers. The problem for many trainers is that a good presenter, facilitator or deliverer of training (Implementor) may not be an equally good investigator (Identifier) of training needs.

If, however, a trainer has difficulty with one or more roles she or he needs to complement it in some way. For example, an in-house trainer may identify the training need and then hire an external trainer to design and deliver the training.

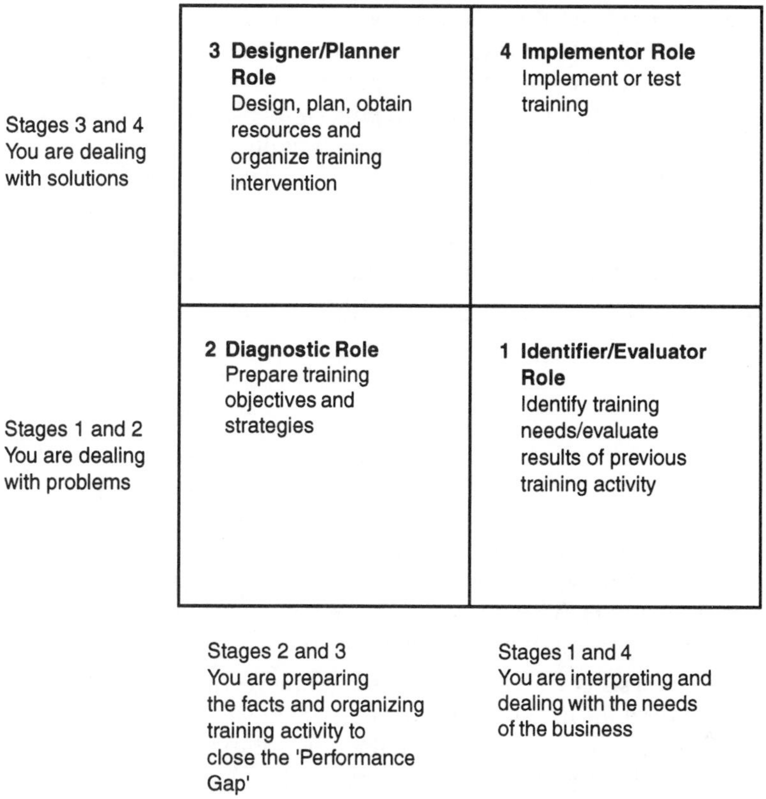

Stages 3 and 4 You are dealing with solutions	**3 Designer/Planner Role** Design, plan, obtain resources and organize training intervention	**4 Implementor Role** Implement or test training
Stages 1 and 2 You are dealing with problems	**2 Diagnostic Role** Prepare training objectives and strategies	**1 Identifier/Evaluator Role** Identify training needs/evaluate results of previous training activity
	Stages 2 and 3 You are preparing the facts and organizing training activity to close the 'Performance Gap'	Stages 1 and 4 You are interpreting and dealing with the needs of the business

FIGURE 3.1 The Training Cycle Window, showing trainer roles and training tasks

THE TRAINING CYCLE WINDOW AND THE TNA

The Training Cycle Window can be described in four stages as shown in Figure 3.1. In addition to the training activities, the diagram shows the core training roles which support each activity, namely:

Stage 1: Identifier/Evaluator Role.
    Identify training needs/evaluate results of previous training.
Stage 2: Diagnostic Role.
    Formulate training objectives, strategies and policy.
Stage 3: Designer/Planner Role.
    Design, plan and organize training intervention.
Stage 4: Implementor Role.
    Implement or test training.

After implementation, the process is repeated thus:

Stage 5: Evaluate results/identify needs.
Stage 6: Reformulate training objectives and policy.
Stage 7: Replan.
Stage 8: Implement or test new training activity.

The stages are again repeated as the process demands.

The four roles that support each part of the Window make us aware that for each stage a different emphasis and different skills are required. Common to all the stages can be the need to participate and agree with users the progress at each step. Although individual circumstances will dictate the level of user involvement, increasingly today the sheer cost of training will require user agreement at each point.

For a closer examination of the Training Cycle Window, let us examine each stage in some detail.

Stage 1: Trainer adopts 'Identifier/Evaluator Role'

In this role, in order to identify training needs, the trainer will need to demonstrate ability to:

- Listen.
- Observe.
- Question.
- Record.
- Evaluate.

To undertake this role the trainer will need to suspend judgement in order to gather data about training needs by listening, observing, questioning, recording, evaluating and agreeing the findings with others. The method that is adopted to achieve this is called a Training Needs Analysis. Prior to carrying out a TNA we note:

1 A Training Needs Analysis is undertaken to discover performance shortfalls or discrepancies (see Chapter 9 for list of techniques).
2 A training intervention, however, may not be the only solution (Chapter 2) and the trainer must expect to identify many non-training needs.
3 External and internal influences may need to be studied, in addition to the performance problem areas, to discover where possible the links between the causes and the effects. (See Note 3.3, p. 37.)

The Training Needs Analysis

When undertaking a TNA the trainer must decide between at least five approaches, namely:

1 The Organization-wide TNA.
2 The Performance Management TNA.
3 The Priority Review TNA.
4 The Self-help Support TNA
5 The Functional Versatility Chart TNA.

If we look at each one of these TNAs separately, we will see that the scale, approach and resources required to undertake each will vary considerably.

1 The Organization-wide TNA. Sometimes called the Global Review, this requires that the whole organization is studied, and detailed training needs for each function and employee be prepared. Although part of the Industry Training Board philosophy (1964–1980s), not everyone was convinced that such a high level of bureaucracy was applicable. Another approach called Organizational Development (OD), advocated by training consultants, also adopted the same model. In this case the emphasis was on developing the organization (via networks of teams) to cope more effectively with internal and external change. Today, organizational development has been partly superseded by Organizational Re-engineering and

Total Quality Management (TQM). Although the focus of TQM is on quality, there is still a requirement for a large-scale training needs analysis. Whereas re-engineering is primarily about rethinking the way the organization can be structured to achieve greater efficiencies, there will still be a need for widespread training. For further discussion about OD, TQM and re-engineering, see Note 3.2 (page 36).

The only drawback of across-the-board Training Needs Analysis is the mechanistic way it is sometimes handled. When examining the *Glossary of Training Terms* description of Training Needs Analysis, we note that it describes the total organizational TNA approach, which stipulates:

> The Organization-wide TNA involves an examination of the organization's present operations, expected operations and manpower requirements in order to identify: the number of staff; manpower categories needing to be trained and/or retrained; and individual training needs which will enable a person to reach the required standard of performance in the current or the future job.

As well as being able to interpret the business plan, in order to examine operational training needs, trainers will also make themselves aware of the 'context' of their study. This is because it may add to the understanding of the causes of performance discrepancies. In addition it may help the trainer to decide upon training methods and timing. If, for example, top management adopts an autocratic style of managing their staff, this may help explain reasons for fluctuations in performance. In this case, any intervention to correct the performance shortfall will need to match the pervading style of management, and fit in with any workload pressures. If we work from 'outside to inside', the aim is to detect whether external factors can in some way influence internal performance. A list of these external and internal factors that can affect training can be found in Note 3.3 (page 37), and are applicable to all types of TNA.

2 The Performance Management TNA. To identify the training needs in this case, the trainer often makes use of the findings from a key results performance review/staff appraisal. As the performance review involves comparing actual standards of performance against a required standard of performance (job description), the difference can be indicative of training needs. Such a review is undertaken between managers and their staff, usually yearly but may be more frequent. The merit of the approach is that it is focused on work-related issues. There is sometimes a danger that trainers and managers end up matching a variety of training needs with aggregate solutions: this is where we can end up with 'time management' for everyone. To be effective in this case, the trainer must adopt the role of a process consultant; that is, be able to interpret performance shortfalls across a wide range of situations, and be able to advise on appropriate individual solutions.

With the wider use of NVQs, this enables training needs to be determined by comparing the required competency standard against the individual's actual standard. While competences may not replace the performance review, they may provide a useful mechanism for identifying training needs.

3 The Priority Review TNA. For this approach the problems and issues facing an organization are prioritized. Likewise, training activity is focused on satisfying priority or critical training needs. This approach is useful when financial resources are scarce or when an organization is in start-up or survival mode. Over a period, the danger is that the longer-term development of people gets forgotten, as does the training of all those that provide a variety of vital (but not critical) support services.

4 The Self-help Support TNA. To achieve this, the organization will likely see itself as a learning organization (Jones (1992), Pedlar (1988), Garratt (1989), Wood (1988)) and will likely be supporting self-development or continuous development activity. Individuals will be adopting an independent approach to training and developing themselves. Training, development and work will blur into one and will be ongoing. In terms of Training Needs Analysis, this is the responsibility of functional and line managers. For the trainer, the broad role becomes one of a 'network support, information specialist and signposter'. That is, the trainer helps achieve the organization's human resource strategy, and supports progress towards it within each function of the organization.

5 The Functional Versatility Chart TNA. (See also Chapter 9.) Of all the TNA approaches this is the most common and easiest to prepare within a busy work setting. To prepare: enter names of team/department/unit in a column down the left side, and enter 'tasks to be done or skills to be acquired' along the top of a sheet of paper or display board. When comparing each person against the list of skills, individual and team profiles of accomplishment will emerge. To record that a person either has or does not have some skill, either a tick and cross can be used, or the skill level can be scored from 1 to 10.

It is not uncommon for such Functional Versatility Chart TNAs to be used as a visual wall display record of staff achievement. To sequence, target, date and monitor the training activity, a Training Plan can be prepared based on the TNA ratings.

Whatever method of TNA is used, the next stage is to diagnose the information.

Evaluation. To determine the effectiveness of previous training activity, the assessor (who should be a different person from the trainer) will determine how well the 'performance gap' has been closed. If resources do not allow for a trainer and assessor, the trainer may undertake both roles. The reason for splitting the training/assessing task is to avoid the difficulty for the trainer of assessing the effectiveness of his/her 'own work'.

To evaluate the effectiveness of training at all levels requires that the trainer is able to:

- assess the accuracy of training objectives and how well training activity has been designed (assessing use and choice of *inputs*);
- assess how well training matches the learner's needs *during training*, and assess how well knowledge, skill and understanding are being gained (assessing the *processes* at work);
- assess how effective training has been, immediately *training has finished*, and assess how well knowledge, skill and understanding have been gained (assessing the *products* of training);
- assess how well a learner is able to correctly *apply* new knowledge, skill and understanding to the work situation (assessing the *outputs* of training);
- assess how well a learner can *transfer* such knowledge, skill and understanding to new situations, and assess what impact such performance has on organizational *outcomes*;
- carry out a cost-benefit analysis. See also Table 3.1. For more information on assessment of training see Chapters 5 and 6.

Stage 2: Trainer adopts 'Diagnostic Role'

In this role the trainer prepares training objectives, strategies and policies. This requires the ability to:

- Think logically.
- Think creatively.
- Analyse.
- Reflect.

This role calls for judgements to be made. The trainer must be able to think both logically and rationally, be able to analyse problems, be able to use well-developed reflective skills and be able to agree the findings with others. At this stage the whole training effort will need to be defined. For example:

Training objectives will be prepared based on business plan objectives and detailed information from the training needs analysis which may be undertaken. Questions that arise when preparing training objectives include:

- What present operations will be affected?
- What new operations will be established?
- What manpower groups/individuals will be affected?
- What performance is required?
- What is the actual performance?
- What standards must be achieved?
- What conditions will people work and be trained under?

An example and further notes for preparing training objectives are shown below.

Example: a training objective for a production operation

All production personnel will be trained:

- to operate *all* production machinery and equipment (*performance*: what is done);
- to produce X units per hour, within one month (*standard* to be achieved), and expressed either quantitatively (accuracy/quality/quantity/time) or subjectively (personal judgement);
- use A, B, C, D type production machinery and equipment, at the new E, F, G site (broad *conditions/constraints* under which performance takes place).

The above method for structuring an objective is known as the Majer (1962) Type. In Appendix 7 the Miller (1962) Type and the Davies (1971) Type Objectives can also be examined, and in Appendix 8 the domains of learning are listed. The main reason for stating objectives is to eliminate ambiguity. When required performance levels are not met, the reason, if not within the individual, may be traced to changes in standards and conditions, for example. See also Chapter 6 for further examples of Majer Type objectives and more discussion on standards.

Training strategies will identify the steps to be taken to support the achievement of training objectives. See example below of a training strategy for implementing a customer service initiative into a large retail store.

Example: a training strategy

The Training Strategy sets out the major steps to support and achieve the training objective.

Example: strategy for customer service

With due regard to all the factors for implementing a customer service programme, it was decided to pilot it first. The broad strategy was as follows:

*   *Stage 1*, inform all managers of the initiative (month 1);
*   *Stage 2*, pilot the initiative in five departments and train managers (months 1, 2 and 3);
*   *Stage 3*, generate interest in the project by inviting non-participating managers to examine the process and the results (during months 2 and 3);
*   *Stage 4*, arrange for the Chief Executive to vet the pilot and give the go-ahead to implement the programme in more departments (end of month 3);
*   *Stage 5*, prepare examples of good customer service programmes and issue, as required (months 3 and 4).

Training policy may comment on:

*   induction training;
*   specific on-job training;
*   management training, at all levels;
*   developmental learning opportunities, including use made of day-release and technology-based-training (TBT);
*   use made of work-related project work;
*   use made of NVQs;
*   health and safety training.

Smaller organizations by comparison often adopt an *ad hoc* approach, have no written policy, and satisfy training and education needs as they arise or not at all.

Having prepared the objectives the next stage is to design and plan the training event.

Stage 3: Trainer adopts 'Designer/Planner Role'

For this role the trainer designs, plans and organizes training interventions. Ability is required to:

*   Plan use of resources.
*   Plan/organize events.
*   Communicate training intentions.
*   Design training interventions in detail.
*   Create an effective climate for change and learning.

The trainer now requires to engage his/her proactive skills. This involves being able to plan the use of resources, plan events, participate with others, communicate training intentions, design training interventions and create an effective learning climate. Having been guided by the Business Plan, undertaken a Training Needs Analysis, and prepared and agreed the Training Objectives, the Training Plan which is used to describe, for example, how the organization-wide training needs are to be satisfied, now requires to be constructed. If the Objectives indicate *what* is to be done, the Training Plan will describe *who, what, how, where, when* and *why* training will be undertaken. The Training Plan schedules training activity and may comment on:

- number of people to be trained and educated by type of learning, job classification, department and method of learning, with reference to:
  - senior management;
  - middle and first-line management;
  - trainers;
  - graduates;
  - operational staff;
  - trainees under agreement;
  - youth training;
- specific individual programmes;
- use to be made of specific schemes, such as Investors in People;
- planned dates and duration of activity;
- standards of performance or competence to be achieved;
- how training and education will be assessed;
- costs involved, which will be used to prepare the Training Budget.

The factors that may assist with the design of a training intervention are dealt with in Chapters 5, 6, 7, 8, 9 and 10.

There is no fixed approach to presenting Training Plans, although for convenience a tabulated approach is often preferred. The structure of the Training Plan (by division or activity) will need to reflect the needs of the organization. By adopting the same process a trainer can also prepare either a Training Programme which describes how a person will be trained, and usually states: time required/training objective/type of training/location/trainer responsible; or a Lesson Plan which describes how an off-job training event is to be undertaken by the trainer, and usually states: the trainer's objectives/lists notes, props and visual aids required/times of each training session/a list of 'What to do' for each session.

Training Programmes (TPs) and Lesson Plans (LPs) are used to explain learning steps and guide demonstration of required work performance in a manner that best facilitates learning. TPs and LPs are useful because they structure the beginning, middle and end of a learning process. In particular, TPs and LPs identify the important relation between trainer, learner and how learning can be achieved. In addition, TPs and LPs can make reference to operational procedures, and can also be used to monitor and assess the learner's performance.

Stage 4: Trainer adopts 'Implementor Role'

Here the trainer implements or tests out training activity. Skills required include ability to:

- Deliver training interventions on/off-job using a variety of training techniques and interpersonal/group skills.
- Create a climate where people can learn to close the gap between actual and required performance within planned times.

This is the training role that most people see. This is where the trainer either directly delivers the training or acts as a facilitator of it. Crucial to this role is the ability to create a climate where others can learn effectively. For successful delivery and implementation the trainer must understand:

- the learning needs.
- how to close the 'performance gap'.
- the dynamics of the learner's situation.

Understanding the learning needs

Here we need to understand what is meant by the learner's actual performance. Will, for example, required performance be met through a training intervention or will performance be increased through better motivation or through more effective use of resources? (See Chapter 2.)

Understanding how to close the 'performance gap'

This requires understanding the effectiveness of training options available, to determine the most suitable method (see Chapter 10 and Appendix 11). It also requires knowing who will help bridge the gap between off-job learning (if appropriate) and on-job application.

Understanding the dynamics of the learner's situation

This requires practical awareness of the training resources available including time, cost, equipment, involvement of others, venue for training, and effectiveness of trainers. It requires understanding the dynamics of the work situation, including knowing who *cares,* who *knows* and who can *change things,* and includes being clear about job and role requirements. It requires understanding how supportive or non-supportive the organizational culture is to various types of training activity to identify what is practical; (see Chapter 7).

TRAINING AND DEVELOPMENT NATIONAL STANDARDS (TDLB)

The Training and Development Lead Body's (TDLB) 'National Standards for Training and Development 1995' states the key purpose of training and development is to 'develop human potential to assist organizations and individuals to achieve their objectives'. In a wider sense, the TDLB standards describe the full function of training. These standards give:

- five main areas of competence;
- fourteen sub-areas;
- thirty-two 'Units of Competence' (or the *job* that the candidate does);
- seventy-eight 'Elements of Competence' (where an element is a *task* which the candidate should be able to do), not including MC1 options.

In addition, there are about eight 'Performance Criteria' for each element (which show the expected *standards* to be achieved), and there are a number of 'Range Statements' for each element (which describe the different *circumstances* under which it would be reasonable to expect the activities to be demonstrated).

However, the Standards do not fit easily within all types of organizational cultures, and it can take some effort to fit the Standards to a particular training job (bearing in mind that like other jobs, training jobs also vary considerably in their emphasis and content). Also, the Range Statements can seem inappropriate to the realities of the workplace for some people.

Within the NVQ/SVQ structure there are two levels of qualifications: Level 3 and Level 4 (see also Appendix 1).

In addition to providing the most comprehensive listing of training activities, the Standards with their performance criteria and range indicators can have other uses. They can, for example, be used to prepare job descriptions; for recruitment and selection; for training, staff development, appraisal and assessment, and for organizational review.

Training Cycle. With regard to the Training Cycle, we note that, in essence, TDLB recognizes that the Cycle comprises the same important stages as described here.

TRAINING SUB-ROLES

By comparison to the Main Training Roles described in this chapter, the TDLB's descriptions are very precise and, if allowed to be, very constraining. As discussed earlier, the Training Cycle reminds us of the tasks necessary to undertake the complete training function. While some trainers will have full responsibility for all facets of training, others will support particular stages of the Cycle. When charged with managing the complete training effort, the Training Cycle structure can be useful for defining what is required of the trainer. The following allocation demonstrates how it is possible to identify Sub-roles at various stages of the Cycle.

Stage 1: Identifier/Evaluator Role

Main role: Identifier/Evaluator. *Sub-roles:* Training Analyst; Mentor; Counsellor; Coach; Process Specialist.

Stage 2: Diagnostic Role

Main role: Diagnostic. *Sub-roles:* Training Director; Strategist; Researcher; Writer; Tutor; Adviser.

Stage 3: Designer/Planner Role

Main role: Designer and Planner. *Sub-roles:* Planner/Organizer; Developer of Curriculum; Administrator/Resource Allocator; Co-ordinator of Open Learning; Training Manager; Programme Designer/Planner; Information/Signposter Specialist; Network Specialist.

Stage 4: Implementor Role

Main role: Implementor. *Sub-roles:* Direct Trainer; Instructor; Team Builder; On-Job Trainer.

Stage 1 is repeated: Identifier/Evaluator Role

Main role: Identifier/Evaluator (with initial emphasis on evaluation). *Sub-roles:* Assessor of Training; Evaluator.

All facets of the Training Cycle

For training jobs that embrace all facets of the Training Cycle we have, for example: Facilitator; Interventionist; Change Agent; Consultant.

SUMMARY

In this chapter we saw how training can be regarded as both reflecting current business plans and supporting existing training needs. The trainer must be careful to check that existing training needs still support current business plans. It is possible that training programmes started some years or even months ago may now be obsolete. In terms of documentation some organizations may require training objectives, a training strategy, a training plan, a training budget and a training policy. In the smallest of companies, good practice suggests that, via national initiatives like 'Investors in People', and the Department of Trade and Industry (DTI) and Employment Department (ED, now DFEE) documentation, the minimum requirement ought to be a Training Plan.

We discovered that we can think of training as a cycle of activity, which in turn requires a different Training Role to be performed at each stage of the cycle. The stages of the cycle can be described as:

- Stage 1: Identifier and Evaluator Role.
- Stage 2: Diagnostic Role.
- Stage 3: Designer and Planner Role.
- Stage 4: Implementor Role.

Stage 1: Identifier and Evaluator Role

We noted that the key to effective training is the proper identification of training needs. It was noted that to ensure successful training results, trainers must understand how both external and internal forces impinge on the training effort. For outside providers in particular, the nuances, history, power figures and the finer points of the organization's philosophy and culture will not be immediately apparent; this information will need to be properly communicated to them.

Stage 2: Diagnostic Role

The trainer needs to analyse the content and context of training and prepare training objectives in order to communicate intentions, and compare progress. Three ways of writing objectives were presented along with a synopsis of learning domains and levels which are located in Appendices 7 and 8.

In terms of skills, the trainer needs to exhibit both solid rational and logical thinking along with an ability to be creative, in order to analyse problems, prepare objectives and foresee solutions.

Stage 3: Designer and Planner Role

This is where the trainer will prepare training plans, training programmes and lesson plans. Depending on resources and expertise available, trainers have a choice of preparing and tailoring their own programmes or modifying off-the-shelf materials to suit their requirements. In general, there has been a swing in the 1980s and 1990s away from use of public courses to in-house tailored events.

Stage 4: Implementor Role

This is the point where training is delivered and where the trainer creates a climate where learners can learn effectively. To be effective at this stage the trainer must understand the learning needs, understand how to close the 'performance gap' and understand the dynamics of the learner's situation.

Stage 1 is repeated: Identifier and Evaluator Role

By coupling the results of evaluation with identification of training needs, Stage 1 is repeated and the Training Cycle continues.

TDLB National Training Standards

With reference to the TDLB National Training Standards, we noted that the Standards provide us with the most comprehensive job description for training yet. Although the sheer size of the document may prevent use of it for some, the Standards can have a number of uses including using them as a checklist for identifying the training needs of trainers.

Training sub-roles

To assist with the management of the training effort, we found it is possible to identify how training sub-roles can support various training jobs for each phase of the Training Cycle.

NOTE 3.1: THE PARALLEL BETWEEN BUSINESS PLANNING AND USING THE TRAINING CYCLE

Business planning

When preparing a business plan (sometimes called a Strategic Plan) it is usual to examine present and past performance, objectives and strategies, and also to examine external and internal opportunities, strengths, weaknesses and threats. It is then possible to exploit the organization's strengths and market opportunities.

Key planning and controlling documents

If we compare the preparation of the organization's and the Training Function's 'key planning and controlling' documents, the result will be as shown in Table 3.1. If we also consider 'how' we prepare these 'action documents', we can say that :

- *for the organization*, the quality of these 'action documents' may depend on the effectiveness of the 'problem-solving' and planning processes used;
- *for the Training Function*, the quality of these 'action documents' may depend on how well the 'training cycle' process is followed.

A brief description of the 'action documents' listed in Table 3.1 is shown below.

Organizational problem-solving

This is how the organization problem-solves and plans its activities. The organization (size/product or service complexity/intensity of competition/dynamics of the marketplace/the organizational culture), and the experience of the top management team, will determine how members approach organizational problem-solving and planning. For example: do managers tend to be reactive and solution-centred, or do managers study the problem first and adopt a problem-centred approach and prepare plans of action? To determine the organization's objectives, strategies and plans: do top management try to shape the organization's future, or do they leave things simply to market forces? Whatever methodologies or rules of thumb an organization uses, the approach will influence

TABLE 3.1 Comparing organization and training function 'Planning and Control' documents

ORGANIZATION	TRAINING FUNCTION
Business (or Strategic) Planning activity involves top, middle and functional management, using appropriate:	Training activity is designed to support the business plans and satisfy current training needs. To achieve this, Functional Management use:
• Problem-solving and planning methodologies	• The Training Cycle
and is guided by:	and is guided by:
• A corporate mission statement	• The corporate mission statement
and prepares:	and prepares:
• Objectives (long/intermediate/short)	• Training objectives (long/intermediate/short)
• Strategy (corporate/business/functional)	• Training strategy (to support all levels)
• Plans (long/intermediate/short)	• Training plans (to support all levels)
• Policies (corporate/business/functional)	• Training policies (to support all levels)
• Procedures/rules (corporate/business/functional)	• Training procedures/rules (to support all levels)

all members at all levels. For the Training Function in particular, the question is 'What sort of problem-solving and planning processes are used?'

The Training Cycle

This is how the Training Function problem-solves and plans training activity. The Training Cycle is used by organizations who value using a systematic method. The Training Cycle is described below and can work at two levels.

1 It can be used on a *macro* level to indicate the sequence of stages that need to be carried out to support the whole Training Function, that is to:
   • identify Training Function Needs;
   • prepare Training Function Objectives;
   • prepare Training Function Strategy and Plans;
   • implement Training Function Strategy and Plans;
   • evaluate how well the Strategy has been implemented.

2 It can be used on a *micro* level to provide a structure to assess, say, individual, group, departmental or divisional training needs as follows:
   • identify needs;
   • prepare training objectives;
   • prepare training plan;
   • implement training plan;
   • evaluate success of training plan.

Mission statement

This is what we stand for. For Campbell (1990) a mission statement should reflect the organization's

- *purpose* (why the organization exists);
- *strategy* (commercial logic);
- *behaviour standards* (how employees behave);
- *values* (beliefs that underpin the organization's management style, its relation to stakeholders and its ethics).

When the strategy and top management are changing, and where there are strong differences between top management members, a mission statement will not be appropriate.

Objectives

This is what we want to achieve. Objectives can be classified as:

- *short-range,* less than one year;
- *intermediate* range, one to three years;
- *long-range,* over three years.

Top management will develop long-range objectives, and divisional and operational management usually assist with intermediate and short-range objectives. Training Objectives will be designed to support the long-term, intermediate and short-range business objectives.

Strategy

This is how we get there. The strategy indicates how the objectives will be achieved. Three types of strategy are:

- *Corporate Strategy.* This addresses what businesses an organization will be in and how resources will be allocated (top management/three to seven years).
- *Business Strategy.* This focuses on how the Strategic Business Unit (SBU)/profit centre or single product organization will compete within a given business (middle management/one to three years).
- *Functional Strategy.* This focuses in detail on how each function will achieve its strategy (functional management/zero to one year). Functions can include:
  - Product lines.
  - Geographic area.
  - Type of customer.
  - Marketing strategy.
  - Finance strategy.
  - Production strategy.
  - Personnel strategy.
  - Training strategy.

Plans

This is what must be done in detail to achieve the strategy. Plans are prepared to support the three types of strategy and can include corporate plans, business plans, and function and training plans. When preparing Training Plans, a major input may comprise the action to support all functions of the business. Another element may comprise the recent findings of a Training Needs Analysis (TNA) of the organization, which has identified current needs.

Although Functional Training Plans (and Functional Strategies) are operational in nature (zero to one year), they are designed to support the long-range requirements.

At this detailed planning stage, business and functional budgets are prepared, including the Training Budget which may include educational activities.

Policies

These are the boundaries that we work within. Policy is a general guide which constrains or directs achievement of objectives. It is common for large organizations to have policies to cover all areas of the business. When constructed, policies may comprise summary, purpose, responsibilities, specific procedures, general guidelines/special considerations, appendices with notes and samples of forms that must be used. Larger organizations are likely to have a Training Policy which may also encompass educational requirements.

Procedures/rules

These are the very specific boundaries that we work within. Policies, procedures and rules have in common that they all seek to limit opportunities for individuals to make poor decisions. Procedures and rules differ from policies in their specificity. *Procedures* can form part of the policy and can exist separately as a Standard Operating Procedure, for example. To accomplish some task, a step-by-step approach is usually described, allowing for little or no deviation. *Rules* like 'No Smoking' do not permit any deviation. Unlike procedures, rules do not necessarily specify sequence.

Training documentation

With regard to the range of training documentation that can be prepared, this can include:

*   *Training Objectives* (what must be achieved long-term/intermediate/short-range?)
*   *Training Strategy* (what key steps are necessary to achieve the objectives?)
*   *Training Plans* (who must be trained in detail to realize the mission, achieve the training objectives and achieve the training strategy? And what/how/where/when and why will this training activity be carried out?)
*   *Training Budget* (what resources are required/available?)
*   *Training Policy/Procedures/Rules* (what are the boundaries?)

NOTE 3.2: TQM, RE-ENGINEERING AND ORGANIZATION DEVELOPMENT

As reference was made in this chapter to Total Quality Management (TQM), Re-engineering and Organization Development (OD), the following descriptions and reading lists are provided.

Total Quality Management (TQM)

For Bendell (1991) 'Total Quality Management is seen as primarily a management-led approach in which top management commitment is essential. The emphasis is on quality in all aspects and functions of the company operation, company wide, not just the manufacturing function or provision of a major service to the external end-user. Employee awareness and motivation are essential.'

Quality Gurus include: *Early American* – Deming, W. E.; Juran, J. M. ; Feigenbaum, A. V.; *Japanese* – Ishikawa, K.; Taguchi, G.; Shingo, S.; *New Western* – Crosby, P.; Peters, T.; Møller, C.

Business Re-engineering

According to Obolensky (1994) 'Business re-engineering is what an organization undertakes to change its internal processes and controls from a traditional vertical, functional hierarchy, to a horizontal cross functional, team based, flat structure which focuses on delighting customers.'

Organization Development (OD)

To Beckhard (1969), OD is defined as 'An effort planned, organization wide, and managed from the top, to increase organization effectiveness and health through planned interventions in the organization's processes using behaviourial-science knowledge.'

Readers will also see a much more detailed description of OD, with a reading list, in Chapter 10.

In 1981, March identified the death of OD and Smith raised a number of important shortcomings. In particular it was suggested that 'love and trust models' must be replaced with much more realistic concepts. OD is still practised, however, and practitioners have modified their approach.

TQM has gained its own momentum since the 1970s, and has proved itself as a company-wide tool for enhancing quality.

With its emphasis on improving 'processes' at all levels in the organization, re-engineering comes closest to stealing the clothes of OD.

In broad terms, TQM, re-engineering and OD, are all major tools for creating organizational change.

NOTE 3.3: LIST OF EXTERNAL AND INTERNAL INFLUENCES THAT CAN AFFECT TRAINING

External contextual influences

- Suppliers.
- Competitors.
- Marketing intermediaries (e.g. advertisers).
- Clients.
- Public agencies (e.g. press/financial community/government agencies/general public).
- Macroenvironment (demography/law/politics/technology/culture/economics).

Internal contextual influences/forces

As indicated by:

- Key historic organizational developments.
- Organizational heroes and villains.
- Organizational culture(s) and values.
- Organizational politics.
- Business mission, objectives, strategies, plans, policies and procedures.
- Organizational structures.

- Succession plans.
- Manpower plans.
- Non-compliance with job descriptions.
- Current training plans.
- Employee turnover records.
- Industrial tribunal records.
- Disciplinary/grievance records.
- Performance assessment records.
- Accident records.
- Health and safety records.
- Customer complaint records.
- Lack of flexibility.
- Levels of waste used.
- Delays caused by errors.
- Output records.
- Absenteeism records.
- Maintenance costs.
- Ineffective use of systems/procedures.
- Excessive hold-ups.
- Poor communications.
- Ignorance of policies/rules.
- Difficulty in mastering new jobs.
- Quality standards not met.
- Lack of interest in the job by staff.
- Not securing repeat business.

REFERENCES AND FURTHER READING

Training Cycle/trainer role

Campbell, A. and Tawadey, K. (1990) *Mission & Business Philosophy*. Oxford: Heinemann Professional Publishing Ltd.

Easterby-Smith, M. and Mackness, J. (1992) 'Completing the Cycle of Evaluation'. *Personnel Management 24, 5*, 42–45.

Garratt, B. (1989) *The Learning Organization*. London: Fontana.

Holden, L. and Vivian, Y. (1992) 'Does Strategic Training Policy Exist? Some Evidence from Ten European Countries'. *Personnel Review 21, 1*, 12–23.

Jones, A. M. and Hendry, C. (1992) *The Learning Organization: A Review of Literature and Practice*. London: The HRD Partnership.

Pedlar, M., Burgoyne, J. and Boydell, T. (1988) *The Learning Company Project*. Sheffield: Training Agency.

Pepper, A. D. (1992) *Managing the Training and Development Function*. Aldershot: Gower.

Taylor, S. (1992) 'Managing a Learning Environment'. *Personnel Management 24, 10*, 54–57.

Tharenou, P. (1991) 'Managers' Training Needs and Preferred Training Strategies'. *Journal of Management Development 10, 5*, 46–59.

Webb, S., Smith, A. and Townley, A. (1991) *Training Policy and the Boardroom*. London: Industrial Society (IS Training Survey 1).

Wood, S. (ed.) (1988) *Continuous Development: The Path to Improved Performance*. London: Institute of Personnel Management.

Total Quality Management (TQM)

Early American

Feigenbaum, A. V. (1993) *Total Quality Control*. New York: McGraw-Hill.

Juran, J. M. *et al.* (1980) *Quality Planning and Analysis: From Product Through Use*. New York: McGraw-Hill.

Walton, M. (1989) *The Deming Management Method*. London: Mercury Books.

Japanese

Bendell, T. *et al.* (eds) (1989) *Taguchi Methods: Application in World Industry*. Bedford: IFS Publications.

Ishikawa, K. (1995) *What is Total Quality Control? The Japanese Way*. UK: Prentice-Hall.

Shingo, S. (1986) *Zero Quality Control: Source Inspection and the Poka-Yoke System*, (trans). Cambridge, Mass.: Productivity Press.

New Western

Crosby, P. B. (1984) *Quality Without Tears*. New York: McGraw-Hill.

Møller, R. (1987) *Personal Quality*. Denmark: Time Management International A/S.

Peters, T. *et al.* (1982) *In Search of Excellence*. Harper & Row.

The Quality Gurus (1995) *Department of Trade & Industry*. DTI Publications. Tel: 0171-5100144.

Business Re-engineering

Burke, G. and Peppard, J. (1995) *Examining Business Process Re-engineering*. London: Kogan Page.

Colson-Thomas, C. (1992) *Transforming the Company*. London: Kogan Page.

Colson-Thomas, C. (ed.) (1994) *Business Process Re-engineering: Myth and Reality*. London: Kogan Page.

Hartle, F. (1995) *Re-engineering Your Performance Process*. London: Kogan Page.

Johansson, H. J. *et al.* (1995) *Business Process Re-engineering*. Chichester: John Wiley & Sons.

Obolensky, N. (1994) *Practical Business Process Re-engineering*. London: Kogan Page.

Oram, M. and Wellins, R. S. (1995) *Re-engineering's Missing Ingredient: The Human Factor*. London: Institute of Personnel & Development.

Spencer, L. M. Jr. (1995) *Re-engineering Human Resources*. New York: John Wiley & Sons Inc.

Organizational Development (OD)

See Chapter 10 for list of references.

March, P. (April 1981) *The Death of OD*. Organization Development Newsletter.

Smith, S. (February 1981) *Changing Views of OD*. Organization Development Newsletter.

4

Training – using the open system approach

INTRODUCTION

To view training as an open system can provide us with some very real insights into how to manage the training process. As will be shown in Chapter 5 it can prove useful when designing training initiatives and evaluating the results of training.

In this chapter we will see how we can conceive of resources needed for training as 'inputs' to the system of training. How we use these resources can be identified as the 'process' of training. When we examine what comes out from the training activity, we can identify not one, but three very distinct levels of results.

To evaluate the effectiveness of training, we can compare the actual result against the required result of training (also described as the 'performance or training gap', Chapter 2). The desired result of training can be referred to as the 'training objective', the experienced worker standard' or the 'required standard' to be achieved. When using TDLB terminology, the required result will be indicated by the achievement of 'performance criteria' which satisfy 'range indicators'.

As the effects of training (results) are discharged into the environment and as training needs (inputs) stem from the environment, we will recognize how vital the environment is to the interpretation and success of training activity. To make sense of this whole connected activity, we will see how 'linking to the environment' makes the difference between working in an open rather than a closed system.

INPUT/PROCESS/RESULT

As shown in Figure 4.1, the system of training is first described in terms of inputs, processes and results. Thus we get *means* (inputs – resources to be used – and processes – how inputs are managed) and *ends* (results at three levels: immediate results; intermediate results; and ultimate results).

If we now examine these components of training in more detail we have:

Means

Inputs

Inputs include training needs and all the resources that can be used to satisfy those needs:

- Identifier/Evaluator Trainer Role (identify training needs/evaluate effectiveness of previous training).
- Diagnostic Trainer Role (prepare training objectives).
- Designer/Planner Training Role (design/plan/obtain resources).

See the Training Cycle Window, p. 23.

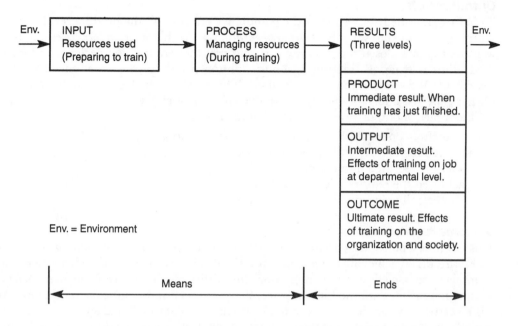

FIGURE 4.1 Showing the input, process and results in relation to training

Processes

Processes refer to how inputs are selected and managed:

- Implementor/Trainer Role (deliver training). See p. 23.
- How is the training method helping the learner to gain the required knowledge or skill?
- Is interaction between learners, trainer and others sought to enhance the learning. If not, why not?
- Is the learner to be consulted about if and how much the training experience is closing the 'training gap'?

Ends

Product results

These are immediate results or sum of the inputs and processes or when 'training has just finished'. Sometimes the results of training are assessed by comparing the differences between a pre- and post-test. Examples of product results include:

- The learner was trained to the 'experienced worker standard', within a training environment.
- The learner operated the system, within a training context.

Output results

These are intermediate results or the cumulative effect of all the product results when 'learning is applied to the job' at *departmental* level. At this stage we are assessing how well the training closed the 'training gap' and met the required job performance standard. This is what all training is about: training people to the experienced worker standard (EWS) or the 'required' standard. This is where the trainer can demonstrate his/her expertise and gain the support of management at all levels.

Examples of output results include that the learner:

- successfully operated the system within the work situation;
- achieved his/her departmental objectives:
  - sold the required number of products;
  - achieved the required departmental net profit;
  - successfully developed effective working relationships.

Outcome results

This is where a person's departmental performance or the total of the training effort has a direct result on achieving *organizational* ultimate objectives. It is also where there can be impacts on society, such as improving the quality of life for people in that society. Although outcomes are the highest prize, they are much more difficult to measure. At this level so many variables can be at work that singling out causes and effects can be near impossible. When, say, a company is charged with meeting a nationally recognized standard of quality, credit for achieving such a standard can go to the trainers, the system co-ordinators and everyone involved in the project. The fact that a newly trained manager helps to solve a problem for one of its clients, and two years later that client introduces more business to the organization is difficult to track and to claim it is a result of training.

Examples of outcome results include:

On the organization:

- the learner or learning group demonstrated that their efforts have contributed to achieving organizational objectives:
  - to reach the required quality standard;
  - to increase productivity per employee;
  - to obtain repeat customer business;
  - to increase organizational net profit.

On society:

- increased employment has reduced those receiving welfare benefits;
- reduced pollution levels (locally/nationally/internationally).

In addition to the effects of training on the organization and on society, the means and ends can also be examined *on the individual,* as shown in Note 4.1 on page 46.

In Note 4.2 (page 47) examples of how to use the Means/Ends Model strategically are shown.

MEASURING PERFORMANCE USING THE CONTROL FUNCTION

To measure performance, as shown in Figure 4.2, a person checks progress by comparing his/her 'actual' performance against 'required' performance. If some adjustment is needed, then corrective action will be taken, which will impact on the inputs or processes. Typically, a learner will ask the trainer questions, will practise some task longer

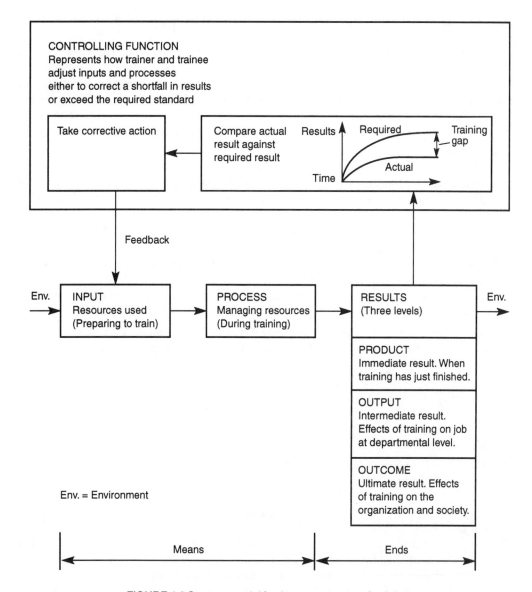

FIGURE 4.2 Systems model for the management of training

or will study harder to correct any shortfall in performance. For the trainer, it is his/her duty to encourage learners to continually monitor and correct their progress in this way. To not compare progress is to work within a closed system rather than an open one. In summary, only continued questioning, effort and openness will close training gaps.

Although people use the control function in the same way, what will vary is how 'actual' and 'required' performances are defined. A training need exists when the gap between 'actual' and 'required' performance (i.e. training gap), can be most economically matched by a training intervention. It is at this stage that the trainer needs to carefully interpret the description of 'actual' and 'required' performance by the learner and the learner's manager. Differences in the description of performance are not uncommon, and will require the trainer to use both sound analytic and social skills to determine the way forward.

When delivering training, the experienced trainer will continuously compare 'actual' and 'required' performance, and will make decisions and take action by adjusting the 'means' at his/her disposal. Failure to close the 'training gap' may be due, for example, to *inputs* (the learner's cultural preferences/emotional states/learning styles/previous learning experiences; the accuracy of the training needs analysis; the content of the training) or *processes* (the delivery of the training; the level of learner/trainer interaction).

FEEDBACK

While the term feedback is associated with normal two-way communication, it also has a specific meaning in systems terms. When adopting the specific meanings of feedback for training, we use such phrases as:

- *positive feedback*, which is where the *trainer* will confirm if the 'actual' level of learning is on course, to achieve the 'required' standard;
- *negative feedback*, which is where the *trainer* will ensure that 'actual' learning will progress at the same rate for all learners;
- *feeding forward*, which is where the *learner* will identify the 'required' (or future) learning requirements.

The above terms are fully explained in Notes 4.3, 4.4, 4.5 and 4.6 (see pages 48–53).

As shown in Figure 4.2, feedback is generally thought of as the vital mechanism that connects all the system activities. Without feedback (communication) any system will not receive new inputs or be kept updated, and must, by definition, be closed rather than open.

The idea that there is such a thing as feed forward as well as feedback reminds us that we are dealing with human systems.

THE ENVIRONMENT

The difference between an open and a closed system is that a closed system is not exposed to the forces of the environment, whereas an open system is.

In the sense that all inputs come from the environment, some will be *known* inputs (training facilities), *partly known* inputs (learners) and some will be *unknown* inputs (a training need only brought to light when training is underlaid). The trainer attempts to limit major disturbances to the training event due to partly unknown and unknown inputs. As part of the Training Needs Analysis and design of a training event, the experienced trainer reduces 'unknowns' to a minimum by asking:

1 The learner:

- What are the learner's suggestions for closing the 'training gap'?
- What are the learner's expectations?
- Does the learner see training as a punishment rather than as an investment in the learner's development and career?

2 The learner's immediate line manager:

- How does the learner's line manager view the need for training?
- What results does the line manager expect to emerge immediately or later?
- How will the manager help the learner to apply the new knowledge, skills and attitudes to the work situation?
- What training methods should be used, according to the line manager, and why?

3 The trainer:

- Will a thorough Training Needs Analysis be undertaken?
- Will the learner's actual and required performance be identified and agreed with the learner's line manager?
- How can the learner transfer his/her learning to the workplace?
- Will the trainer identify the results required and stipulate how the results of training will be measured?

4 People external to the organization:

- How will the following external factors affect the design of the training programme:
  - competitors;
  - customers;
  - suppliers;
  - retailers for organization;
  - political system;
  - people and groups in society?

The importance of the environment

If the trainer operated with little reference to the environment, the trainer could be said to be functioning in a relatively closed manner. Whereas the design of a computer program or a filing system is designed largely as a closed loop, people by contrast are forever interacting, changing and reviewing their options. In this sense, for training to be effective, it must remain open and responsive to the factors that are shaping successful performance. The importance of the environment for the trainer is that:

- inputs are derived from it;
- the results of training are discharged into it and training effectiveness is assessed by it (when *applied* to the job and *transferred* to ever new situations);
- the perceived reality of it, with its work-related demands, constraints and choices (see Chapter 8), will remain with the learner throughout the learning experience, and will act as a benchmark by which most things will be compared;
- if interpreted correctly, the environment can be used to assist the development of learners and resolve their difficulties;
- it helps to focus on the impact of outcomes for the organization, which are critical for success, and beyond this it helps to focus on the outcomes for society;
- it can be used as a friend if consulted, or be experienced as a foe if not.

SUMMARY

We discovered that the open system model can mirror the management of training activity.

Foremost, we discovered that the open system model is very useful for stimulating our strategic and operational thinking. For example, to discuss training in terms of means (inputs and processes) and ends (results), can provoke debate and challenge perceptions about what training is appropriate and how it can be effectively delivered.

The open systems view of training indicated that we can consider such components as:

- *inputs:* resources needed;
- *processes:* how inputs need to be managed;

- *product results:* the immediate results or when training has just finished;
- *output results:* the intermediate results or when applying new skills and knowledge to the work situation;
- *outcome results:* the ultimate results or the total effect of the learner's contribution to satisfy organizational objectives;
- *performance measurement:* describes how comparison between 'actual' and 'required' performance (the *training gap*) can be understood via the *control function* which regulates:
  - *positive feedback:* a mechanism for assessing that progress is on course, as the learner approaches the 'required' standard;
  - *negative feedback:* sometimes employed by trainers to keep all learners moving at the same pace, but which, if used inappropriately, may be indicative of poor training needs analysis, poor training design and/or delivery difficulties;
  - *feeding forward* where, for example, the learner reviews the 'training gap' and re-sets or confirms the 'required' standard (EWS/training objective) to be achieved;
- *the environment:* which can be seen to influence both the beginning and end of training, and which must never be ignored.

For the trainer, this methodology is a very useful tool for the trainer's kit bag. Such methodology has limitless applications, and can be used to explain how training activity is connected, and can be used as part of work-related problem-solving with line management. See also Chapter 8.

The value of adopting a systems approach is in the useful questioning that such a model induces. If, for example, the learner's line manager is ignored when training plans are prepared, this could have a detrimental impact on the trainer and the credibility of the training function. If we know the line manager expects some tangible practical result to occur, the trainer may be able to integrate on-job project work into the programme.

Contingency plans. From the mode of questioning that comes from carrying out a Training Needs Analysis, the trainer will be in a position to prepare contingency plans where appropriate. Sometimes a trainer can try out or pilot a training programme and 'iron out' the bits that do not work well. Even under these circumstances, experienced trainers will have contingencies for training different learning groups, and for exploiting different learning opportunities.

See also Note 4.6 (page 53) which discusses learning and the idea of feeding back and feeding forward.

NOTE 4.1: EXAMPLES OF INPUT/PROCESS/RESULTS ON THE INDIVIDUAL

When analysing inputs, processes and results, the examples below remind us that as well as the effects of vocational training on the organization and society, personal objectives can also be examined in this way.

Example 1: Individual desires new job
Means
- *Input.* Person desires to improve career prospects.
- *Process.* Person studies appropriate course.

Ends

- *Product result*. Person passes examination.
- *Output result*. Person obtains certificate or graduates.
- *Outcome result*. Person improves career prospects.

Example 2: Individual desires new job

If we take the next step with the individual we get:

Means

- *Input*. Person has desire for new job.
- *Process*. Person job searches vigorously.

Ends

- *Product result*. Person granted job interview.
- *Output result*. Person receives and accepts job offer.
- *Outcome result*. Person enjoys new job challenges and better quality of life.

Example 3: Individual fitness

If the individual then went on to improve their fitness, we get:

Means

- *Input*. Person desires to improve their fitness.
- *Process*. Person follows keep-fit programme.

Ends

- *Product result*. Person masters keep-fit programme.
- *Output result*. Person develops strong muscles, loses or gains weight or improves their stamina.

Outcome results

on the individual:

- person achieves their desired level of fitness;
- improves their quality of life;
- enhances their self-confidence.

on society:

- person helps others to seek fitness;
- person's relationships with others have led to improved quality of life.

NOTE 4.2: USING THE MEANS/ENDS MODEL STRATEGICALLY

The effect of the systems approach has prompted us to ask useful questions. By extending the analysis, we can begin to provide a guide to the design of training initiatives. The following examples indicate how the Means/Ends Model can be used in a strategic sense.

Example 1: Train or recruit

How can supervisors improve their budgetary preparation and control skills?

Question A: Examine the means (inputs and processes)

Why don't we design and provide training events within a training environment?
Why don't we train supervisors in their job environment?

Question B: Examine the ends (results required)

Why don't we from now on recruit supervisors who are already experienced, and thus reduce future training expenditure?

Question C: Examine means and ends

Why don't we provide line management with training resources and direct them to close the training gap by whatever means appropriate?

Example 2: Traditional job description (means) versus key results (ends)

When examining how well a person performs in the job, we can either look at the inputs (means) and describe what is to be done, or we can identify the results required in the job (ends). In this case the 'traditional job description' lists inputs (means) and the 'key result job description' defines a range of results (ends). As a matter of interest, the key result job description is today widely used, and the traditional approach has mostly been discarded as a tool for performance assessment.

Example 3: Competences (means or ends?)

Although there is some debate about it, the MCI, NVQ and TDLB competency programmes are said to be 'results-led'. That is, they focus on what is performed (ends). This is because Knowledge (K) + Skills (S) + Experience (E) can be quantified. For the Management Charter Initiative (MCI), as shown in Appendix 2, Competence = K + S + E + Personal Qualities (PQs). This is where PQs reflect personality and ability to act decisively. In this sense PQs are both the 'means' and 'ends', as they 'carry' and 'integrate' performance, from desire to learn (input/means) to transferring performance to any situation (outcome/ends). Competences then, are not just measuring results, they are most importantly reflecting 'processes of behaviour' or 'means'.

The benefit of examining means and ends from a strategic or 'helicopter stance' is to enable us to interrogate our overview. Such fundamental questioning, although not meant to be provocative for its own sake, can address cherished assumptions and prejudices.

NOTE 4.3: POSITIVE FEEDBACK

A mechanism for assessing if the 'actual' level of learning is on course, as the learner approaches the 'required' standard. See Figure 4.3.

Using an engineering example, positive feedback acts in the same direction as the measured deviation. The braking system of, say, a motor vehicle provides positive feedback: the harder the brake pedal is pushed, the harder the brakes are locked. For a sales manager, the increase in sales may reflect the increase in advertising expenditure, with the result that advertising may be increased again to achieve higher sales.

Positive feedback in a training context is about assessing whether training is on course during the training process, where the objective is to make the training as effective as possible, and where learner comments can be favourable and/or unfavourable. Positive feedback is a mechanism for assessing that progress is on course, as the learner approaches the 'required' standard. Assessment can be carried out using questionnaires, interviews and observation techniques.

A potential danger of positive feedback involves learners wanting to go beyond the 'required' (EWS) objectives. While in some cases training at a higher level may be permissible, the trainer and the learners may not have properly prepared themselves for an 'extension'. In this case, the trainer must *always* review the situation carefully and only proceed with great care. If further learning proved too difficult, for example, not only could the trainer risk undermining the learner's sense of achievement and confidence,

POSITIVE FEEDBACK (Is 'actual' level of learning on course?)

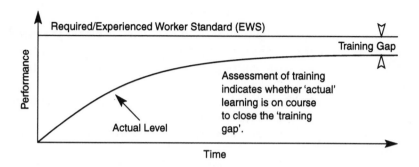

NEGATIVE FEEDBACK (Trainer controls progress of all learners.)
Used to keep all learners at the same stage on the learning curve.

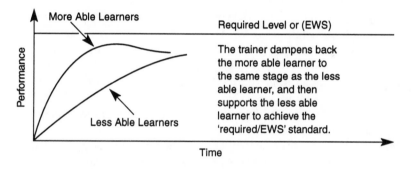

FEEDINGFORWARD (Learner identifies the 'required' level of
learning for future training.)

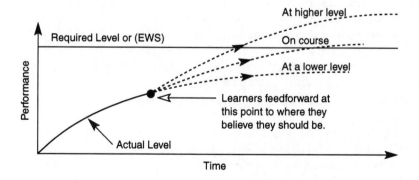

FIGURE 4.3 Showing positive feedback, negative feedback and feedingforward

the trainer could be said to have broken his/her 'contract of learning'. If the training proved dangerous (on an Outward Bound course, for example, or using machinery), the trainer could be subject to penalties imposed by a country's legislation on such matters.

Example

When seeking positive feedback, the trainer seeks to confirm whether the 'actual' level of learning is on course. The learner says, for example:

1 'I like this training but I wish the trainer would move the material along faster', which means:
   • 'I want more training' (thus indicating training is on course which is positive feedback, and there is high demand for training);
   • 'Please change the way the training is delivered' (so an adjustment in delivery is required).
2 'This training is not matching my training need'. The learner may be saying: 'Let us examine the "mismatch" and resolve it' (thus indicating training is not on course, which is positive feedback.

NOTE 4.4: NEGATIVE FEEDBACK

This is where the trainer will ensure that 'actual' learning will progress at the same rate for all learners. See Figure 4.3.

Using the engineering analogy, negative feedback dampens and reduces fluctuations around a norm or standard. When, for example, production levels are above plan, negative feedback signals that inputs, such as the number of operators, may need to be reduced. Stock control systems can be explained as operating around a preferred standard. If too much stock is present, the negative feedback will dampen the fluctuation to the planned stock level.

For training, the 'norm' is the 'actual' level of learning of the less able learner. In this case, the trainer ensures that all learners progress at the same rate. When applied to a group of learners, this means that the more able learners are held back (their efforts are dampened) for the sake of the less able. Needless to say, the more able become frustrated, and the less able can sometimes be made to feel guilty because they have a learning need! Although many readers will recognize this approach as traditional teacher-centred learning, it does, nonetheless, still have a part to play when training mixed ability groups or when training for critical procedures. The trick, perhaps, is to involve everyone in the learning process rather than alienate sub-groups. When self-paced learning technologies are not available, and when the need is to train learners who possess a mix of learning abilities, some options may include:

• Train the whole group a step at a time, and empower the more able learners to assist the less able.
• Use the learning difficulties as a learning experience in themselves for all to share.
• Train in smaller groups where individual learning speeds may be similar.
• Build-in frequent evaluation and summaries of key points.

Negative feedback differs from positive feedback in that:

• *negative feedback* is governed by the trainer; that is, the trainer dampens the rate of learning of the more able learners in order to keep pace with less able performers, but when used inappropriately, the use of such feedback may indicate faulty Training Needs Analysis and/or delivery;

* *positive feedback* is a mechanism, used by the trainer, for assessing training during the training process, and will confirm if the 'actual' level of learning is on course.

Contrary to popular usage of the terms, positive feedback is not about favourable comment, and negative feedback is not about unfavourable comment.

NOTE 4.5: FEEDING FORWARD

This is where the learner identifies the 'required' (or future) level of learning. See Figure 4.3.

With liquid industrial processes, any deviation from the 'required' standard from one treatment to the next can be fed forward. This means that adjustments can be made 'up-the-line', in advance of the faulty chemical batch entering the system.

Feeding forward

In addition to positive feedback (reporting on what 'has happened'), it is also possible for the learner to feed forward information about learning that 'is required', before and during training and development activities. Examples of learners feeding forward include:

* learners identifying their 'expectations' (future);
* learners identifying 'how well' the training programme will match the learner's training needs, based on experience to date (future);
* learners identifying how back home 'job requirements' are likely to be satisfied (future).

The results of the feed forward information will enable any corrections to the training programme to be made, and also the learner's expectations to be addressed forthwith (and any mismatch be dealt with immediately).

Feed forward questions

When training, learners can be encouraged to ask such 'feed forward questions' as:

Before training:

* Will the content of this training satisfy my training and job needs? (Evaluating all stages of Figure 4.1.)

During training:

* Will the quality and content of the training which I am experiencing, continue to satisfy my training and job needs? (Evaluating training during the *process* stage.)

After training:

* Will the learning that I have received (i.e. training has just finished) equip me better to do my job? (Evaluating training at the *product* stage.)

At work:

* Will I be able to *apply* this learning to my work situation? (Evaluating at the *output* stage.)
* Will I be able to *transfer* this learning to any new work situation? (Evaluating at the *outcome* stage.)

If there are shortfalls in closing the training gap, is this because the learner:

- Is not satisfying his/her social needs to interact with others?
- Is experiencing poor delivery of the training?
- Considers the content of training is not appropriate?
- Has no opportunity to benchmark his/her progress and observations against other learners?
- Maintains that accommodation, meals and the learning environment are of a poor standard?
- Has failed to correctly identify his/her training needs?

Is it, on the other hand, because the trainer has failed to correctly identify training needs, or failed to prepare the learner for training? When in the work situation, is it because the learner's manager has failed to provide 'application' opportunities?

As shown above, feeding forward, as well as positive feedback, can be used as part of training design and as a proactive evaluation process.

Example 1: Problem-solving

This technique can also be used when problem-solving. When, for example, a team was experiencing some communication difficulties, the input/process/results model was used. As the 'outcomes' in any system are critical for future survival and success, the team asked '*How* is it possible to achieve the outcomes?' By feeding forward what had to be achieved (i.e. to gain repeat business, the ultimate result or *outcome*), the team then worked backwards to find solutions at each stage of the model. One solution was to communicate customer needs faster to production planning. To do this involved creating a desire to plan better (changing the *input* stage) and activating a system of planning (improving the *process* stage).

Example 2: Decision points

As well as examining each stage of the input/process/results in detail, Frank Dick (former British Athletics Coach) also used the idea of feed forwarding in terms of 'decision points'. When, for example, planning for the selection of coaches and athletes for tournaments he would ask himself such questions as:

- Where will the tournaments be held?
- What will the climate and conditions be like?
- Will our athletes be able to function well under these conditions? If not, what must we do?
- How old will our athletes be?
- How old will the competitors be?
- Do we need to start coaching our keenest youngest athletes now, so that, in five or ten years' time they will be in their prime condition?
- What do we need to do, to be successful at the tournament after the one we are currently planning for?
- Which of our coaches will be best suited to the various tasks?
- Do we need to better develop our coaches?

By feeding forward how things are likely to be, Frank Dick would then work backwards to match what was necessary for success.

Example 3: Appraisal

When, during appraisal, the appraiser asks the appraisee to consider where they see themselves in one, two, three, four or five years' time, the appraiser is using the feed forward technique. To complete the process, however, the next stage is to examine how the future can be achieved.

Example 4: Setting objectives

When preparing objectives for any situation, the technique of feeding forward is employed. In the case of business planning, for example, the 'How do we get there?' is achieved by preparing a *strategy* (main steps), followed by preparation of *plans* that link each strategic step together.

NOTE 4.6: SELF-PACED LEARNING

While it does not follow that a group of learners have to share similar learning abilities, the positive feedback of a learning group (en-mass), is more likely to occur when this is the case. This is why, in the main, trainers select learners who share similar learning experiences and patterns, when engaged in traditional trainer-led activity. When assessing whether learning is on course with a mixed ability learning group, the *positive feedback* and *feeding forward* response will indicate that members learn at different rates. And without extra trainers, the task of trying to satisfy the various needs will be near impossible. It is under these circumstances, in fact, that *negative feedback* is employed, and exercised as creatively as possible.

To confront the fact that we each do learn at different rates, one answer is 'self-paced' learning. Such learning can be undertaken using computer-based learning, programmed learning texts and guided self-development, for example. From their books and courses Majer and Pipe satisfied self-paced learning through the use of what they call Criterion Referenced Instruction (CRI). Here the learner studies a subject (text/video/role play/conversation), carries out a test with criteria to achieve, and undertakes self-evaluation when complete. A facilitator is available if anyone gets stuck, and monitors the results of the test and the self-evaluation. A typical CRI course could have many tests and self-evaluations, and the learner will likely need a course map to guide progress. When finished, the idea is that the learner goes back to work, goes home or carries out private study. The drawback of CRI and other programmable methods is the cost of preparing and validating such materials. What all the above individual self-paced learning methods have in common is that the learner is in control of his/her learning, and they all recognize the power of positive feedback to drive the learner towards his/her learning goals.

Accelerated learning

As a further support to the idea of positive feedback and in contrast to the dampening effect of negative feedback, 'accelerated learning' focuses on individual learning potential. Accelerated learning suggests that we can learn far more effectively than we do. See Buzan (1974, 1977a, 1977b), Rose (1985) and Brown (1977).

REFERENCES AND FURTHER READING
Basic

For introduction to ideas about management information systems.
Lucey, T. (1981) *Management Information Systems*. Winchester: D.P. Publications.
For introduction to systems of solving problems.
Kaufman, R. (1979) *Identifying and Solving Problems: A System Approach*, 2nd edn. San Diego: University Associates, Inc.

Advanced

For example of a management systems problem-solving technique.
Checkland, P. (1981) *Systems Thinking, Systems Practice*. Chichester: John Wiley & Sons.
Application of systems ideas to engineering/management problem.
Jenkins, G. M. (1969) 'The Systems Approach', *Journal of Systems Engineering*, (Autumn) *1, 1*, 3–49.

Various writers on systems

Edited by Open Systems Group (1987) *Systems Behaviour*, 3rd edn. London: Harper & Row.
Schoderbek, C. G., Schoderbek, P. P. and Kefalas, G. A. (1980) *Management Systems: Conceptual Considerations*. Dallas: Business Publications, Inc.

Majer and Pipe/Criterion Referenced Instruction (CRI)

Majer, R. F. and Pipe, P. (1970) *Analyzing Performance Problems*. CA: Fearon Publishers, 6 Davis Drive, Belmont.
Majer, R. F. and Pipe, P. (1975) *Preparing Instructional Objectives* (2nd Ed.) CA: Fearon Publishers, 6 Davis Drive, Belmont.
Majer, R. F. (1979) *Applied CRI*. CA: Available from Majer Associates Inc. 13245 Rhoda Drive, Los Altos Hills.

Accelerated learning

Brown, M. E. (1977) *Memory Matters*. Canada: David & Charles.
Buzan, T. (1974) *Use Your Head*. London: BBC Publications.
Buzan, T. (1977a) *Speed Memory*. Canada: David & Charles.
Buzan, T. (1977b) *Speed Reading*. Canada: David & Charles.
Rose, C. (1985) *Accelerated Learning*. Buckinghamshire: Topaz Publishing Ltd.

5

Design and evaluation of training

INTRODUCTION: INITIAL DESIGN AND EVALUATION CONSIDERATIONS

Based on discussions with experienced trainers, all agree that there are a number of considerations that must be made when designing and evaluating training. Experienced trainers will argue, for example, that there may not be a single evaluation method that will be adequate for the assessment of training effectiveness. Whereas then the experienced trainer will build in a number of evaluation methods when designing the training, a less experienced trainer may not.

Another consideration is the extent to which evaluation can enhance management commitment to training. Again, the experienced trainer will, from the outset, ensure that management will, at least, be informed about the effectiveness of training, and where possible will be directly involved in setting and measuring training standards achieved. By comparison, the less experienced trainer may not see how management involvement can lead to the very necessary management support.

It is examples like those above that form part of the necessary preparations for designing training interventions and selecting training methods. Further examples can be found in Note 5.1, page 61.

TRAINING DESIGN AND EVALUATION: SOME DESCRIPTIONS

Training design also involves identifying what it is that can be evaluated. One is simply the mirror of the other. Although the design stage embraces evaluation, they represent two different activities and are separated by time. A description of 'training design' and 'evaluation' is given below.

Training design

For a micro view, training design will focus on Stage 3 of the Training Cycle, p. 23. For a macro view (broad initial considerations), training design can embrace all stages of the Training Cycle (i.e. how will we identify training needs, prepare training objectives, decide learning methods and deliver the training activity?).

Evaluation

The process of assessing training in terms of:

- achieving its laid-down objectives;
- costs and benefits (direct, indirect, social, financial).

It can be directed at any part of training activity (inputs), delivery (processes) and subsequent performance (results), and can be applied to the total training operation. Also see Chapter 4.

Unplanned learning

While it is important to design training activities to meet learning needs, it is possible for significant learning to occur which has not been planned. Such learning may be the result of interaction with others, or the learner may be awakened in some way. It is not uncommon, for example, for unplanned training to have a positive effect on departmental climate and/or organizational culture. That unplanned changes will happen means that, as far as is practical, such change should be considered when designing the training and evaluation material. Whether the changes are desirable or not, better training will result if evaluation instruments are in place, and not added as it suits.

Micro and macro evaluation

Training design and evaluation can be carried out at a micro and macro level. At the *micro* level, evaluation would take the form of pre- and post-questionnaires and learner comments, for example. At the *macro* level, evaluation can take the shape of an Evaluation Audit. This will examine what was done with evaluation information each time a training event was held. In addition, it will assess how well the training operation itself was managed, compared against its own brief, all training activity and indirect results.

Training Cycle

An interesting feature of the Training Cycle (Stage 1: Training Needs; Stage 2: Training Objectives; Stage 3: Planning; Stage 4: Implementing Training), is that it can be used to evaluate individual training courses and programmes at the (micro) level of training and also to evaluate the training function itself at the (macro) level of training.

Assessment of training effectiveness

A description which is interchangeable with Evaluation is Assessment of Training Effectiveness. This description is commonly used and is used throughout this book.

THE OPEN SYSTEMS DESIGN/EVALUATION MODEL

Based on our understanding of the previous chapter, we will see how the 'open systems approach' can again be adopted to make ready sense of the five stages of design and evaluation, as shown in Figure 5.1, and described as:

- Input Design/Evaluation.
- Process Design/Evaluation.
- Product Design/Evaluation.
- Output Design/Evaluation.
- Outcome Design/Evaluation.

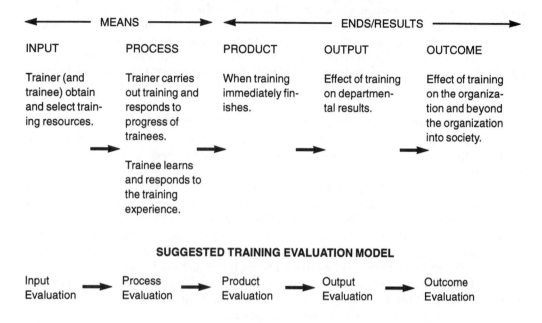

FIGURE 5.1 Training and evaluation model

Input design and evaluation (Identify training needs, prepare objectives, devise and organize programme)

Both design and evaluation at this stage are concerned with *what* and *how* information is obtained, and with understanding the factors that influence the training need. Questions that can be asked at this stage may include:

- How did the need for training arise?
- Has the trainer the right level of expertise?
- Is the trainee willing to learn?
- Will the departmental climate and the organizational culture support or not support changes in behaviour as a result of training?
- Is the training remedial, maintenance or development?
- What are the areas of learning? Is it knowledge, affective or psychomotor for example? (See Appendix 8.)

For a more comprehensive list of questions see Note 5.2, page 63.

Process design and evaluation (How resources and expertise are being used and deployed)

This concerns:

- whether the ongoing training event is achieving its specified objectives;
- how training resources are being used;
- how well training is being delivered;
- whether the learner is finding the experience useful.

Training design and evaluation can take the form of ongoing formal and informal review sessions. At this stage, evaluation is focused on the reactions of learners in terms of their attitude, feelings, liking for the experience and factual observations. This can include, for example, group discussions, formal tests and informal over-the-bar conversations. The objective of such activity is to determine the effectiveness of training as it is taking place and to implement design improvements, if so needed. Questions that can be asked at this stage can be found in Note 5.3 (see page 65).

Product design and evaluation (When training is just finished)

This involves designing evaluation instruments to determine how well the 'training gap' has been closed, and using these results to evaluate what has been learnt when training has just finished.

Product Evaluation will record the learner's 'reaction', and will measure changes in knowledge, skill and attitudes, for example, as soon as a training event has been completed and before the learner leaves the training situation.

Evaluation will measure changes in learning compared against the learning objectives. This is where the learning objective reflects the 'required' performance to be achieved. Examples of evaluation instruments are listed in Note 5.4 (see page 66).

Not forgetting the definition of evaluation, notice will also be given to detecting indirect learning. This, for example, can be allowed for in open-style questionnaires and recorded as part of discussion and written comments.

If only the learner's 'reactions' are sought at this stage, the danger is that either very 'happy' or 'sad' responses may be recorded. The 'halo-effect' which reflects last-minute good feelings rather than an overall reaction is well known. Depending on the people involved, end-of-course reviews can be influenced by social considerations. Shall I, for example, score high and feel able to walk away with a smile, or shall I score as I feel, and risk having to explain myself? Where possible, such learner reactions as these need to be considered as part of design.

Another factor that can mislead the trainer with high scoring is known as the 'Hawthorne effect'. This can heighten motivation when a person or group feel they are singled out for special attention.

Output design and evaluation (Job performance)

Here, training design will be aimed at deciding how to measure the application of learning from training to job performance. For example (using feed forward questions, see Chapter 4): Will learning take place to the 'required' job performance standard and if not, why not? If not:

- Will it be because the learner lacked confidence?
- Will it be because the line manager failed to assist with providing adequate opportunities for applying the new skills?
- Will it be because the line manager was not briefed as to his/her facilitator role?

As well as design questions, the reader can see that they pose evaluation responses as well.

In addition to achieving the training objectives, the learner may have agreed with his/her manager other results. For example, the learner may be eager to apply his/her learning in some specific way to the job. Such on-job objectives could be part of the 'training contract' and part of evaluation, if so agreed. On the other hand, such on-job benefits may be classified as 'indirect' results if they were not part of the training activity. In short, Output Evaluation measures how well learning has been applied to the job, and also how well on-job objectives have been achieved either directly as part of training, or indirectly as a consequence of it. For a list of measures to evaluate the impact of training at the workplace, see Note 5.5, page 66.

Outcome design and evaluation (Impact on organizational performance and benefits to society)

When evaluating results at this stage, it is the cumulative effect of all output results on the organization and society that can be assessed.

At this ultimate level of performance, it is recognized that cause and effect may not be easily trackable, and there may be a high level of performance complexity which is impossible to dissect. If, for example, quality standards are improved via a planned training programme, a direct link can be made to the training effort. If, on the other hand, organizational sales and profit margins increased:

- Was this due to the newly trained sales teams?
- Was this due to the fact that the managing director recently visited the client company?
- Was this due to the factors inside the client's organization of which little may be known?

Is there, in short, a direct (training) or indirect (director) link or was it due to chance (client factors)? Because so many people inside and outside the organization can influence organizational results, and because so much of the cause–effect picture is unknowable, there can sometimes be a genuine problem for evaluation at the Outcome level.

Examples of what can be measured may be similar to departmental measures, but will occur at a higher organizational level and beyond this into society. Such (direct and indirect) changes can occur, for example, at the organization level with increased repeat business, and within society, with more people contributing to society.

For an extended list of ultimate results, see Note 5.6, page 66.

TRAINING DESIGN CRITERIA

An assumption that many designers of training activities make, is to strive for training which is 'general, accurate and simple'. Although felt by many to be intuitively correct, the fact is that only two of the three design elements are possible to achieve. If designers want to achieve 'Generality' and 'Accuracy', then the third ingredient will be 'Complexity' and not 'Simplicity'. See Note 5.8, page 67, for more discussion of the four design possibilities. The topic is also briefly mentioned in Appendix 2, page 219.

EVALUATION MODELS

As we compare the five evaluation models (Figure 5.2: Warr, 1970; DoE, 1981; Hamblin, 1974; Kirkpatrick, 1974; Suchman, 1967), against the five-stage Training Design and the Training Evaluation Models, we notice considerable similarities. For the discerning reader, the search for the differences between these models will provide some useful insights.

Nearly all the writers above agree that it is useful to evaluate:

TRAINING	DESIGN	MODEL		
MEANS		ENDS/RESULTS		
INPUT Preparing to train	PROCESS During training	PRODUCT When training has just finished	OUTCOME Effect of training on job at departmental level	OUTCOME Effect of training on job at organizational level and beyond into society

TRAINING	EVALUATION	MODEL		
Input Evaluation	Process Evaluation	Product Evaluation	Output Evaluation	Outcome Evaluation

OTHER EVALUATION MODELS

Warr (1970)	CIRO	EVALUATION	METHOD	
Context Input	Reaction	Immediate	Intermediate	Ultimate

DoE framework (1981)				
	Internal validation	External validation		

△   △   Evaluation   △   △   △

Involves determining direct, indirect, social and financial costs and benefits

Hamblin (1974)				
	Reaction	Learning	Job Behaviour	Organization Ultimate

Kirkpatrick (1974)				
	Reaction	Learning	Behaviour	Results

Suchman (1967)				
		Immediate	Intermediate	Ultimate

FIGURE 5.2 Training and evaluation model compared against other evaluation models

- how well the Training Needs Analysis was carried out (or *inputs*);
- the learner's reaction during training and immediately it finishes (or *processes*);
- what has been learnt after the training finishes, and called here immediate results (or *products*);
- how well the learner has applied the learning to the job, sometimes referred to as job behaviour, and called here intermediate results (or *outputs*);
- how the effects of training may have contributed to improving organizational performance, and called here ultimate results (or *outcomes*).

Beyond organizational performance, is the impact that the organization can have on the community and the environment. For many organizations, evaluation may also embrace the effect training can have on society. See also Note 5.7 (page 67) for further discussion of evaluation methods.

SUMMARY

The terms Training Design, Evaluation and Assessment of Training Effectiveness were described, and it was considered how design and evaluation could be thought of as mirror activities. Although design comes first, the later evaluation processes should be considered at the design stage. Although separate activities, the results of the evaluation can be used to improve the design of training in the present and at a later stage.

The Systems Design/Evaluation Model, Figure 5.1, is based on the open systems concept and comprises:

- *Input design/evaluation* (How training activity is designed.)
- *Process design/evaluation* (How resources are being used.)
- *Product design/evaluation* (When training just finishes.)
- *Output design/evaluation* (How training contributes to job performance.)
- *Outcome design/evaluation* (How training contributes to organizational performance and how it benefits society.)

At each stage in the Systems Design/Evaluation Model, examples were given of the type of analysis undertaken, type of design criteria sought, type of evaluation instruments used and type of results examined.

It was noted that design, evaluation and the Training Cycle can be understood at the micro and macro level.

In Figure 5.2, five evaluation frameworks were compared against the Suggested Systems Design/Evaluation Model. Based on this comparison, the Systems Design/ Evaluation Model appears to act as a unifying structure for these frameworks, and provides a focus for the synthesis of ideas regarding design and evaluation activity.

NOTE 5.1: SOME CONSIDERATIONS WHEN DESIGNING TRAINING ACTIVITIES
Continuous process

To be effective, evaluation must be designed as part of a continuous learning process.

Working alliance

To be successful, evaluation must be designed to include a working alliance between trainer, learner and management. For co-operation to be forthcoming, each person must be fully aware of the objectives of the training intervention. Dissatisfaction, due to a failure to brief the learner, could impair the learning process, and thus impede the intended change in behaviour.

No single evaluation method

No single evaluation method may be adequate for the total assessment of training.

Specific, not general

Evaluation needs to be specific, not general, if it is to be of help to improving later activities.

Help trainer

Evaluation is not only designed to assess training and its effects, it is a means of helping the trainer to assess his/her skills and performance.

Avoid grapevine communication

Evaluation overcomes the dangers inherent in grapevine communication.

Management support

When evaluation can demonstrate that it is making a real contribution to achieving departmental and/or organizational objectives, management support for training will become a near-automatic response.

Sometimes costly

Training programmes are so diverse in type and use, that preparation of new evaluation methods can be a costly activity.

Can infer a direct or indirect threat

Since evaluation attempts to measure the degree of change, it can infer a direct or indirect threat to anyone who is being assessed. It is such considerations as these that argue for effective design of evaluation instruments. This is where just 'bolting on' an evaluation tool could generate hostility to an otherwise successful training event.

Open system

Evaluation confers on training the quality of an 'open system' rather than a closed one.

Positive feeding back and feeding forward

As shown in Chapter 4, evaluation makes use of both positive feedback and feeding forward. *Positive feedback* assesses whether the 'actual' level of learning during training is on course, or how well at the end of training, the training objectives have been met. *Feeding forward* asks the learner to identify expectations (future focused), assesses how well the training programme will match the learner's actual or perceived training objectives (future focused), and assesses how well job requirements are likely to be satisfied (future focused).

NOTE 5.2: QUESTIONS FOR EVALUATING 'INPUTS' TO TRAINING
Training need
- How did the need for training arise?
- What information needs to be collected?
  - Business, manpower and succession plans?
  - Work-related records and reports?
  - Results from assessment centre/psychological instruments?
- What training analysis techniques can be used? (See Chapter 10.)
  - Questioning and listening techniques?
  - Task/job analysis?
  - Work samples?
  - Diary method?
  - Survey technique?
  - Critical incidents?
- What instruments are needed for evaluation?
  - Pre- and post-knowledge tests?
  - Skill performance test?
  - Attitude survey?
  - Fact-finding questionnaire?

Trainer
- Has she/he the right level of expertise?
- Will his/her personality be appropriate?
- Has she/he the motivation to succeed?

Learner
- Is the person willing to learn?
- What match is required between the training material and the learner's intellectual level, background and experience?
- What is the learner's preferred style of learning? (See Chapter 7 and page 161.)
  - Is the learner action-focused and so prefers practical exercises?
  - Is the learner system-driven and prefers a structured exercise?
  - Is the learner team-orientated and so prefers a discussion exercise?
  - Is the learner individualistic and so prefers self-development activity?

Organization
- Will the departmental climate and the organizational culture support or not support changes in behaviour as a result of training?
- Will the range of management styles indicate a range of preferred training methods? For example, will action-orientated training fit easily with conservative bureaucratic management styles?

Content
- Will the subject matter indicate if knowledge and/or skill acquisition and/or attitude change is required? When addressing 'customer service', for example, will training need to address changing the attitudes of learners? And if so, will this prove more challenging than imparting knowledge and skill?

- Will the subject matter suggest what training methods should be used to deliver and apply it? For 'selection interviewing', for example, will the learner need to practise the interviewing process?
- Will the subject matter indicate how the training material can be scheduled? For the 'disciplinary interview', for example, training might follow recognized disciplinary stages.

Nature of training need

The design of a training intervention can vary depending on the nature of the training need. For example, the nature of the training need could reflect a *remedial* situation, where things have gone wrong; a *maintenance* situation, where updating of skills is required; or a *development* situation, where it is felt that the individual, team or organization will benefit from acquiring and practising new skills within the context of work. In turn, this will either shift performance to a higher level, or will contribute to a more rounded outlook and approach, and hence contribute to long-term effectiveness.

This is where *remedial* training may need to be highly structured and intense; *maintenance* training may be directed at building upon existing skills; and *development* may be aimed at integrating and building upon various skills in the work situation.

Focus of training

Is training focused on:

- the individual;
- relationships;
- the group/team;
- inter-group processes/relationships;
- the organization;
- the effects of training on society?

By examining who will be involved in the training, the trainer will be better able to select appropriate training methods. Also see Chapter 10 and Appendix 11.

Areas of learning

As shown in Appendix 8, areas of learning can include:

- psychomotor, concerned mainly with manual skills;
- cognitive, concerned with knowledge of procedures, rules, issues;
- affective, concerned with beliefs, attitudes and feelings;
- interpersonal, concerned with person-to-person skills;
- self-knowledge, concerned with personal growth and awareness of one's own strengths and weaknesses.

Such a classification is very useful when preparing learning objectives, but as Gage (1979) noted, the behaviours listed are not isolated one from the other. When training the swimming pool high diver, the trainer, although focused on the psychomotor skills, will not ignore the cognitive and affective elements. In fact, perhaps a lot of time will be spent on the affective (attitude/feeling) or Personal Qualities areas in particular.

Learning methods and level of learning

In Chapter 10, a classification of training methods and level of learning has been prepared. This is where level of learning refers to:

- *knowledge,* learning to recall facts;
- *understanding,* able to explain and justify;
- *application,* able to use concepts or techniques in a prescribed way;
- *transfer,* able to select appropriate concepts or techniques, and modify or create a new approach where there are no right answers.

Group size

- How many people are to be trained?
  - Individual, 1–2 persons. Using for example: development assignments; programmed learning; instruction; coaching; mentoring.
  - Small group, 3–16 people. Using for example: discussion leading method; role playing, case studies; experiential exercises.
  - Large groups, 17–24 people. Using for example: case studies; syndicate methods; lectures.
  - Aggregate groups, 25-plus people. Using: lectures; talks; buzz groups.

NOTE 5.3: QUESTIONS AND INSTRUMENTS FOR EVALUATING THE 'PROCESS' OF TRAINING

Questions

- Is this training method promoting the learning that was planned?
- How well is the training being delivered?
- Is interaction between learners, trainer and others being achieved?
- Is the content of the programme matching the training need?
- How well is the training enabling the learner to deal better with his/her perceived reality of the work situation?
- How comfortable is the learner in terms of the quality of learning materials, accommodation, meals and other matters?
- Are the learners finding the experience worthwhile?

Evaluation instruments

Evaluation instruments can include:

- Knowledge/skill/attitude pre-tests.
- Ongoing tests and surveys.
- Ongoing fun quizzes.
- Ongoing individual/group/formal/informal discussions.
- Progress made and recorded by the learner.
- Independent observers.
- Continuous assessment methods.
- Self-pacing learning programmes.
- Ongoing use of questionnaires.

NOTE 5.4: EVALUATION INSTRUMENTS FOR MEASURING THE 'PRODUCTS' OF TRAINING

Evaluation can be concerned with, for example:

- Questionnaires:
  - quantitative (numerical, attitude measurement);
  - qualitative (open-ended, projective).
- Post-test which can embrace knowledge, skill and attitude factors.
- Specific skill performance test.
- Fun quiz.
- Formal/informal discussions.
- Training assignments.
- Independent observer findings.
- End-of-course reviews, including:
  - assessment about the usefulness of training methods;
  - assessment about how training was delivered.

NOTE 5.5: LIST OF MEASURES FOR EVALUATING THE 'OUTPUTS' OF TRAINING

Examples of *departmental* measures designed for Output Evaluation include (direct and indirect):

- Job performance measures:
  - increased net profit;
  - reduced customer complaints;
  - increased productivity per employee;
  - reduced absenteeism;
  - reduced labour turnover;
  - reduced accident frequency;
  - reduced pollution;
  - increased repeat business;
  - reduced running costs;
  - reduced wastage.
- Retention test (similar to post-test).
- On-job coach findings.
- Periodic or annual performance appraisal.
- On-job work-related project re Action Learning (Chapter 10).
- Action plan, prepared at end of training.
- Formal/informal discussions with learner, learner's manager and colleagues.
- Cost/benefit analysis, at a departmental level.
- Job behaviour ranking instruments.
- Questionnaires.

NOTE 5.6: EXAMPLES OF 'ULTIMATE' TRAINING RESULTS

At the organization level:

- All the factors listed previously but at the higher organizational level.
- Increased repeat business.
- Increased net profit (i.e. contribution of all departmental net profits).
- Improved social benefits, due to:

– formation of social club;
– access to keep-fit facilities;
– flexible working;
– supportive organizational culture.

Within society:

• Reduced air/river/noise pollution (locally/nationally/ internationally).
• Fewer people receiving benefit.
• More people contributing to society.
• Improved quality of life in community.
• Fewer people injured at work, because effective safety standards were introduced.

NOTE 5.7: EVALUATION STRATEGIES

In his book, Bramley (1986) identifies five strategies for evaluation, namely:

Quantitative approaches:

• the goal-based approach (discussed here);
• the systems approach.

Qualitative approaches:

• the goal-free approach;
• the professional review approach;
• the quasi-legal approach.

In this chapter we have been concerned with the universally adopted goal-based approach. Although the method of evaluation in this chapter can be described as quantitative, it does contain qualitative measurements, such as seeking learner's reactions and seeking comments from work colleagues.

Most trainers find that the *quantitative* dimension provides the *facts*, and the *qualitative* information provides the very necessary glue of *understanding*.

NOTE 5.8: TRAINING DESIGN CRITERIA

As mentioned earlier, a common mistake of designers of training activity is to assume that it is possible to achieve 'generality', 'accuracy' and 'simplicity' as a design mix. Although it goes against one's intuition, it is only possible to achieve two of the three design elements at any one time.

As shown in the Design Window, Figure 5.3, the design mix means that: if *accuracy* and *simplicity* are required, the design of the training will be *specific*. *Example 1:* The instructions (accurate/simple) for using a public telephone (specific). *Example 2:* When the instructions are accurate and simple because a specialist is being hurriedly trained to support recent developments, but the training is not sufficiently specific. This is when gas fitters install appliances incorrectly and end up killing people, for example.

If *accuracy* and *generality* are required, the design will need to take account of the resulting *complexity*. Although not always acknowledged, examples can apply to any training activity where due emphasis has not been placed on the complexity that results from striving for accuracy and generality. *Example 1:* For most traditionally taught management education and training activities, the designers/educationalists/trainers usually fail to respond to the complexity of the topic at hand.

Typically for management education courses (DMS/MBA), *accuracy* is achieved by learning the detailed techniques of each discipline and *generality* is achieved by focusing

The Training Design Window reminds us that the design of training activities must match the nature of the subject matter, and that
design *cannot be* accurate, simple and general but training
design *can be*:

(1 & 2) – accurate, simple and specific;
(3 & 4) – accurate, general and complex;
(2 & 4) – simple and general, with a danger of being inaccurate;
(1 & 3) – specific and complex, with a danger of being inaccurate.

2 SIMPLE The nature of the subject matter can be dealt with simply.	**1 SPECIFIC** The subject matter is specific.
4 GENERAL The subject matter can be dealt with generally.	**3 COMPLEX** Learning must match the complexity inherent in mastering the subject matter.

**ACCURACY
IS
SOUGHT**

There is a danger that the result of 1 & 3 and 2 & 4 may lead to
inaccuracy, so further steps will be required to prevent this
occurring. That is, 1 & 3 will induce high preparation cost to cope
with the subject matter's specificity and complexity, and 2 & 4 will
require additional support (such as instructor guidance) to
provide reference points to cover for the lack of structure and
detail.

FIGURE 5.3 Training Design Window

on the core disciplines of finance, marketing, production and human resources. *Example 2:* When examining competency-based training structures (NVQ/MCI/TDLB) we observe that *accuracy* is sought via the 'performance criteria and evidence' elements and *generality* is sought via the 'roles, range statements and units of competence'.

Missing from the design mix, in both examples, is *complexity*. Missing is:

* the large variety of 'ifs and buts', contingencies and circumstances that form the knowledge, create the understanding and enable effective performance;
* being able to understand the shape of the 'whole';
* being able to identify the shape of the systems of knowledge and skills that are connected to the subject matter at hand;
* being able to see above and around the forest as well as the trees.

If *simplicity* and *generality* are sought, there will be a likely danger of *inaccuracy*, due to the lack of detail and structure. That is, training activity, based on such design criteria, will likely not be able to provide the learner with sufficient guidance to cope with real-world situations. *Example:* A training initiative based on these criteria would mirror the instruction to go to Broken Hill which is 'over there'. In reality, Broken Hill is in Australia which is thousands of miles from here, and to get there will require that I do this, this and this, and that it will cost this, and it will mean . . . In other words the initial instruction (based on simplicity and generality) lacks sufficient detail, so that further support is required to make sense of the instruction.

If *specificity* and *complexity* are sought, there will be a likely danger of *inaccuracy* due to the high level of detail that will be required to be learnt. In addition, there will be a high cost associated with meeting such design criteria. *Example 1:* The flight simulator which is used to train and monitor the performance of aircraft pilots is an example of the high cost involved in overcoming inaccuracy because specificity and complexity of design are sought. *Example 2:* For the few blue-chip organizations that can afford it, they endeavour to train their managers to achieve *specificity* and *complexity* and overcome *inaccuracy* by providing intensive off-job and on-job training, rigorous reporting and continuous assessment regimes, and highly effective mechanisms involving coaching, mentoring, one-to-one instruction and access to a wide variety of other support networks. *Example 3:* Where *specificity* and *complexity* are sought, this can only be supported by thorough training, guided experience and continuous assessment to overcome *inaccuracy*. When such support is lacking or not available, poorly supported managing directors can seriously damage or collapse the organizations they are fronting, and also poorly supported scientific and technical specialists design systems that fail, provide advice that is flawed and fly aircraft that crash.

REFERENCES AND FURTHER READING

Training design

Binsted, D. S. (1978) 'The Design of Management Learning Events: A Framework'. *Journal of European Industrial Training 2, 5.*

Binsted, D. S. (1980) 'Design For Learning in Management Training and Development: A View'. *Journal Human Resource Development 4, 8.*

Binsted, D. S. (August 1980 and Spring 1981) 'The Design of Learning Events for Management', Parts 1 & 2. *Management Education and Development.*

Binsted, D. S. and Stuart, R. (1979 and 1980) 'Designing "Reality" into Management Learning Events', Parts I, II, III. *Personnel Review 8, 3 & 4 and 9, 1.*

Bloom, B. S., Engelhart, M. B., Furst, E. J., Hill, W. H. and Krathwohl, D. R. (1956) *Taxonomy of Educational Objectives. The Classification of Educational Goals Handbook 1: Cognitive Domain*. New York: Longmans Green.

Cramp Algorithm (1969) Industrial Training Research Unit (ITRU), Lloyds Bank Chambers, Hobson Street, Cambridge CB1 1NL. Tel: 01223 66814. For industrial skills.

Gage, N. L. and Berliner, C. (1979) *Educational Psychology*, 2nd edn. Chicago: Rand McNally.

Huczynski, A. (1977) 'Organizational Climates and the Transfer of Learning'. *British Association for Commercial and Industrial Education Journal*, June.

Huczynski, A. (1978) 'Approaches to the Problems of Learning Transfer'. *Journal of European Industrial Training 2, 1*.

Krathwohl, D. R., Bloom, B. S. and Masia, B. B. (1964) *Taxonomy of Educational Objectives, Handbook 2: Affective Domain*. New York: David McKay Co. Inc.

Pedler, M. (1974) 'Learning in Management Education'. *Journal of European Training 3, 3*, 182–94.

Salzberger-Wittenberg, I. *et al* (1983) *The Emotional Experience of Learning and Teaching*. London: Routledge and Kegan Paul.

Stiefd, R. T. (1979) 'Learning Transfer Strategies in Management Training'. *European Training 3, 1*.

Wallen, N. E. and Travers, R. M. W. (1963) 'Analysis and Investigation of Teaching Methods' in Gage, N. L. (ed.) *Handbook of Research on Teaching*. Chicago: Rand McNally.

Pre-course learning

Ausubel, D. P. (1965) *Educational Psychology: A Cognitive View*. New York: Holt, Rinehart and Winston.

Davies, I. K. (1976) *Objectives in Curriculum Design*. London: McGraw-Hill, Chapter 10.

Hartley, J. (1973) 'The Effect of Pre-Testing on Post-Test Performance'. *Instructional Science 2, 4*, 193–213.

Hartley, J. and Davies, I. K. (1976) 'Introducing New Materials: the Role of Pre-tests, Behavioral Objectives, Overviews and Advance Organizers as Pre-instructional Strategies'. *Review of Educational Research 46, 2*.

McDonald-Ross, M. (1973) 'Behavioral Objectives – a Critical Review'. *Instructional Science 2, 1*, 1–52.

Post-course learning

Farnsworth, T. (1968) 'After the Course is Over – Dynamism or Despair?'. *Personnel and Training Management*, February, 26–8.

O'Neill, H. and Loew, H. (1975) 'The Anatomy of a Problem: Follow Up Training in Analytical Trouble Shooting'. *Industrial and Commercial Training*, February, *7, 1*, 27–31.

Weiss, E., Huczynski, A. and Lewis, J. (1980) 'The Superior's Role in Learning Transfer'. *Journal of European Industrial Training 4, 4*, 17–20.

Evaluation

Bramley, P. (1986) *Evaluation of Training: A Practical Guide*. London: British Association for Commercial and Industrial Training.

Bramley, P. and Newby, A. (1984) 'The Evaluation of Training: Clarifying the Concept'. *Journal of European Industrial Training 8, 6*.

Easterby-Smith, M. and Mackness, J. (1992) 'Completing the Cycle of Evaluation'. *Personnel Management*, May.

Easterby-Smith, M. and Tanton, M. (1985) 'Turning Course Evaluation from an End to a Means'. *Personnel Management*, April.

Glossary of Training Terms (1981). London: HMSO.

Hamblin, A. C. (1974) *Evaluation and Control of Training*. London: McGraw-Hill.

Harrison, R. (1988) *Training and Development*. London: Institute of Personnel Management.

Hesseling, P. (1966) *Strategies of Evaluation Research*. Van Gorcum.

Jackson, T. (1989) *Evaluation: Relating Training to Business Performance*. London: Kogan Page.

Jones, J. A. G. (1970) *The Evaluation and Cost Effectiveness of Training*. London: Industrial Training Service.

Kersley, G. (1982) *Costs, Benefits and Productivity in Training Systems*. Reading, Massachusetts: Addison-Wesley.

Kirkpatrick, D. L. (1967) 'Evaluation of Training' in Craig, R. L. and Bittel, L. R. (eds). *Training and Development Handbook*. New York: McGraw-Hill.

Mackenzie, D. D. and Harris, R. (1982) *Judging People: A Guide to Orthodox and Unorthodox Methods of Assessment*. Maidenhead: McGraw-Hill.

Mumford, A. (1980) *Making Experience Pay*. London: McGraw-Hill.

Plett, P. and Lester, B. (1991) *Training for Older People*. Geneva: International Labour Office.

Rackman, N. and Morgan, T. (1977) *Behaviourial Analysis in Training*. UK: McGraw-Hill.

Rae, L. (1991) *How to Measure Training Effectiveness* (2nd edn). Aldershot: Gower.

Reid, M. A. and Kenney, J. (1987) 'Selecting and Evaluating Training Strategies'. *Personnel Management Handbook*. Aldershot: Gower.

Rowe, C. (1992) 'How Useful Was It? The Problem of Evaluating In-House Training Programmes'. *Industrial and Commercial Training 24, 7, 14–18*.

Suchman, E. A. V (1967) *Evaluative Research*. Russell Sage.

Tracey, W. R. (1968) *Evaluating Training and Development Systems*. American Management Association.

'Training Evaluation: An IRS Survey' (1992) *Employee Development Bulletin 29, 2–12*.

Warr, P., Bird, M. and Rackham, N. (1970) *Evaluation of Management Training*. London: Gower Press.

Whitelaw, M. (1972) *The Evaluation of Management Training – a Review*. London: Institute of Personnel Management.

Woodward, N. (1975) 'Cost/Benefit Analysis of Supervisor Training'. *Industrial Relations Journal 6, 2, 41–7*.

'Workplace Training and Assessment' (1990) *Employment Gazette 98, 3, 121–4*.

6

Effective learning strategies

INTRODUCTION

If we examine the process of 'instruction' as a vehicle for helping others to learn, we will discover that the fundamental ideas, ingredients and strategies for learning are applicable to almost any learning intervention.

Throughout instruction, we shall examine how the able instructor can employ not one but six different learning strategies. If we look first at the ingredients for learning we see that effective learning requires:

- *a willing learner*, because if somebody does not want to learn, they won't;
- *an able instructor;*
- *clear objectives,* because in both cases the alternative is not sustainable on moral, ethical, lawful or 'professional practice' grounds;
- *access to learning strategies,* because the trainer must be ready to respond as flexibly as possible to the learner's style of learning, the learner's learning difficulties and the learning opportunities as they arise.

As most trainers will agree, effective training is directly related to the quality of preparation. As far as practical, this means:

1 *Preparing the learner to learn by:*

- understanding the learner's difficulties and aspirations in relation to the training need;
- individual counselling;
- assisting the learner's line management to prepare for behaviour changes when the learner 'returns' to the workplace;
- subjecting learners to 'warm-up' sessions focused on tension relief and relaxation;
- learner undertaking prior study to bring the learner up to a 'common level', to assist with an 'accelerated start' or to provide an 'experience base' from which to comment, question and reflect.

2 *Creating an effective learning climate by:*

- helping learners to feel relaxed enough to 'learn', and yet 'ready' to challenge their own and other people's ideas;
- helping learners to change without damage to the individual's reputation and self-esteem;
- paying attention to the learners' emotional state and their level of competence.

3 *Preparing effective learning materials*

As we saw in Chapter 5, three of the four training stages are devoted to preparation of learning materials. The old maxim that to be able to teach a subject you must first study it thoroughly, could not be truer. Even with 'ready made' learning packages, the trainer can support them only if she/he has used them and understands the learning boundaries of the programme.

Below is a list of practical observations and good practices that find common agreement amongst experienced instructors.

A WILLING LEARNER

Voluntary

Remember: learning is a voluntary process. If a person decides not to learn, there is little anyone can do.

Doing

Many of us learn best by doing. Whatever a person learns, he/she must learn for him/herself, no one can learn for him/her.

Rate of learning

Each person learns at his/her own rate.

Reinforcement

A person learns more when each step is immediately strengthened or positively reinforced.

More or less permanent

Remember: learning is a *more or less* permanent change in behaviour as a result of experience. If a task has not been performed for some time, be prepared to help the person learn again.

Why

Explain *why* a job is performed; this helps connect the mental and physical requirements of the task and brings meaning and relevance together to form a whole.

Enjoyment

We learn when we enjoy it, and in this sense, encouragement helps and discouragement usually hinders the learning process.

Involvement

We learn when we can use our mind, body, values, feeling, intuition, imagination, senses – sight/sound/hearing/touch/smell.

Growing

We learn when we know we are developing and growing as a person.

Objectives

We learn when we have objectives that are demonstrably achievable.

Check starting point

A person can learn only in relation to what he/she already knows. When training, check and test out the starting point of the person's knowledge, skill and attitude.

Fully train each step

Full, rather than partial mastery of each step, makes total learning more meaningful.

Simple to complex

If a person is learning a procedure of tasks, proceed from a whole view, to a more detailed view, and then back to a whole view. Where there is complexity, then proceed from the simple to the complex. Reassure the person that it takes several attempts to learn a whole chain of tasks.

Quality

When discriminating between acceptable and unacceptable quality, take time to explain, show and allow the person to experience the differences. When ready, allow the person to discriminate between good and bad quality, and let the learner use his/her own words to describe the differences. This is vital.

Diagrams

Be prepared to use diagrams, pictures and flow charts to help with learning quickly and effectively.

Use learner's insight

Be prepared to ask learner to contribute towards new ways of learning.

Mistakes

We learn from our own and others' mistakes and from trial and error experiences.

Below is a list of practical observations and good practices that find common agreement amongst experienced instructors, regarding 'An Able Instructor'.

AN ABLE INSTRUCTOR
What is instruction?

Instruction is a process which involves:

- the skilled performer, called instructor, helping the less skilled performer, called learner or trainee, to master and apply some task to an 'experienced worker standard', as quickly as possible;
- creating planned learning situations using on- and off-job opportunities for learning;
- the instructor providing a safe and supporting learning climate;
- the instructor preparing and following an Instruction Schedule (see below).

What are the hallmarks of an effective instructor?

Safety
Where safety is concerned, instructors have a statutory obligation to train without causing harm to learners, themselves and others.

Flexibility
Effective instructors use instruction methods which are *flexible,* can be *adapted* to suit circumstances, offer *choice,* and take advantage of learning *opportunities.*

Self-motivated
Instructors have a duty to get themselves properly motivated.

Attitudes
Effective instructors know that, for some people, the process of learning may change negative attitudes about the task to be done, themselves and others.

Rewarding experience
Like other helping processes, effective instructors treat the whole amazing process of learning as the fantastic, creative, rich and rewarding experience it is.

Instructors learn
Effective instructors are effective learners.

Opportunities
As well as preparing carefully designed training programmes, effective instructors create and use opportunities for learning, for example:
- Let's watch the experienced performer in a busy period.
- Let's have a go at a less busy time.
- Let's use the equipment when we will not be disturbed.
- This has just come up. What would you do? For these reasons, this is how we handle it here.

Supportive climate
Effective instructors know that learning is best undertaken under a supportive training and working climate.

From dependence to autonomy
As a person matures, she/he becomes more independent towards the learning and contributes towards it. A person not only learns material that she/he feels is relevant, but the person learns to make decisions and to suffer the consequences of those decisions.

From ignorance to insight
A learner must decide when newly acquired ideas and skills are applicable and when they might need to be modified.

From a negative self-image to a positive one
In some cases a learner may feel inferior to other learners and the trainer at the start of

training. Not only must the trainer be concerned with getting the training material right, but must always be ready to help learners build a positive self-image. Effective instructors know that plenty of encouragement and positive rewarding helps learners through this self-image barrier.

From a need for certainty to a tolerance of ambiguity

When learning a new procedure or skill, there is a tendency for learners to seek absolute certainty. If learners can mature so as to tolerate ambiguity, they will be better equipped to deal with novel situations and will have the confidence of their own convictions. For instructors, the message is 'Be careful about teaching absolute answers, when situations do not support it.'

What is an instruction schedule?

An Instruction Schedule is a detailed breakdown of a specific skill for the purpose of instruction. It aims to set down the best learning sequence in order to help the trainee master new skills and stipulates key points in the job. (It is not the same as a Lesson Plan which provides the trainer with a complete plan for the conduct of a session, usually, for a group of trainees.)

Below is a list of practical observations and good practices that find common agreement amongst experienced instructors regarding preparation of 'Clear Objectives'.

CLEAR OBJECTIVES

To help the trainer and learner to be successful, the trainer must ensure that the learner knows what performance is expected. To guide the trainer and help the learner compare his/her performance against what is expected, one good practice is to communicate the training objectives. As suggested by Majer (1962), the training objective (Chapter 3) can be written thus:

- What is to be *performed*? To drive a car or write a report for example?
- What *standards* are to be achieved? Can the standards be described either objectively or subjectively, or both?
- What *conditions* will exist, when the task is carried out, including both physical and psychological? For example, to drive on the motorway, drive in snow or drive in summer weather, all involve driving but under very different conditions?
  - To avoid: 'I didn't know you wanted me to do that.' Make sure the learner knows what is to be *performed*.
  - To avoid: 'I didn't know you wanted me to phone everyone on the list.' Make sure the *standards* are clear.
  - To avoid: 'Yes, I know a car's a car, but this car is automatic. I've never driven one of those before.' Make sure the *conditions* under which training occurs, mirrors what is later expected, and does not prevent transfer of skills.

In Appendix 7 two other methods of preparing objectives are shown. Using the Majer type objective, the following example will help demonstrate its use.

EXAMPLE 1: OPERATING OVERHEAD PROJECTOR

After demonstration and practice, the learner will be able to:

Performance

Operate overhead projector.

Standard

Follow Health and Safety Office Procedures.
Follow retrieval and unpacking of projector procedure.
Set up projector 1 metre from screen.
Operate projector and display a clear image, using sample overhead.
Provide an unobstructed view when the room is fully occupied.
Follow packing and storing procedure.

Conditions

Follow safety procedures.
Use Store Room 5.
Use Lecture Room 104 (4 metres x 5 metres) equipped with black-out facilities, electrical sockets and 30 chairs; layout, as shown.
Use ABC type projector.
Use sample overhead.

More will now be said about standards as this is often the key element in most situations. Below is a list of practical observations and good practices that find common agreement amongst experienced instructors, regarding preparation of Standards of Performance.

GUIDELINES FOR PREPARING STANDARDS OF PERFORMANCE

Seek where possible to be objective by describing the standard in terms of:

- time;
- quantity;
- quality;
- costs;
- accuracy;
- completeness/error rate;
- safety.

The idea of being objective is to limit misunderstanding and to focus attention on achieving the required performance. When it is only possible to infer a standard: *seek contrast* by comparing acceptable and unacceptable standards.

- In engineering, for example, metal surface finish has long been measured by matching the actual surface finish against a gauge of surface finishes.
- When setting up an overhead projector, it is common practice to contrast a poor display against an acceptable one, in order to suggest the standard to be achieved.
- When describing how to provide the right quality of service, for example, explain and demonstrate both acceptable and unacceptable standards.
- To fix the learning, arrange for the learner to practise performing the desired standard. Where learners experience difficulty in understanding the difference between

acceptable and unacceptable standards, get them, where safety and ethics will allow, to experience both standards. Sometimes it may be necessary to 'feel' the difference in order to understand what is required.

Use experts. Arrange for the learner to: either work alongside role models (or effective 'Sit-By-Nellys'); or be instructed, coached, mentored or guided in order to identify the 'experienced worker standard' and discover how it is to be achieved.

Seek repetition. When it is necessary to chain together a series of physical or mental skills, repetition of physical actions and mental processes may need to be used. For public performers, such as actors and broadcasters, this becomes the only technique that works.

Subjective scoring. In Example 2, Hosting and Chairing Meeting (see page 79), an attempt is made to describe standards as objectively as possible. When, however, it comes to assessing actual performance, the problem arises that one is left with mental impressions instead of physical evidence. One way to resolve this difficulty is to use a Subjective Scoring Sheet as shown in Table 6.1. In this case, the assessor has scored 7 on both the 1 to 10 scales. The Scoring Sheet in this example is part of a larger assessment. In addition to scoring, it would be useful for the learner to have some idea of 'signals missed' and those which were 'responded to' so that a useful picture of the 'performance gap' can be established.

Another way to capture performance is to video or record the sound only. In this case the visual record will facilitate a more thorough analysis of Table 6.1.

TABLE 6.1 Subjective Scoring Sheet – showing two parts of a larger Subjective Scoring Sheet

10	Responded extremely well at all times. Clients were fully satisfied.		10	Posture successfully matched client requirements, at all times.
9			9	
8			8	
(7)			(7)	
6			6	
5	Missed 50 per cent of client requests/signals.		5	Occasions when posture failed to match 50 per cent of client responses.
4			4	
3			3	
2			2	
1	Showed little response to client requirements.		1	Posture failed to match client signals.

Responsiveness to client requests/signals for help, support, guidance, clarification, recognition.

Posture at meeting
Includes all non-verbal signals, including correct eye contact to suit national customs.

EXAMPLE 2: HOSTING AND CHAIRING MEETING

After demonstration, practice and shadowing effective performers, the learner will:

Performance

Host and chair meeting with clients.

Standards

Host at arrival:
Satisfy 'Office Dress/Appearance' standard.
Arrange transport requirements, well in advance of meeting.
Greet clients using their cultural customs.
Welcome clients, and in the event of a fifteen-minute delay, delegate an effective substitute, and inform clients of any changes.
Escort clients to room.
Make clients comfortable and put at ease:
– show where washrooms/cloakrooms are located;
– offer refreshments;
– show where telephones are located;
– guide clients to seating places.

Chair meeting:
Welcome clients and make introductions.
Explain purpose of meeting.
Read through agenda, and suggest time required for each item.
Action each agenda item, agree objectives, deadlines and allocate responsibilities.
Close meeting and thank clients for their contributions and for attending.
Be responsive to client requests/signals and ensure your body posture matches client expectations.

Host at departure:
Ensure clients have all their possessions.
Escort clients to 'Client Service Area', as required.
Action transport requirements, as required.
Escort clients to reception/car park.
Leave clients using their cultural customs of departure.

Conditions

Carry out within ABC Organization.
Use Room 3.
Liaise, three days in advance, with Mr Smith for Client Service area and transport support.
Liaise, three days in advance, with Mrs Sharpe, for Reception Services.

LEARNING STRATEGIES

When asked to describe the method for instructing others, many people will make two assumptions. One, there is only one method. Two, there are only two stages, namely: 1. the instructor demonstrates (*show*); 2. the learner has a go (*do*). Further examination will reveal, however, that 3. the learner mentally records, reflects upon and plans around the 'have a go' experience (*think*).

When observing effective instructors, we not only discover a three-stage instruction method, but each stage is topped and tailed by *informing* and *debriefing*. And it is this that can be critical to the whole learning process. Another equally important factor to instructing is the initial 'getting to know you' period. Like interviewing and other social processes where people meet, first impressions can dramatically influence the final results. Time genuinely spent, therefore, on making each other feel comfortable, when first meeting, is an investment that must not be ignored.

If we take the three-stage instruction sequence (*show/do/think*) and then consider the sequence of options, the result will be as shown in Figure 6.1. As the reader will see, of the six instruction strategies, two can be referred to as 'traditional' instruction and four can be described as 'discovery' approaches. Let us now examine how each instruction method can be carried out.

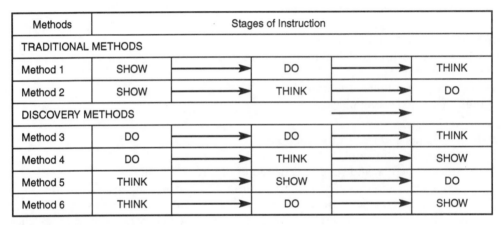

Methods	Stages of Instruction				
TRADITIONAL METHODS					
Method 1	SHOW	⟶	DO	⟶	THINK
Method 2	SHOW	⟶	THINK	⟶	DO
DISCOVERY METHODS		⟶			
Method 3	DO	⟶	DO	⟶	THINK
Method 4	DO	⟶	THINK	⟶	SHOW
Method 5	THINK	⟶	SHOW	⟶	DO
Method 6	THINK	⟶	DO	⟶	SHOW

EXAMPLE
The diagram below shows the sequence of instruction for Method 1, which includes topping and tailing each stage by informing and debriefing

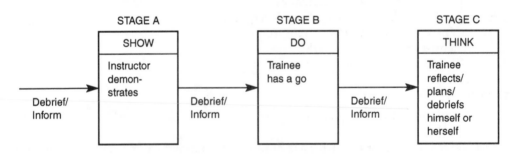

STAGE A	STAGE B	STAGE C
SHOW	DO	THINK
Instructor demonstrates	Trainee has a go	Trainee reflects/plans/debriefs himself or herself

Debrief/Inform → Debrief/Inform → Debrief/Inform →

FIGURE 6.1 Six instruction strategies

METHOD 1: SHOW/DO/THINK (Traditional)

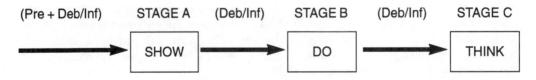

(Pre + Deb/Inf)   STAGE A   (Deb/Inf)   STAGE B   (Deb/Inf)   STAGE C

⟶ SHOW ⟶ DO ⟶ THINK

This first method of instruction represents the typical view of instruction. The instructor shows, the learner has a go and then the learner thinks about, reflects on and helps to mentally fix the learning.

When to use this method

- When it is paramount, for safety or cost reasons, that the task must be strictly followed.
- When the learner prefers to be told exactly what to do.

Preliminaries – driving a car

Invest time

Good morning. My name is . . .
How was your journey this morning?

Debrief learner – previous learning

Tell me about your previous driving experience?
What did you expect to achieve (performance)?
Tell me about what you are good at and less good at?
Tell me about any problems.
What bits did you not pass on?
What would you like to practise?
How would you sum up your driving ability?
What would you like to do when you pass your driving test?

Inform learner

This is what we will do today.
I will fully demonstrate how to reverse, then I will do it again more slowly in stages.
This is what I would like you to observe.
This is why it is done like this.
This is the knowledge that must be acquired and applied.
Imagine yourself on the motorway. What is your role as a driver? Yes, and I would add . . .
How can we make this role become a reality? Yes, and I would add . . .
What is my role as a driving instructor? Yes, and I would add . . .
What is your role as a learner? Yes, and I would add . . .

Stage A (Show): Instructor demonstrates to learner

First, safety. You *must always* . . .
This is how and why I prepare to reverse.
As I demonstrate, I will talk you through it.
You notice a vehicle approaching. I am going to stop because . . .
Please notice how I line up the back of the car with the kerb.

Debrief learner

What are your immediate reactions?
How did it compare with your experience?

What did you learn from observing?
What seemed easy/difficult? Why?
What did I do (*perform*)?
What are the *standards* I achieved?
Under what *conditions* did I achieve this?
How would you evaluate my performance?

Inform learner

What is the final result you want?
Talk me through 'reversing' stage by stage.
Start safely.
Very good.
If another vehicle approaches, what will you do?
If you feel undecided, say so straight away.
In the last resort I will use the dual control.

Stage B (Do): Learner has a go

Talk me through it, as you practise.
When comfortable, proceed.
Take some deep breaths.
Tell me how you feel.
Take it gently.
That's very good.
When you experience sensations of awkwardness and achievement – it means you are learning.
Please enjoy this moment. This is a time when you can gain real insight into how you learn to learn.

Debrief learner

That was excellent.
Tell me how you felt.
Tell me what you did (*performed*).
Tell me what *standards* you achieved.
How did the *standards* compare to the required standard/my demonstrated standard?
Describe the *conditions* you were working under.
What might happen under different *conditions*?
Tell me about the bits that need working on.
How can you use your strengths to improve skill areas that need developing?
Why are you skilled at this, and less skilled at that?
Which part do you enjoy most/least?
What can we learn from this?
How would you evaluate today's lesson?
What would you like to do next time?

Inform learner

Compared against my instruction plan for today, this is how I evaluate your progress.
I would like to congratulate you about today's performance. You have demonstrated a real desire to learn and to master driving skills.
I have not only learned a great deal, but I have also enjoyed the whole process.
Next time we meet:

> plan how you would tackle a reverse drive up a hill;
> find out what to do when the right/left indicating lights fail.

Stage C (Think): Learner – reflects/plans

The learner will consciously and unconsciously:

- continue to mentally fix the learning;
- reflect on what needs to be done to improve performance;
- congratulate self on achievements;
- in some cases, match poor self-image with poor performance;
- mentally 'practise' successful driving strategies;
- discover things that can be discussed openly about how to improve;
- continue to keep 'private' other things which affect performance (and which must remain private, until the learner is ready to share such thoughts, feelings, fears, expectations, hopes, assumptions);
- in some cases, assess wrongly, a good performance as a poor one, and vice versa.

The value of the instructor informing and debriefing the learner at all stages is to help the learner accurately assess his/her own performance.

When the instructor resumes training, she/he will start with a debrief about what has been learnt, and what unfinished business remains.

If you would like to explore the other five instruction strategies, see Note 6.1 (page 84). It is suggested that as an exercise, you consider how all these strategies, and the discipline of debriefing and informing, can be applied to other training techniques, such as coaching and role playing.

SUMMARY

In this chapter it has been suggested that the ingredients to assist learning are:

- a willing learner;
- an able instructor;
- clear objectives;
- access to learning strategies.

To assist the willing learner and the able instructor, a list of good practices were identified. For clear objectives, one method involved seeing the objective in terms of:

- *performance* or what is to be done;
- *standards* to be achieved;
- *conditions* under which the training will take place.

Of the three components, setting standards requires particular attention and often proves the most difficult to prepare. In this regard, the idea of:

- contrasting good and bad standards;

- 'discussing' what good standards are;
- subjective scoring;
- using role models as standard setters are all attempts at 'fixing' the standard for learners and trainers.

Based on the simple idea of instructing others, it was shown how six different learning strategies could be deployed to suit the learning situation. Using the example of instruction, it was shown how the usual *Show/do/think* could be undertaken in terms of:

- Show/think/do.
- Do/show/think.
- Do/think/show.
- Think/show/do.
- Think/do/show.

We also noted that vital to helping the learner understand is the process of 'informing and debriefing'. When these general learning sequences and patterns of questioning and feedback are applied to other learning situations (coaching, group work, case studies, role playing etc.), the trainer should find a marked improvement in the quality of the training delivery and the learning. For trainers, the task of reflecting upon how the strategies for instruction can be applied to other learning methods should prove worthwhile. For example, do I 'tell', as a trainer, or do I ask the learner what she/he knows or believes and start from there? In this way, the trainer can gradually build upon existing knowledge, skill and confidence.

NOTE 6.1: INSTRUCTION METHODS 2, 3, 4, 5 AND 6
METHOD 2: SHOW/THINK/DO (Traditional)

By changing the sequence of instruction to *show* (A), *think* (C), *do* (B), Method 2, although still traditional, can be explored. As much of the *debriefing* and *informing* sequences will be repeated as in Method 1, we will focus here on the core method. Assuming the Preliminary Stage has been undertaken, as before, Method 2 looks like this.

When to use this method
- When flexibility in the procedure can be justified on safety and cost grounds.
- When it is necessary to explore alternative procedures, and through practice, discover the tried and tested advantages and limitations.
- When learners need convincing through experience, after receiving some initial guidance.
- When learner is required to work out and plan alternative procedures.

Task: planning a route

Debrief learner
Inform learner

Stage A (Show): Instructor demonstrates (similar to before)

Debrief learner
Inform learner (Instructor says:)

- I want you to plan a route from 'here' to 'there'.

Stage C (Think): Learner – reflects/plans

Learner works out a number of options and decides best route.

Debrief learner (Instructor says:)

- Are there any difficulties?
- What are the factors you are considering?
- What have you learnt?

Inform learner (Instructor says:)

- Now drive the route you have chosen.

Stage B (Do): Learner has a go

Learner says:

- I realize now that if I had gone round the town centre, traffic would be less congested.
- It has made me think about the build-up of traffic at peak times during the day.

Debrief learner (Instructor says:)

- What would you now do differently?
- How long will it take you to match the 'knowledge of roads' with 'times of peak travelling' with 'local conditions'? Why? So from now on, how will you plan to match all these requirements?

METHOD 3: DO/SHOW/THINK (Discovery)

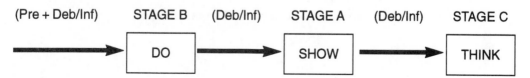

If we now consider the above sequence, we obtain Method 3 which can be called a discovery method of instruction. Again, if we assume the *preliminary* stage has been undertaken, the following example shows the sequence.

When to use this method

- When it can be justified for the learner to have a go, prior to being shown acceptable procedures.
- When the trainer and learner are prepared to accept alternative ways of doing something.
- When, in some cases, the learner is allowed to explore the limitations of alternative approaches (under supervision), so that the advantages of the recommended method can be clearly demonstrated, and also time and other resources are not wasted later (because close supervision is not possible).

Task: writing report

Debrief learner
Inform learner (Instructor says:)

- Using your experience, write a damage assessment report.

Stage B (Do): Learner has a go

- Learner writes report.

Debrief learner (Instructor says:)

- What factors did you consider?
- Who are you writing for?

Inform learner (Instructor says:)

- This is how we do it.
- This is why we do it.

Stage A (Show): Instructor demonstrates

- Watch as I assess the damage to the car.
- Notice, I start with the bodywork first.

Debrief learner (Instructor says:)

- How does this compare with your approach?
- What are the *standards* I achieved?

Inform learner (Instructor says:)

- Write down the items that must be commented on in the report.

Stage C (Think): Learner – reflects/plans

Learner compares his/her actual approach against the 'experienced worker standard', and works out what must be learnt.

METHOD 4: DO/A – THINK/C – SHOW/A (Discovery)

Still in the 'discovery' mode, consider the above sequence.

When to use this method

• When it is safe and cost-effective to use.
• When it would prove useful for the learner to 'discover' and demonstrate his/her experience and abilities through doing and evaluation.

Task: collating and interpreting

Debrief learner
Inform learner (Instructor says:)

• Take these 100 car insurance claims and decide how you would process them and interpret them.

Stage B (Do): Learner has a go

Learner sorts documents.

Debrief learner (Instructor says:)

• Tell me why you chose to collate the claims like this?
• What criteria did you use to interpret them?

Inform learner (Instructor says:)

• Think about the collating procedure you have chosen, and consider if it is the most effective arrangement.
• What claims would receive priority clearance?

Stage C (Think): Learner – reflects/plans

Learner is allowed to question experienced workers to discover how experts collate and interpret insurance claims.

Debrief learner (Instructor says:)

• What are the experts' overall aims?
• What are the standards they are trying to achieve?

- What criteria do they use?
- Why did your results differ from those of the experts?

Inform learner (Instructor says:)

- This is what I am going to do.

Stage A (Show): Instructor demonstrates

- This is how we collate and interpret the information.

Debrief learner (Instructor says:)

- Having compared your approach with the experts' method, please explain why you think the experts' method is preferred.
- What aspect of all this has been of most value to you?

METHOD 5: THINK/SHOW/DO (Discovery)

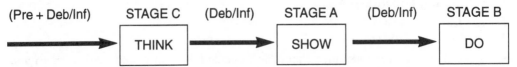

For this option, the learner is encouraged to think and plan first.

When to use this method

- When it is safe and cost-effective to use.
- When it is important to know the learner's actual skill level.
- When it is not possible to allow the learner to practise first.

Task: fault finding

Debrief learner
Inform learner (Instructor says:)

- I am going to present you with a number of mechanical motor vehicle faults, and I want you to tell me how you would go about identifying the problem. Here are some tools and testing instruments you can use.

Stage C (Think): Learner – reflects/plans

Learner reflects, thinks and plans how to diagnose the fault.

Debrief learner (Instructor says:)

- I would agree with your diagnostic approach. I would add that instead of using this instrument, I would use this one for this reason.

Inform learner (Instructor says:)

- Watch as I talk my way through this demonstration, using this instrument.

Stage A (Show): Instructor demonstrates

- Can you see how easy it is to manipulate this instrument?
- Can you see how clear the reading is?

Debrief learner (Instructor says:)

- What is the advantage of using this instrument compared to the one you wanted to use?
- What standards did I achieve?

Inform learner (Instructor says:)

- Diagnose this fault using both your instrument and this one.

Stage B (Do): Learner has a go

Learner says:

- I see what you mean, I never took the trouble to compare these two testing devices.

Debrief learner (Instructor says:)

- Tell me what the difference is between these two ways of testing.
- Which one gives more accurate results? Why?

METHOD 6: THINK/C – DO/B – SHOW/A (Discovery)

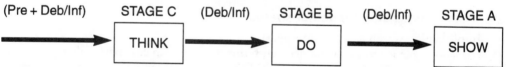

The learner is encouraged to think about how to do the task, and then do it.

When to use this method

- When it is safe and cost-effective to use.
- When it is important to assess learner's reasoning and application skills.
- When it is important to know the learner's actual skill level.
- When it is important for the learner to explain and demonstrate where he/she is having difficulty.

Task: rectifying a fault

Debrief learner
Inform learner (Instructor says:)

- Find the fault in this car and rectify it, using these tools and instruments.

Stage C (Think): Learner – reflects/plans

Learner plans how to diagnose fault.

Debrief learner (Instructor says:)

- Do you remember what we did last week, how the spring flew off when . . .?
- What is the standard you are aiming for?

Inform learner (Instructor says:)

- Go ahead. Carry out the diagnosis and rectify the fault.

Stage B (Do): Learner has a go

Learner diagnoses fault and rectifies.

Debrief learner (Instructor says:)

- What have you learnt from spending time:
  – planning?
  – using the best tools for the job?
- What have you done (*performed*)?
- What *standards* have you achieved?
- What are the *conditions* (type of car/in workshop) you are working on/under?

Inform learner (Instructor says:)

- This is how I would diagnose and rectify the fault.

Stage A (Show): Instructor demonstrates

- In particular, watch as I take this apart.
- It is good practice to cover the floor with this dust sheet in case parts fall out.
- If a part is lost, a complete new unit will have to be purchased, so always take great care at this stage.

Debrief learner (Instructor says:)

- Compare your approach against my method.
- Why do I recommend my method?
- What standards did I achieve?

REFERENCES AND FURTHER READING

Instruction

Gilbert, T. F. (1962) 'Mathetics: The Technology of Education'. *Journal of Mathetics 1*, 1–73.
Industrial Training Research Unit (1976) 'Choose an Effective Style: A self-instructional approach to the teaching of skills'. Industrial Training Research Unit Research paper TR9.

Majer, R. F. (1961) 'On Sequencing of Instructional Content'. *Psychological Review 9*, 405–414.
Winfield, I. (1979) *Learning to Teach Practical Skills*. London: Kogan Page.

Training objectives/learning

Berger, M. (1977) 'Training and the Organizational Context'. *Journal of European Industrial Training 1, 2*.
Bloom, B. S. (1956) *Taxonomy of Educational Objectives, Handbook 1, Cognitive Domain*. New York: McKay.
Davies, I. K. (1971). *The Management of Learning*. Maidenhead: McGraw-Hill.
Gagné, R. M. (1977). *The Condition of Learning*. USA: Holt, Rinehart and Winston.
Gronlund, N. E. (1978) *Stating Behaviourial Objectives for Classroom Instruction*. London: Macmillan.
Krathwohl, D. R., Bloom, B. S. and Masia, B. B. (1964) *Taxonomy of Educational Objectives, Handbook 2, Affective Domain*. New York: McKay.
Majer, R. F. (1962) *Preparing Objectives for Programmed Instruction*. San Francisco: Fearon.

Older/adult training

Belbin, R. M. (1969) *Employment of Older Workers. No. 2, Training Methods*. Paris: Overseas Economic Country Development.
Belbin, E. and Belbin, R. M. (1972) *Problems in Adult Retraining*. London: Heinemann.
Plett, P. and Lester, B. T. (1991) *Training for Older People*. London: International Labour Office.

7

Matching training interventions to organizational culture, management style and motivation

INTRODUCTION

The idea that organizations can be driven by their own cultures must be of interest to anyone trying to influence the macro or micro level of organizational effectiveness. The following maxims may help explain this observation.

1 That organizations can be guided in how and what things are done by a predominant culture.
2 That within an organization can be nested various sub-cultures which can influence people in different directions.
3 That organizational cultures prefer to employ training methods that reflect their own image.
4 That pure forms of the culture may not exist, the core ideas make useful benchmarks by which to make comparisons with real situations. That is, in the same way that recruitment makes use of an 'ideal' person specification by which to compare 'real' candidates.
5 That to understand organizational culture is to understand how this can influence: management style; motivational stimuli employed; preferred training methods adopted; internal relationships and external responses.
6 That such ideas can help explain departmental differences in ethics, values, attitudes, behaviour and work practices.

In this chapter, an attempt is made to provide connections between some of the common findings and ideas that underpin our thinking on these subjects. It is important to make these connections because they can help us compare our actual findings against the framework suggested here. For example, to know that power cultures may favour action-focused training methods, can be more than helpful to the trainer, and can be the difference between a most useful learning experience and a completely disastrous one for the learner.

ORGANIZATION CULTURES

The work of Harrison (1972, 1986, 1992, 1993) and Handy (1978) provide us with one way of understanding the factors that influence behaviour in organizations. In outline four types of organization culture have been identified, and are known as:

- Power Cultures.
- Role Cultures.
- Achievement Cultures.
- Support Cultures.

Power Cultures

These are decisive, focused and strong. They are based on survival and possess strength, decisiveness and determination. Typically, top management embody this culture, and they set an example and provide direction. Power cultures empower through identification with a strong leader. They disempower through fear, and through inability to act without permission. A power culture tends to induce a 'power management style'.

Like the Role Culture it also tends to favour McGregor's (1960) Theory X management attitude, and supports Herzberg's (1974) Hygiene Motivation Factors, for example.

Role Cultures

These are reliable, rational and systematic. They are based on security and provide order, stability and control. The civil service is one example. Role cultures empower through systems which serve the people and the task, thus reducing confusion and conflict. They disempower through restricting autonomy and creativity, and erecting barriers to co-operation. Such a culture induces a 'role management style'.

Achievement Cultures

These are committed, idealistic and energetic. They are based on self-expression and seek members' growth, success and distinction. Examples would include aerospace organizations. Achievement cultures empower through identification with the values and ideals of a vision, through the liberation of creativity, and through freedom to act. They disempower through burnout, stress, treating individuals as an instrument of the task, and through inhibiting dissent about goals and values.

Managers in this culture, usually exhibit an 'achievement management style'. Like the Support Culture, they favour McGregor's (1960) Theory Y management attitude, and support Herzberg's (1974) Motivators.

Support Cultures

These are co-operative, responsive and caring. They are based on community. They seek mutuality and integration and provide a high quality service. An example would be a specialist management consultancy organization. Support cultures empower through co-operation and trust, and by providing understanding, acceptance and assistance. They disempower through suppressing conflict, preoccupation with process, and through conformity to group norms. Managers usually match such a culture with a 'support management style'.

MANAGEMENT STYLES

What management style signals to the trainer

The term management style is not as superficial as it first seems. If we say it refers to how managers manage others, we have said a great deal in a few words. The 'how' is important because, like the motivational stimuli that can be employed to motivate others, it signals:

- an attitude;
- a point of view;
- a way of thinking and working;
- how a relationship is to be formed;

and can be directly linked to managerial effectiveness.

For these reasons, the trainer when designing training interventions will consider different implementation strategies, depending on the situation. For example, the trainer will endeavour to match the training activity to the management styles prevailing (short-term); and the trainer will spend time training the managers to accept training interventions which would otherwise not sit easy with them (long-term).

The alternatives to these strategies, when there is a mismatch between training and management style, will include: management will ignore and not support the training effort; management will highlight any shortcomings in the training which in turn will reflect badly on the trainer and the learner; managers will witness the results of training and will support it.

While the first two responses are to be avoided, the third will involve a calculated risk which only the most experienced (or inexperienced) trainers will take.

Management style at different organization levels

If we examine management at different levels in the organization, we become aware that they each must face in, at least, two directions. For example:

- the chief executive faces the board of directors and the shareholders;
- the functional director faces middle management and the chief executive;
- the middle manager faces his/her functional department and the functional director;
- the first line manager faces his/her team and the middle manager.

That many of these managers will work across departmental and divisional boundaries, and will work with suppliers, customers and even competitors, adds other important dimensions which must also be considered. From all of this we can deduce that managers must employ different management styles in order to cope with the variety of interactions.

Example 1

Let us take the example of middle management within an airline service which reflects a predominant power culture, but where other sub-cultures are nesting within it. In this case:

- the accounts manager (inhabiting a role sub-culture) will likely display a role management style to department members, but may use an accommodating power management style to promote effective communication when facing the functional director;
- the public relations officer (from a support sub-culture) will likely use a supporting, delegating, sharing management style to team members, but again use an appropriate power management style for effective communication when facing the functional director.

Example 2

If the accounts manager (role), as in Example 1, used a power management style to manage department members, this would likely result in crossed transactions and confusion, as manager and members struggled to understand the other's attitude and direction.

Example 3

If the accounts manager, again as in Example 1, used a role management style to converse with his/her immediate manager who was using a power management style, the same result would occur as in Example 2.

As with transactional analysis, Examples 2 and 3 are indicative of crossed transactions or crossed communications, and the result will usually be confusion.

The range of management styles

For the trainer and for the design of training events, the above examples show that managers may need to use a range of management styles to match:

- individual team member requirements, especially their level of maturity and competence;
- the management style (or attitude) of their immediate manager;
- the management styles of colleagues, from other departments, when working across boundaries;
- the management styles of those external to the organization;
- the management styles of those in working parties, when contributing as a member.

Summary of main points

From the level of possible activity indicated above, it is fair to comment that most managers will need to employ more than one management style. We can therefore see:

- how the predominant organizational culture and the sub-culture can induce different management styles to be used;
- that, in general, there can be danger in 'mixing' management style transactions, for example, a role style matches a role function and a power style does not;
- that managerial effectiveness (for communication and results) can be dependent on the competence of deploying appropriate management styles;
- that trainers must adapt their own 'management support styles' when dealing with the styles of other managers;
- that in the equation somewhere will be the manager's own level of competence, striving to find a way forward and perhaps battling with his/her own management style preferences;
- that when assisting managers with a training needs analysis, for example, these factors will play a part in the analysis and in the delivery of training;
- that when training, training methods may need to match the organization's culture and the variety of management styles that exist.

MOTIVATION

Within the section 'Full description of the Unifying Window' in this chapter (page 102), examples of motivation theory will be linked to descriptions of management style, organizational culture and appropriate training method. For example, McGregor's (1960) Theory X can be linked to Power and Role organizational cultures and management styles, and McGregor's (1960) Theory Y can be linked to Achievement and Support organizational cultures and management styles. This 'match', and others that are listed, has been observed by a number of writers, for example Hersey (1982), and is based on general attitudes which are common to each theory and description. For anyone trying to compare 'theory' against practice, this sort of synthesis should prove useful for integrating ideas across a number of areas. When studying how people are motivated, it is important to remember that we are studying a number of interrelated factors, and not just some isolated thing called motivation. For example, when studying motivation, we embrace:

- How people communicate with each other (communication and interpersonal skills).
- People's attitudes towards each other (management style, perception and assumptions).
- How rewards and punishments are distributed (organizational assumptions and procedures).
- How an organization's culture can influence a person's level of energy (organizational history, attitudes, structure and values).
- How events and people outside work can affect a person's desire to perform well (individual outside work influences).
- How a person perceives and values behaviour and achievement of results (individual and group predispositions).
- How a person values feedback about his/her behaviour and results (individual and group predispositions).

For the trainer, there are two issues here. First, that the trainer needs to be aware of the motivation theory, and second, that the trainer needs to understand that people's motivation is interconnected with everything else. Regarding the first point, the location of motivation theory is set out under the 'Full description of the Unifying Window'. Regarding the second point, the reader can compare him/herself and others against the following list of factors that can motivate people at work.

- Do key people create the right climate for working and training effectively?
- Do key people ensure that the right people are in the right jobs?
- Do people take account of social and domestic influences?
- Do people communicate effectively at all levels?
- Do key people handle changing situations with care? Do they seek the involvement and participation of those concerned?
- Do key people note that 'the things that get rewarded get done'? Is the organization rewarding:
  - Those that achieve?
  - Risk taking?
  - Working smarter?
  - Team work?
  - Individual commitment?
  - Quality work?
  - Effective behaviour?
  - Effective decision-making?
  - Creative work?
  - Those who set and monitor standards of work performance?
  - Those who simplify work systems?
  - Those who provide opportunities for others to develop?
  - Those who train, coach and mentor others who are less skilled?
- Do key figures set a first-class example?
- Do key people 'listen' to others?
- Do key people seek other people's views?
- Do key people reinforce good work, to encourage it to be repeated? To achieve this, does the organization:
  - Give money?
  - Give recognition where due?

– Give time off?
– Give prizes?
– Provide enjoyable activities to celebrate?
– Provide opportunities to achieve promotion?

Exercise 1

For yourself, or as part of a group training exercise, ask 'What is rewarded?', 'What should be rewarded?'; then, compare the two.

Exercise 2

'Why don't managers reinforce good work more often?'

Exercise 3

Why is it, that the hardest and the simplest thing of all is 'to give others recognition for work well done'?

When considering what causes dissatisfaction and what perhaps restrains well-motivated behaviour, consider:

- Does the organizational culture support training activity?
- Are the management styles appropriate for the people being managed?
- Is the level of organizational bureaucracy appropriate for the tasks and people involved?
- Do the terms and conditions of employment discourage well-motivated performance?
- Is inter- and intra-group/department conflict stifling good performance?
- Is the work interesting or challenging enough to lift performance? If it is not, will job restructuring (Chapter 10, item 56) help to widen people's responsibility and allow them to use their initiative by using:
  – Job rotation?
  – Job enlargement?
  – Job enrichment?
  – Semi-autonomous work groups?

When considering factors which may either contribute to satisfaction or dissatisfaction at work, consider for example:

- What overall effect does inter-team competition have on people's performance?
- What effect do high levels of change have on people's contribution?
- What effect does high work pressure have on people's output?
- What effect does strong management have on people's desire to want to do well?

Exercise 1

What factors cause dissatisfaction at work?

Exercise 2

Do the factors identified in Exercise 1, restrain well-motivated behaviour?

Exercise 3

Which factors may either cause satisfaction or dissatisfaction? Why?

TRAINING METHODS

Example

'Why was it,' a young graduate said to me, 'that the organization sent me away on an outdoor leadership course, for which I was encouraged to prepare a "back-home action plan"? And, having produced and explained the plan to my line manager, he just poured cold water over it. I just feel the whole training effort has been a waste of time.'

Was the manager's response just an isolated reaction or was it part of something bigger? In this case, all the graduates who attended felt the same way about their back-home experiences. When we discover that this took place in a large traditional retailing organization, the manager's behaviour becomes a little clearer to understand. The retail industry, like the oil, banking, civil service and insurance industries are system driven. That is, all organizational activity is subservient to making the system work. The manager's reaction was 'cool' in this case, because the managers knew that to create change in such an organization would require adhering to well-established bureaucratic procedures. On top of this, the managers knew that to make significant changes to systems could take years. Rather than explain this situation to the young graduate, the manager's response was not to show enthusiasm for the graduate's ideas. The analysis of this situation would indicate that:

- the choice of training intervention did not match the organization's culture; that is, the over-riding role culture did not support unplanned change;
- the managers who had absorbed the culture knew this;
- as part of the graduate's learning and 'conditioning' process, the managers in this case decided to react in a way that mirrored the organization's cultural response, which was to not respond.

As the example above demonstrates, certain training interventions may not accord with the expectations of the cultural tasks of the organization. When this occurs, transfer of learning to the workplace will either be blocked or hindered.

As organizations become flatter and operate more horizontally, more managers are experimenting with a wider set of management styles. As Likert (1961) and Halpin (1959) discovered, managers are increasingly using role and achievement management styles.

For the trainer, the questions 'What training methods are likely to be valued?' and 'What training methods may not be valued?' are worth asking as part of the Training Needs Analysis. The framework of answers suggested here can only be indicative of what to expect: they are, therefore, not meant to be prescriptive. For example, pure organizational cultures may not exist, and managers today may be experimenting with more than one management style and using a wider range of training methods.

For descriptions of training interventions, the reader can consult: Huczynski (1983) who lists an encyclopedia of approaches, *The Glossary of Training Terms* (1981), and the *Further Education Staff College Guide* (1989). A description of training methods in relation to organizational culture is described by Ferdinand (1988) and is expanded in Chapter 10.

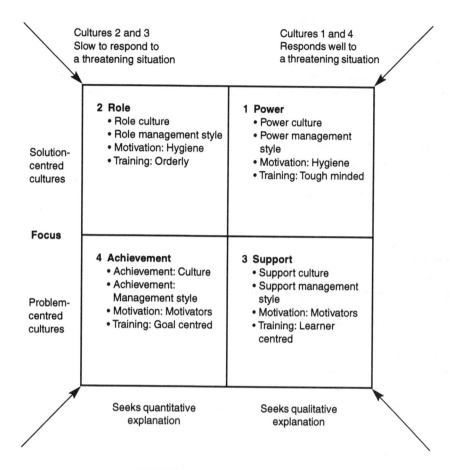

FIGURE 7.1 The Unifying Window

STRUCTURE OF THE UNIFYING WINDOW

Figure 7.1 represents an initial synthesis of ideas that management writers and practitioners have been presenting over the years. The idea of the synthesis is to provide an understanding of how the whole works, rather than just its parts. To know separately about management styles and motivation theory is one thing, but to know that organizational culture may induce certain management styles, and may employ certain motivation stimuli, is something else. To know that certain types of training may be favoured by different types of organizational culture is something else again.

However, the ideas suggested by the Unifying Window do not make diagnosis of training needs and transfer of skills from a training to a work environment any easier to accomplish. All the Window can do is to outline a way of thinking about the sometimes conflicting factors involved. In this sense, the Window can help us become more adept at seeing the trees as well as the wood. Above is an outline of the Window quadrants and structure of the Window and this is followed by fuller descriptions.

Quadrant 1

1A Dominant culture: *Power*.
1B Dominant management style: *Power*.
1C Preferred motivation employed: *Hygiene*.
1D Preferred type of training: *Tough minded*.

Quadrant 2

2A Dominant culture: *Role*.
2B Dominant management style: *Role*.
2C Type of motivation employed: *Hygiene*.
2D Preferred type of training: *Orderly*.
Handy (1978) believes that as much as 80 per cent of many organizations reflect a role culture.

Quadrant 3

3A Dominant culture: *Achievement*.
3B Dominant management style: *Achievement*.
3C Type of motivation employed: *Motivators*.
3D Preferred type of training: *Goal-centred*.

Quadrant 4

4A Dominant culture: *Support*.
4B Dominant management style: *Support*.
4C Preferred motivation employed: *Motivators*.
4D Preferred type of training: *Learner-centred*.

The initial similarities between the above factors in each quadrant can be seen in terms of whether the culture is biased toward *solution-centred* behaviour or *problem-centred* behaviour. All organizations will be comprised of both, because the two construct a whole for complete problem-solving. There can, however, be a tendency for organizations to embrace one side more than another.

Example

An hotel owner (power culture) is able to respond quickly to a customer complaint (threat from environment), because there is a range of remedies or solutions that can be used to solve the problem. The hotel manager, firstly and perhaps mostly, operates in a solution-centred mode. By comparison, the aerospace production manager (achievement culture) will also respond quickly to problems as they occur. In this case, the manager must, because of the huge costs involved, ensure that the cause and nature of the problem are thoroughly investigated before solutions are sanctioned. In this example, the manager is not able to select from a range of off-the-shelf solutions. The aerospace production manager is first of all problem-centred.

Main observations of Figure 7.1

The problem/solution focus

Role and *Power* cultures can be thought of as *solution-centred*. Management in such cultures will limit self-regulation by the team, but will be highly self-regulated themselves.

Such management behaviour could be said to be autocratic and Theory X-biased: McGregor (1960).

Achievement and *Support* cultures can be seen as *problem-centred*. Management seek self-regulation by the team. Management behaviour could be described as democratic and Theory Y-focused: McGregor (1960).

Attitude towards situations (internally and externally)

Power and Support cultures seek to limit feedback by team members. *For power,* managers know which solutions to adopt, which in turn induces short-term thinking patterns, and does not encourage the training and development of team members. *For support,* the manager is prepared to train and develop team members to solve problems, which in turn induces longer-term thinking approaches (but there comes a time when team members take over and little feedback is required).

The difference between short-term and long-term thinking is the difference between *telling* (power) and *delegating* (support), and is the difference between management attitude adopted – Theory X/autocratic (Power); Theory Y/democratic (Support).

Role and Achievement cultures seek feedback from team members. *For Role,* managers co-ordinate team member action and they use systems and procedures to select solutions; *for Achievement,* managers harness team effort by participating in the problem-solving process.

For Role, the individual is subordinate to the system; for Achievement, the individual's contribution counts, but only within the consensus of the team. For Role, the manager seeks an aggregate approach to selecting solutions. For Achievement, the manager recognizes that individual problems require individual explanations. Although individuals within Achievement cultures are often experts, individual contributions must satisfy the team's (aggregate) position. Within Role the individual thinks via interpretation of the system procedures, and within Achievement the individual thinks via his/her specific knowledge and skill. In both cases, the 'individual' is subordinated; one is restrained within a system, and the other is restrained within the bounds of his/her expertise.

Other observations of Figure 7.1

Internal integration

Whereas Role and Power induce a high level of internal integration and co-ordination of effort, Achievement and Support do not. This is because, for Power, control emanates from the top end, and for Role the system guides everything. For Achievement, flexible structures may make co-ordination difficult. For Support, common goals may elude Support individuals, which in turn makes co-ordination difficult.

Dealing with environmental complexity

In this case, Achievement and Support cultures deal more effectively with environmental complexity and change than Role and Power. This is because:

- the situation matches the problem-solving team (Achievement) and the individual's expert (Support) *modus operandi*;
- the channels of communication soon become overloaded for Power, and their sheer lack of experience in this area means that change will be slow;
- for Role, the system takes time to reprogramme, hence like a giant ocean liner, change in direction is slow.

Responding to a threatening environment

When responding to the usual competitive environment, Power and Achievement cultures can respond well. They 'do things right' by instinct and willpower. Role and Support cultures are slow to respond to a threatening environment. They 'do the right things' through systems and working together. This is because:

- Power is always ready to fight and win the usual battles.
- Achievement, although slower than Power, will respond competently after jointly agreeing their action.
- Role will be slow to realize any external threat and equally slow to mobilize troops to meet the external threat, partly because its focus is internal rather than external, and partly because the system requires re-directing.
- Support will likewise be slow to realize and mobilize troops, partly because it lacks a common goal and partly because it is more used to serving others than worrying about its own survival.

FULL DESCRIPTION OF THE UNIFYING WINDOW

Quadrant 1

1A Dominant organizational culture: Power

Organizations with Power cultures deal with breakdown, crisis, policy and direction. They are the home of the entrepreneur. Organizations can include:

- start-up situations;
- hotels;
- restaurants;
- political groups;
- casinos;
- airline services;
- investment banks;
- property companies.

Power sub-cultures within organizations tend to include all top management positions and activities, such as:

- chief executive;
- finance;
- marketing/new products/innovation;
- production;
- crisis handling;
- journalism;
- sales-orientated organization.

Characteristically, in Power sub-cultures:

- people strive for status and influence and endeavour to build close relationships with power figures;
- they work on precedent, or anticipating the wishes and decisions of those in control.

Common features of Power organizations include:

- actions are judged by results;
- they are adaptive and organic;
- management is regarded as an art and a science.

The behaviour of the Power organization can range from:

* effective stewardship, when community-focused, to
* political, when seeking distinction and competitiveness, to
* authoritarian, if seeking stability, to
* exploitive, if seeking survival (the dark side of the Power culture).

1B Management Power style ('This is what I want')

This management style is described by other writers as 'Telling' by Hersey (1982), 'Directing' by Greiner (1972), and is generally described as 'autocratic'.

A feature of the manager using a Power style is that its exact shape can be found to vary. For the chief executive, for example, using a Power management style, his relationship with his next in line can be based on either trust or fear. In either extreme, managers are expected to perform well. Although rewards can be high, so can the price of failure.

In the case where the chief executive says 'I don't care how you do it, but achieve these results', the lieutenant will be trusted and free to secure the ends. In this case managers achieve speed through empathy and not through paperwork systems or tight definitions of jobs. For some managers, where this sort of flexibility is practised, they will say this approach adds a certain excitement to the work.

Strengths
* Managers can unify individual effort behind the vision of the chief executive or leader.
* Managers can provide direction and certainty, and reduce conflict in time of danger and emergency.
* It enables users of the style to move quickly in the market place and make rapid internal change.
* The style can be used:
  – to save time and money in the short term;
  – to provide answers, not ask questions;
  – with individuals or teams who have little ability and who are seldom willing to perform well.

Limitations
* Short-range thinking can be a feature of the Power culture and the Power management style.
* Constructive change can be limited by the vision and flexibility of top management.
* Hands-on control by top management of large organizations can produce confusion and inefficiency.
* Energy can be diverted from work into politics and gaining favour with top management.
* Top management's impulsive seizing of opportunities may disrupt systems, schedules and plans.
* Top management can become isolated, and insulated from bad news.
* Top management can become overloaded which then stalls subordinates' work.
* The worst type of Power style:
  – does not encourage a team to grow, mature, cope and manage itself without a leader;
  – depresses rather than lifts the human spirit;

– doesn't generate team cohesion and a team spirit;
– can induce negative energies into a team;
– is mostly task-focused, rather than task and person-focused.

Darker side of the Power management style
The darker side refers to when the Power management style moves to a more repressive position. When this occurs, perhaps due to a shortage of resources:

- People stop questioning top management, even when they are wrong.
- People are afraid to pass on bad news.
- People give the boss's wishes highest priority, even when this interferes with important work.
- Managers break the rules with impunity and take special privileges.
- People realize, at all levels, that information can be used as a source of personal power.
- Mediocre people can rise by being loyal to those in power.

1C Preferred motivation/attitude employed by the Power management style
- They tend to favour McGregor's (1960) Theory X where
  – a person dislikes work and will avoid it if she/he can;
  – a person would rather be directed than accept responsibility, which she/he avoids.
- They will support Herzberg's (1974) Hygiene Factors
  – which provide short-lived satisfactions, because they become accepted as the norm and may include company policy/procedures/supervision/status/salary/working conditions;
  – which may not make people happy, but they can remove unhappiness.
- They will satisfy Maslow's (1943) level 1 and 2 Needs, which include:
  – physiological needs, 1 (food/drink/shelter)
  – safety needs, 2 (danger/threat/deprivation/security).
- They may favour Job Rotation, where a person performs different jobs at same level.
- They may support Schein's (1970) Rational Economic Man.
- They may support Harris's (1969) 'I'm not OK. You're not OK'.
- They may support Alderfer's (1972) 'Existence'.
- They may support Berne's (1964) 'Destructive Child'.

1D Training methods and the Power manager
Training that may *not* be valued includes structured training and anything bureaucratic. This is why, for example, personnel systems involving considerable amounts of planning and monitoring, such as succession planning and appraisal systems, do not always work well in a power culture. Training that is likely to be valued includes:

- tough-minded activities;
- Outward Bound;
- risk taking;
- trial and error;
- self-development;
- skills of control;
- management development by apprenticeship;
- the discovery method of instruction;

- project work on-job;
- secondment.

Of all the manager types, the Power manager comes in different complexions. At one end can be the more common paternal Theory X manager; at the other end there is the hard-nosed and ruthless autocrat.

The training that is valued above suits more the paternal Power manager. This is where an individual's training tends to be seen from a 'macho' perspective. Such training will reflect the idea of winning, overcoming obstacles and showing initiative. For this type of Power manager, she/he says in effect, I want you to achieve this and this, and how you do it is up to you. In this sense, Outward Bound and discovery learning, for example, parallel this cultural work ethic.

For this type of Power manager who works on the 'edge', relying on intuition, feeling and empathy rather than paperwork and job descriptions, she/he trusts others to come through. To obtain this trust, however, requires a like mindedness, a sense of joining the club and a knowledge or strong feeling that the more junior members can take the heat and handle the risks.

For the extremely hard-nosed Power manager on the other hand, training may not even be on the agenda: you can either do the work or not do it. In this case, training in any planned sense does not occur.

QUADRANT 2

2A Dominant organizational culture: Role

Organizations with Role cultures deal efficiently with the routine, programmable or steady-state activities and are the home of the bureaucrat. Organizations can include:

- oil industries;
- retail industries;
- banking professions;
- life insurance professions;
- civil service;
- hospitals;
- schools;
- fast-food restaurants;
- automobile industries;
- Federal Express (USA);
- McDonald's/Wimpy's.

Role sub-cultures within organizations can include:

- the accounting system;
- wages;
- the secretarial system e.g. switchboard, post room;
- the office services system;
- most of production;
- administrative aspects of sales activities;
- stores controller;
- quality function.

Characteristically, authority tends to be based on formal, legalistic structures, and is exercised through rules, systems and procedures. People at the top tend to be guardians of the status quo and can be prone to nit-picking. Common features of such organizations are that they will seek economies of scale, have long product/service life cycles, will seek predictability and security, will be stable and mechanistic and will view management as a science. The behaviour of the Role organization can range from:

- responsive (Wimpy's, McDonald's), when community focused, to
- iconoclastic (mould breaking, banks and civil service in the 1990s), when seeking distinction and competitiveness, to
- bureaucratic (typically, civil service), when seeking stability, to
- rule driven, when in survival mode.

2B Role management style ('This is how we can co-ordinate our efforts')
This management style is also described as 'Selling' by Hersey (1982), 'Co-ordinating' by Greiner (1972) and is generally thought of as bureaucratic.

Strengths
- Managers in such organizations:
  - design structures and systems that make for efficient operation and reduce time for learning jobs;
  - have clear lines of authority and responsibility to reduce indecision, confusion and conflict;
  - have clear, fair rules and guidelines to protect individuals from exploitation and abusive use of power;
  - endeavour not to 'reinvent the wheel' through their systematic approach.
- The structure, routine and predictability provides security and reduces stress.
- The style:
  - starts to encourage some communication between individuals;
  - allows people to have a say;
  - starts to recognize the individual;
  - can be applicable when the individual or team have some ability and are willing on occasions to perform well.

Limitations
- Managers can be slow to respond to a changing or threatening environment because, firstly, their focus is on managing internal systems and, secondly, changing systems and mobilizing staff can take considerable time.
- Everybody tends to do what the rules say, rather than what is needed.
- Managers tend to take care of their own business, and hence tend not to take care of the whole.
- Managers tend to vigorously guard their divisional and departmental boundaries with the result that operating units tend to become non-co-operating fiefdoms.
- Managers tend to insist on high checking and reporting requirements, which in turn can reduce time for productive work.
- The manager is still very much in control.
- Individuals may be consulted but will be over-ridden, as required.
- The individual or group does not feel fully involved and committed.

Darker side of the Role management style
When the Role management style is threatened in some way, the darker side reveals that:

- people at all levels follow the rules, even when they get in the way of doing the work;
- people at all levels give up making needed improvements, because it becomes so difficult to get approval;
- 'doing things right' becomes more important than 'doing the right things' which in turn amplifies the message, 'Do not deviate from the norm';
- it becomes a sin, at any level, to exceed one's authority or deviate from accepted procedures;
- managers define jobs so tightly that there is little room to contribute individual talent;
- people at all levels are treated as interchangeable parts of a machine, rather than as individuals with special and differing skills and abilities.

2C Preferred motivation/attitude employed by the Role management style
- They tend to favour McGregor's (1960) Theory X. See 1C.
- They will support Herzberg's (1974) Hygiene Factors. See 1C.
- They may satisfy Maslow's (1943) level 2 and 3 Needs, which include:
  – safety needs, 2. See 1C.
  – social needs, 3 (sense of belonging/giving/receiving friendship/social activities).
- They may support Job Rotation and Job Enlargement where job rotation enables people to perform different jobs at the same level and job enlargement enables people to do more of the same.
- They support Schein's (1970) Rational Economic Man and Social Man.
- They support Harris's (1969) 'I'm not OK. You're OK'.
- They support Alderfer's (1972) 'Relatedness'.
- They support Berne's (1964) 'Happy Child'; 'Parent'.

2D Training methods and the Role manager
Training which may *not* be valued includes anything aggressive and which looks risky and is short on structure, or is too individualistic. Training which is likely to be valued includes:

- orderly training with no risk elements;
- objective, structured standardized training for role occupant (not individual);
- counselling to correct deficiencies;
- skills training to provide standard service;
- case study;
- business game;
- education.

Quadrant 3
3A Dominant organizational culture: Achievement
Organizations with Achievement cultures deal with innovation, they are the home of the expert as team player and can include:

- high risk business;
- research teams;
- general management consultancy;
- construction companies;
- aerospace companies;

- advertising agencies;
- entertainment companies.

Sub-cultures can include:

- corporate planning;
- research and development teams;
- organization and methods;
- project teams/task forces;
- marketing product groups;
- computer programmers;
- recruitment officer.

Characteristically, the organization values adaptability and promotes a problem-solving team culture to maintain the flexibility required. The sub-culture's greatest strength is dealing with complex and changing environments.

Common features of such organizations are their short product or service life cycles, they are driven to achieve the over-riding goal, they are adaptive and they enjoy handling variety rather than predictability. Management would tend to be regarded as an art and a science.

The behaviour of achievement cultures can range from :

- co-operative, when community focused, to
- competitive, when seeking distinction, to
- reliable, when stability is required, to
- trial and error approaches, when in survival mode.

3B Management Achievement style ('How can we achieve?')

This management style has also been described as 'Participating' by Hersey (1982), as 'Collaborating' by Greiner (1972) and is generally described as democratic.

Strengths
- There is unity of effort towards mutually valued goals.
- There is a reduced need for high-level controls on individuals.
- There is high internal motivation.
- Maximum utilization is made of members' talents.
- Managers promote high self-esteem in members.
- Managers set an example for rapid learning, problem-solving and adaptation to change.
- People are encouraged to get involved and involvement usually leads to commitment.
- Managers make full use of the opportunities that are present within the team, such as people's ideas, experiences and energies.
- Teams can become self-regulating: they can manage without close supervision.

Limitations
- There can be a tendency to use up and burn out members.
- Narrow views can sometimes reflect the experts' or specialists' *modus operandi*.
- Members can sometimes be arrogant, competitive and ruthless.
- Achievement of goals can take longer compared with the Power manager.

- If seen as a limitation, an investment is required: managers must learn to develop their 'participating skills', for example:
  - listening, supporting, coaching;
  - encouraging team building and team bridging;
  - developing effective problem-solving skills.

The darker side of the Achievement management style
The darker side can be observed when the culture is threatened in some way. Members:
- believe so much in what they are doing that the end comes to justify the means;
- become intolerant of personal needs and sacrifice family, social life and health for work;
- of groups become isolated from others and family;
- of groups tend to only co-operate internally, 'group-think' takes over and criticism becomes stifled;
- have a commitment to excellence at any cost which can lead to waste and inefficiency.

3C Preferred motivation/attitude employed by the Achievement management style
- They favour McGregor (1960) Theory Y, where:
  - work is necessary to a person's psychological growth;
  - under the right conditions a person is motivated by the desire to realize his/her own potential.
- They use Herzberg's (1974) Motivators, which include:
  - achievement/recognition/work itself/responsibility/advancement/growth.
- They enable people to satisfy Maslow's (1943) level 3 and 4 Needs, which include:
  - social needs, 3. See 2C.
  - self-esteem needs, 4 – self-respect/respect of others/autonomy/responsibility /appreciation/recognition/achievement/knowledge/status.
- They make use of Job Enlargement where the individual learns and performs a number of other jobs at the same level. This means that responsibility, at least, will increase; and successful job enlargement can soon lead on to job enrichment.
- They support Schein's (1970) Social Man and Self-Activating Man.
- They support Harris's (1969) 'I'm OK. You're not OK'.
- They support Alderfer's (1972) 'Growth'.
- They support Berne's (1964) 'Parent', 'Adult'.

3D Training methods – Achievement
Training which may *not* be valued includes activity which requires long off-job time, and anything which is too administratively cumbersome. Training which is likely to be valued includes:
- coaching;
- discovery;
- of practical application;
- skills to achieve task;
- informality;
- goal-centred;
- modelling;
- group/team work.

Quadrant 4

4A Dominant organizational culture: Support

Organizations with Support cultures are the home of the expert or professional as an individual star, dealing with one-off support type activities and can include:

- partnerships;
- families;
- small consultancy;
- barristers' chambers;
- spiritually-orientated communities including sects and cults.

Sub-cultures within organizations can include:

- professionals of all sorts;
- computer expert/systems analyst;
- information officer;
- trouble shooter;
- internal consultant;
- public relations officer;
- school teacher;
- antique dealer;
- university professor;
- hospital and R&D consultant;
- aircraft pilot;
- trainer;
- specialist safety officer;
- doctor;
- security officer;
- parliamentary lobbyist;
- legal officer/company secretary.

Characteristically, Support people will be employed for their unique experience and contact with others. Support individuals tend to thrive on interesting work, and then will desire maximum freedom of expression. Members help each other through example, helpfulness and caring. As a rule, Support people can only survive if they are protected from other cultural threats in which they operate.

Interestingly it is the only culture where organizational goals can be determined by individual development needs.

Common features of Support organizations are that they often lack a superordinate goal, and in times of crisis such organizations can fragment quickly. Management tends to be regarded as an art form rather than a science.

The behaviour of the Support organization can range from:

- highly supportive, when community-orientated, to
- elitist, when distinction is sought, to
- conformist, if seeking stability, to
- alienated, from those they are supposed to be serving, when in a survival stage.

4B Dominant management Support style ('I can help you achieve')

This management style has also been described as 'Delegating' by Hersey (1982) and by Greiner (1972).

Strengths
- Managers induce:
  - good internal communication;
  - a high level of commitment to decisions;
  - high levels of co-operation and trust.
- Members:
  - display sophisticated process skills;
  - provide a caring and responsive service;
  - are good at sensing influencing factors in the environment;
  - can work effectively in groups even though they may be required to make a special contribution.
- Members are encouraged to develop themselves by undertaking higher order tasks.
- Managers allow individuals to use their potential.
- Managers raise members' spirits, because people feel they are growing and testing themselves.
- The style can be used with people who show ability and are willing to perform well at all times.

Limitations
- There can be a tendency to put needs of people over the needs of the organization.
- Members may not be strongly task-orientated, and may not deal well with conflict.
- Members can be slow in making decisions.
- Efforts can sometimes be diffuse and unfocused.
- The Support style of management cannot be carried out wholesale, so in this sense it may be limited to people where some element of choice in decision-making is possible.
- There can be a danger of raising job expectations, using this style, so that when such expectations fail to materialize, people leave the organization or become disgruntled.

The darker side of the Support management style
The darker side can emerge as perhaps vital resources are taken away or their influence is diminished. When this occurs:
- issues fester because disagreement is avoided, but this is followed by covert conflict;
- consensus may not by achieved and the group may become indecisive;
- changes may take a long time because of the need to get everyone on board;
- people of unequal contribution are rewarded the same, leading to frustration of the ambitious;
- difficult personnel decisions may be avoided (out of kindness).

4C Preferred motivation employed by the Support style
- They favour McGregor (1969) Theory Y. See 3C.
- They use Herzberg's (1974) Motivators. See 3C.
- They enable people to satisfy Maslow's (1943) levels 4 and 5 which include:
  - self-esteem needs, 4. See 3C.
  - self-realisation needs, 5 (growth/personal development/accomplishment/talents fully used/creativity).
- They make use of Job Enrichment, Herzberg (1974). This is where the individual increases their level of responsibility, authority and power.

- They support autonomous and semi-autonomous work groups.
- They support Schein's (1970) Self-Actualizing Man.
- They support Harris's (1969) 'I'm OK. You're OK'.
- They support Alderfer's (1972) 'Growth'.
- They support Berne's (1964) 'Adult'.

4D Training methods – Support

Training that may *not* be valued includes structured training and tutor-centred training. Training that is likely to be valued includes:

- learning skills which can be transferred;
- learner-centred;
- mentoring and coaching;
- intuitive learning;
- self-development;
- experimentation;
- creative learning;
- 'inward bound'.

DYNAMIC TENSION

For the trainer, an understanding of dynamic tension helps us understand how different forms of co-ordination can pull the organization toward different organizational cultures. Top management, for example, may swing an organization more toward a Power culture than it needs to be, because of its heavily centralized decision-making activity. If unaware of such tensions, the trainer can misinterpret the factors in the organization that may be causing performance shortfalls. If unaware of the tensions, the learner may experience difficulty when applying his/her learning to the work situation.

If an organization is in considerable tension, the trainer should consider the timing for introducing training initiatives. When an organization is stretched beyond its usual limits, both delivery and the results of training may suffer. When training under these circumstances, the trainer may need special support from Power culture figures. For further reading regarding organizational tension see Mintzberg (1979).

The following examples indicate the nature of the tension that can be induced in each of the other cultures.

Source: Power culture

When senior management (Power) co-ordinate all other functions (sub-cultures) through direct supervision, tension can emerge from those being co-ordinated, for example, to adhere to the level of centralized decision-making, and to accept how resources are to be optimized. (Tension can be caused by centralized decision-making.)

Source: Role culture

When the accounts department (Role) standardizes the collection of information from other sub-cultures, tension can result from those being co-ordinated, to conform to new standards. (Tension can be caused through seeking conformity.)

Source: Achievement culture

Tension can be caused when Research and Development (Achievement) hand over their new product for manufacture:

- Production (Role) can find it needs to work to higher quality standards.
- Inspection (Role) can find it needs to use purpose-made instruments for checking measurements.
- Quality Control (Role) can find it needs to adopt new checking procedures.
- Training (Support) can find it needs to train large numbers of staff to achieve higher quality standards.
- Marketing (Achievement) can find it needs to market and sell the new product differently from other products in the range. (Tension can be caused by setting new standards.)

Source: Support culture

When the security manager (Support) improves security procedures, tension can result from the ongoing 'collaboration' that may be required with all other sub-cultures to maintain new internal security standards. (Tension can be caused through seeking collaboration.)

SUMMARY

This chapter has dealt with the idea of how organization culture(s), management style, type of motivation employed and organizational tension can all affect the preparation, the carrying out and the results of training. Although a fairly detailed account has been presented here, the message to the trainer is to ask questions about the context as well as the content of training. In particular:

- How will learners respond to the training messages, which perhaps assume different management attitudes to the ones presently being experienced?
- How will the learner apply the new knowledge and skill correctly to the work situation?
- Who can connect the aims of training with the opportunities within the workplace?
- How will the learner transfer the knowledge and skills to ever new situations?

Organizational culture

The method of viewing organizational culture was based on Harrison's and Handy's work which identified four types of organizational culture. Further to this, they observe that some organizations can be dominated by one particular culture; and nested within an organization are likely to be four types of sub-cultures which will reflect the function of work undertaken (hence production is likely to be dominated by a Role culture).

The significance of culture to the trainer is that it will likely yield clues about attitudes, management styles and preferred methods of training.

Management style

Compared to the autocratic management style of the industrial revolution, and for some time after, today's managers are making greater use of the Co-ordinating and Participating styles, Likert (1961). The reasons for this may include:

- that managers' education and training has improved;
- the maturity level of team members has increased along with their expectations;
- that flatter organizational structures over the last twenty years require that managers must be prepared to communicate and share control more widely than before.

Motivation

In this chapter we have identified how motivation theory can be linked to organizational culture and management style. When training others it is useful to understand:

- What things motivate people at work and lead to feelings of satisfaction?
- What things may cause dissatisfaction at work?
- What things may contribute to both satisfaction and dissatisfaction at work?

A person's level of motivation or energy level is important for the trainer, because it can affect the design of training events; it can affect how training is delivered; and it can also affect how learners can apply and transfer their learning to the workplace.

When assessing how the 'context' of the work environment affects people's motivation, it is useful to ask 'What behaviour gets rewarded?' By default, the answer to the question 'What behaviour does not get rewarded?' will also emerge. Likewise, when asking 'Does the organization support training activity?', the trainer will begin to understand how difficult and time-consuming the training task can be.

Training method

This chapter has suggested that the selection of training methods may need to match the prevailing organizational culture and management style, for successful training results. Chapter 10 takes this idea further, and provides a classification of training methods and organizational cultures.

The Unifying Window

When examining the Unifying Window (Figure 7.1), we noted that it can be examined on a number of levels. In addition to the horizontal and vertical similarities and differences, there is also diagonal common ground. In addition to displaying how it is possible to view pure descriptions of organizational culture and management style, the Window can also be used to examine the 'mixture' of cultures and styles that exist.

Dynamic tension

At any one time an organization's cultures are held in a dynamic tension. As indicated, each culture can induce a different tension within other cultures. For example:

- a Power culture can create tension in the other cultures through centralized decision-making;
- a Role culture can create tension in other cultures through seeking conformity;
- an Achievement culture can create tension in other cultures, by setting new standards;
- a Support culture can create tension in other cultures through seeking collaboration.

Such tension is not easy to determine, because it is often hidden and can form part of the politics and power play within an organization, which often resides at senior level. When training, it is useful to know the nature and degree of tension that exists, as this can influence both the introduction and the results of training.

REFERENCES AND FURTHER READING
Organizational culture
Handy, C. B. (1974) 'Pitfalls of Management Development'. *Personnel Management*, 20–5.
Handy, C. B. (1976) *Understanding Organizations*. 2nd edn. Aylesbury: Penguin.
Handy, C. B. (1978) *Gods of Management*. London: Souvenir Press.
Handy, C. B. (1989) *The Age of Unreason*. London: Hutchinson.
Harrison, R. (1972) 'Understanding Your Organization's Character'. *Harvard Business Review 50, 3,* 119–28.
Harrison, R. (1975) *Diagnosing Organization Ideology. The 1975 Annual Handbook for Group Facilitators*. La Jolla, CA: University Associates.
Harrison, R. (1983) 'Strategies for a New Age'. *Human Resource Management 22, 3,* 209–35.
Harrison, R. (1986) *Understanding Your Organization's Culture*. Berkeley, CA: Harrison Associates Inc.
Harrison, R. (1992) *Diagnosing Organization Culture* (rev. edn). San Diego, CA: Pfeiffer.
Harrison, R. (1993) *Diagnosing Organization Culture, Trainer's Manual*. San Diego, CA: Pfeiffer.
Harrison, R. (1995) *The Collected Papers of Roger Harrison*. Cambridge, Mass.: McGraw-Hill.
Mintzberg, H. (1979) *The Structuring of Organizations*. Englewood Cliffs, N.J.: Prentice-Hall Inc.
Plant, R. (1987) *Managing Change and Making it Stick*. Aldershot: Gower.
Rice, A. K. (1963) *The Enterprise and its Environment*. London: Tavistock.
Schein, E. H. (1958) *Organization Culture and Leadership: A Dynamic View*. San Francisco/London: Jossey-Bass.
Schein, E. H. (1965) *Organizational Psychology*. Englewood Cliffs, N.J.: Prentice-Hall Inc.
Sherwood, J. J. (1988) 'Creating Work Cultures with Competitive Advantage'. *Organizational Dynamics 1, 16, 1,* 2–5.
Williams, A., Dobson, P. and Walters, M. (1989) *Changing Culture*. London: Institute of Personnel Management.

Management style
Blake, R. R. and Mouton, J. S. (1964) *The Managerial Grid*. Houston, Texas: Gulf Publishing.
Cooper, C. L. and Makin, P. (1988) *Psychology For Managers*. London: Macmillan.
Greiner, L. E. (1972) 'Evolution and Revolution as Organizations Grow'. *Harvard Business Review*, July/August, 37–46.
Halpin, A. W. (1959) *The Leadership Behaviour of School Superintendents*. Chicago: Midwest Administration Centre, The University of Chicago.
Hersey, P. and Blanchard, K. (1982) *Management of Organizational Behaviours*. Englewood Cliffs, N.J.: Prentice-Hall.
Hodgkinson, C. (1984). *Philosophy of Leadership*. Oxford: Blackwell.
Likert, R. (1961) *New Patterns of Management*. New York: McGraw-Hill.
Mangerison, C. (1984) *Managerial Problem Solving*. New York: McGraw-Hill.

Reddin, R. (1985) *The Best of Bill Reddin*. Trowbridge: Institute of Personnel Management.

Motivation/Attitude/Systems

Alderfer, C. P. (1972) *Existence, Relatedness, and Growth: Human Needs in Organizational Settings*. New York: Free Press.

Berne, E. (1964) *Games People Play*. New York: Grove Press.

Harris, T. A. (1969) *I'm OK. You're OK: A Practical Guide to Transactional Analysis*. New York: Harper & Row.

Herzberg, F. (1974) *Work and the Native of Man*. London: Crosby Lockwood Staples.

Herzberg, F. (1969) 'Job Enrichment Pays Off'. *Harvard Business Review*, March/April, 61–78.

Likert, R. (1967) *The Human Organization*. New York: McGraw-Hill Book Company.

Likert, J. G. and Araki, C. T. (1986) 'Managing Without a Boss: System 5'. *Leadership & Organization Development Journal 7, 3,* 17–20.

McGregor, D. (1960) *The Human Side of the Enterprise*. New York: McGraw-Hill Book Company.

Maslow, A. (1954) *Motivation and Personality*. New York: Harper & Row.

Schein, E. H. (1970) *Organizational Psychology,* 2nd edn, 50–72. Englewood Cliffs, N.J.: Prentice-Hall Inc.

Motivation

Argyris, C. (1957) *Personality and Organization*. New York: Harper & Row. For maturity continuum.

McClelland, D. C., Atkinson, J. W., Clark, R. A. and Lowell, E. L. (1953) *The Achievement Motive*. New York: Appleton-Century-Crofts.

Maslow, A. H. (1943) 'A Theory of Human Motivation'. *Psychological Review 50,* 370–96.

Vroom, V. H. and Deci, E. L. (1970) *Management and Motivation*. Bungay, Suffolk: Penguin Books.

Training method

Ferdinand, R. (1988) 'Management Training Needs Analysis'. *Journal of Industrial and Commercial Training,* September/October, 27–31.

Further Education Staff College (1989) *A Guide to Work-Based Learning Terms*. London. Training Agency, HMSO.

Glossary of Training Terms (1981). London: Manpower Services Commission, HMSO.

Huczynski, A. (1983) *Encyclopedia of Management Development Methods*. Aldershot: Gower.

Likert, R. (1961) *New Patterns of Management*. New York: McGraw-Hill Book Company.

Richardson, J. and Bennet, B. (1984) 'Applying Learning Techniques to On-The-Job Development: Part 2'. *Journal of European Industrial Training 8, 3.*

8

Investigative, problem-solving or training needs location methods

INTRODUCTION

In this chapter we will examine some problem-solving approaches which can be used by the trainer to assist management with examining work-related difficulties, and to locate training needs buried within work-related problems. Having identified the 'potential training needs' using a problem-solving approach, the trainer will likely identify training requirements in more detail using a Training Needs Analysis (TNA) technique, as shown in Chapter 9.

RECORDS AND REPORTS

Records and reports provide objective but historic evidence of the results of people's performance, and provide clues to potential training needs. As always with training, having located a performance discrepancy, further examination of likely causes and remedies must be undertaken. When investigating the causes of problems, the investigator must remember that it is the past situation which is reflected, and, the current situation may be different again. When examining data over a long period (perhaps one, two, three, four years or more) trainers may need to develop statistical skills to deal with trends and patterns.

When interpreting records and reports it is vital that the context of the situation is fully appreciated and that interpretations of facts are accurate. To learn that no sales staff were available to serve on three occasions, may or may not indicate a potential problem: perhaps on each occasion there was a shortage of staff. And if it is a staff resourcing problem, then it may be a line management matter and not a training one. The following list of items will give some indication of records that can be consulted to determine clues about training needs.

- Complaints (From: Customer Complaint Records)
  - Poor customer service.
  - Late deliveries.
- Output (From: Production/Quality/Financial Records)
  - Low output.
  - Delays caused by errors and mistakes.
  - Excessive time taken to finish jobs or orders or supply parts.
  - Specifications not followed.
  - Standards of quality not met.
  - Frequent bottlenecks in production.
  - Too much waste.

- Organizational (From: Personnel/Communication or Quality Control Records and from minutes/memoranda)
  - Lack of flexibility in labour force.
  - People receiving instructions from more than one person.
  - Poor communications generally.
  - Ignorance of company/department rules.
  - Errors resulting from instructions not clearly understood.
- Employee attitude (From: Personnel/Attitude Survey/Safety Records)
  - Excessive absenteeism or poor punctuality.
  - Excessive number of applications for time off.
  - High labour turnover.
  - Employees' lack of interest in the work.
  - Untidiness of work area.
- Selection/training (From: Training/Production/Maintenance Records)
  - Employees' difficulty in mastering new job or new equipment.
  - New employees who take too long to reach experienced worker standard.
  - Employees' failure to realize importance of minor jobs or details.
  - Excessive maintenance costs.
  - Excessive wear and tear on equipment.
- Health and safety (From: Health/Safety and First Aid Records)
  - High accident frequency.
  - Ignorance of safety rules by employees.
  - Failure to observe known safety rules or use safety equipment.
  - Neglect of minor injuries.

In terms of gaining management attention, historic and factual data is usually a good argument for discussing performance shortfalls.

DISCUSSION LEADING GROUP PROBLEM-SOLVING METHOD

The Discussion Leading Group Problem-Solving Technique is a method of using individual and group expertise to examine problems, consider solutions and identify areas requiring further analysis for training. For the trainer undertaking new activities, for example, there is frequently a need to understand how and what type of change is taking place, and from a training point of view, support it. In such situations the discussion leading technique can be very useful.

This technique involves the group leader acting as focal point for examining change, using a problem-solving process. The group leader leads, presents the problem, asks questions, debriefs and monitors progress to conclusion of the event. The group leader will always be thoroughly prepared, but does not necessarily require special expertise. What is important is that the group leader is able to empower group members to contribute as effectively as possible, within a problem-solving context. Below are listed the elements for handling this approach.

The ingredients for discussion leader

The ingredients for handling this technique include:

- *Briefing* (usual) or *not briefing* members (less common) about problem to be examined.
- The group leader using *questioning techniques* which empower group members.

- The group leader adopting a *problem-centred and solution approach* (either overtly expressed or mentally followed).
- *Debriefing* members.
- The group leader using *no structure* or using *simple procedures or structures*, on which to 'hang' contributions.

The problem to be examined

This can include almost anything. For example:

- working out the business strategy;
- resolving quality problems;
- resolving communication difficulties;
- improving the functioning of existing systems and procedures.

Questioning techniques

These could be:

- Open question: 'What experience do members have of dealing with . . .' (How, when, where, why, who, what).
- Direct question: 'What is your policy on this matter?' 'How would you summarize the points made thus far?'
- Relay question: 'How do the rest of you feel about this issue?'
- Redirected question: 'Mr B, how do you think Mr A's policy of dealing with late payers would work in your department?'
- Leading question: 'Would you rather leave it to market forces, or would you like to control demand using . . . ?'
- Factual question: 'What do you see as the purpose of such a strategy . . . ?'
- Controversial question: 'Do buyers know by instinct which lines are best-sellers?'

Problem-centred and problem-solution approaches

The group leader maps contributions against the need to examine the problem and seek appropriate solutions. This is done, not so much in sequence as in total.

Debriefing members

Questions are asked such as:

- What was our purpose?
- What other information is required?
- Who might be best suited to examine this problem in more detail?
- What would you do next?
- If taking part in a similar exercise, is there anything different you would do?
- How do you feel now?
- What have we managed to achieve?
- What are the implications for training?

Using simple procedures and structures or using no structures

For example:

No structure
A blank flip chart to record information.

Structure used
- The 'Where are we now? Where do we want to be?' method (on flip chart).
- The 'Cause/Effect Fishbone' method.
- The 'Demands/Constraints/Choices' method.
- The 'Post-it' method.
- The 'Input/Process/Results' General Systems method.
- The 'Force Field' method.
- The 'Input/Process/Results' method.

The variety of simple procedures and structures that can be used to locate training needs is considerable, but in most cases the group leader tends to use a simple structure as a 'starting point' which can be discarded, if necessary. In brief, the method for handling each of the above is as follows:

USING BLANK FLIP PAD (No structure)

The leader briefs the team and is prepared to list contributions as they come. It may be that data is recorded in the usual serial manner, or it may happen that a 'pattern' emerges. Note:

- The group leader will require some expertise to handle this unstructured situation.
- Senior management members may prefer this mode of working, where no assumptions are made.
- To assist data recording, the group leader could use
  - the spider diagram method;
  - columns;
  - balloons;
  - a key word approach;
  - member seating plan on flip chart as hook for recording comments.
- There can be a case for gathering and not fully briefing, say, experts or lay people together to examine some problem, but these, although novel approaches, are not common.

THE 'WHERE ARE WE NOW? WHERE DO WE WANT TO BE?' METHOD

This method draws heavily on the 'Performance Gap Curve' which was discussed in Chapter 2. In this case, the group leader draws two boxes, one to the bottom and one to the top of, say, a flip pad, as shown in Figure 8.1. The leader then asks the members to describe the bottom box 'Where are we now?'. Members may reply, for example:

- 'We have no training instructors.'
- 'We have high turnover.'
- 'There is high waste.'
- 'There is no induction training.'
- 'There is only poor "sit-by-Nelly" training.'
- 'Our quality is erratic.'

Having established the 'now' situation, the leader then asks 'Where do we want to be?', which is represented by the box at the top of the page. So, for example, members may state:

- 'We want products which meet our quality standards every time.'
- 'We need to develop a training plan and a supportive training climate.'
- 'We want to gain recognition for the Investors in People award.'

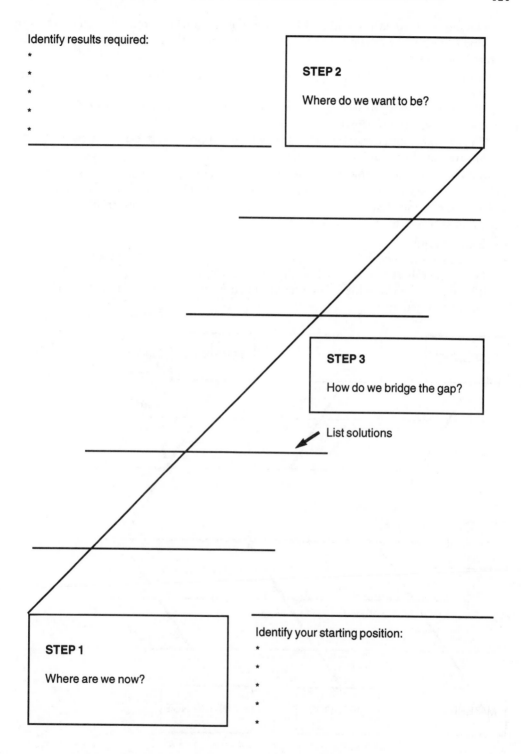

Identify results required:
*
*
*
*
*

STEP 2

Where do we want to be?

STEP 3

How do we bridge the gap?

List solutions

Identify your starting position:
*
*
*
*
*

STEP 1

Where are we now?

FIGURE 8.1 Where are we now? Where do we want to be?

Having established the end and beginning of the journey, the leader then asks, by drawing a line between the two boxes, 'How do we bridge the gap?' Answers to this question may include:

- 'Appoint training instructor to prepare training programmes or maintain training records.'
- 'Run course for all supervisors to make them aware of the shared difficulties we face and how we might resolve them.'
- 'Prepare and agree work procedures which support practices to achieve desired product quality standards.'

In this example, a direct need for training activity emerged. It will, however, need further study based on, say, a job and role analysis. Such analysis may yield a person specification, a job description, a list of job priorities and the pattern of relationships which must be established. Note that this procedure is:

- Easy and quick to use.
- Very useful for obtaining a 'rough draft' for location of training needs.
- Group members find it very friendly to work with.
- The analysis can be achieved on one side of an A4 sheet of paper, in terms of ideas and key points generated.

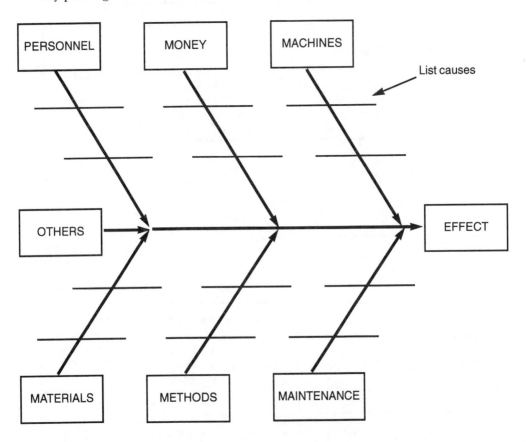

FIGURE 8.2 The Cause/Effect or Fishbone Diagram

THE 'CAUSE/EFFECT FISHBONE' METHOD

The Cause/Effect, Fishbone or Ishikawa diagram, Figure 8.2, has long been associated with the quality circle problem identification process. However, the same simple structure can be used by the group leader to examine problems and identify areas that require training action.

To construct the diagram, it is usual to start with describing the effect of the problem. Perhaps it is a quality problem which is not easily traceable: the leader will describe the effect and enter it in a box, to the left but at the centre of, say, a flip pad. The leader will then draw a horizontal line across the centre of the page joining the 'Effect' box. From this central line, the leader will draw lines at an angle like a fishbone. At the end of each fishbone, the leader will draw boxes labelled perhaps: Machines; Materials; Methods; Personnel; Money; Maintenance.

In this case, there would be three fishbones above the centre line and three fishbones below. At this stage, the leader will ask the members to consider likely causes of the problem which may occur at any of the labelled sites. From member contributions, the causes may have an impact at more than one site, i.e. Machines and Materials.

Although this technique is used to locate causes of problems, it can be used to locate potential areas for training. In both cases further investigation and analysis will be required. In the case of training, a Training Needs Analysis technique may need to be employed. Note that this procedure is:

- Easy and quick to use.
- Useful for locating areas for further investigation.
- The Cause/Effect findings can also be used with statistical methods such as Pareto analysis to determine significance of the causes.
- When, say, considering the effect on an organization, the location of strategic shortfalls may be examined in terms of causes such as: economic; social; political; legislative; technological; markets and geographical.

THE 'DEMANDS/CONSTRAINTS/CHOICES' METHOD

When dealing with people's perception about what 'must be done' and what 'must not be done' to achieve some outcome, all too often the choices can become overlooked. To use this method, the group leader draws a fried-egg shape, as shown in Figure 8.3. The centre (yolk) is marked 'Demands' (what must be done). The outer ring (the white of the egg) represents the 'Choices' (what can be done). Everything outside the egg can be thought of as the 'Constraints' (what must *not* be done).

Demands. These reflect the job requirements and are seen as things that must be done by the job holder.

Constraints. These are the things that can be seen by the job holder to limit or eliminate choice. They are seen as the limits of responsibility by the job holder and represent psychological boundaries and physical forces beyond which a person cannot 'travel'. While some constraints are *imposed,* many can be *self-imposed.* It is often the self-imposed constraints which inhibit clear thinking and exploration of choices.

Choices. These are the things that help us achieve the demands and work within the constraints more effectively than we have done before. The discovery of choices usually comes after the demands and constraints have been examined. To exploit the choices, the leader can also ask members to consider what opportunities there are for doing this.

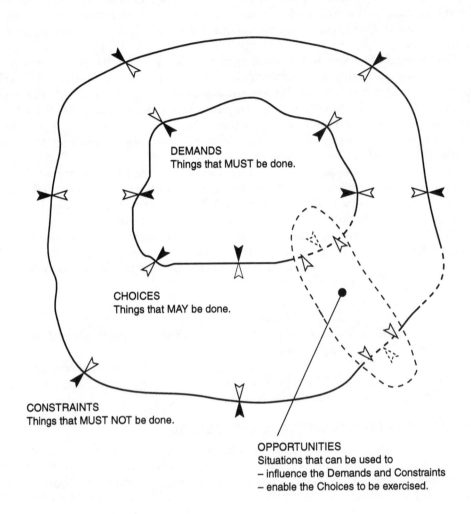

FIGURE 8.3 The Demands/Constraints/Choices Diagram

Sometimes, *opportunities* can be used to 'alter' the demands and the constraints, and thus facilitate choice for the job holder.

Example 1

By reorganizing staff in an accounts office from a traditional structure, where each person specialized, to one where teams coped with all the tasks, the manager achieved the task by:

- creating a vision of what could be done (Choice);
- analysing the situation (Choice);
- making out a case for the changes (Choice);
- negotiating the case (overcame senior management concerns about creating change which could be detrimental for financial reporting if it went wrong – overcame Constraint);
- winning a budget (overcame Constraint);
- involving all members of staff (Choice);
- providing training (Choice);
- having the courage to face the challenge of change (Choice).

The result of all this was:

- improved productivity (supported the Demand);
- improved quality (supported the Demand);
- improved job satisfaction (supported the Demand);
- an improvement in the work climate (supported the Demand).

Example 2

A building developer wanted to build houses on land which contained unique plant life. Conservationists wanted the fields to be left alone.

Demands (What must be done)
- For developers: they must build.
- For conservators: they must save the unique plant life.

Constraints (What must not be done)
- For developers: building must go ahead. They knew they must not break the law to achieve their aims.
- For conservators: they can protest. They decided they must not break the law to achieve their aims.

Choices (What can be done)
- For developers: there was no choice! They decided they would, at least, listen to the opposing arguments.
- For conservators, they considered two strategies: First, *direct action* – protesting, seeking legal injunctions, and generating bad publicity for the developers in the hope that they will back off. Second, *seek opportunity* – to compromise, and involve as many interested parties in discussion to generate more choices and opportunities or to create good/bad publicity.

The final choice

Through discussion with interested parties (creating opportunities), it was arranged, with local authority help, for the top soil (which contains the unique seeds) to be transported to another site.

Analysis of results

When we analyse the results of this approach using the Result part of the Input/Process/Result (Chapter 4) Problem-Solving Model we get:

- Immediate (win/win) result. (Product).
  - Developers can build.
  - Conservators have saved the unique seeds.
- Intermediate (win/win) result. (Output).
  - Developers and conservators received good publicity.
  - Relationships between developers and conservators improved.
  - The developers' new buildings sold quickly and met their expected profit margins.
  - Everyone felt 'good' about this decision.
- Ultimate (win/win) result. (Outcome).
  - Living examples of unique plant life have been kept alive, to be enjoyed by present and future generations of people, and to be studied by scientists at any time.
  - This 'compromise' signalled a new way of negotiating for many similar situations, involving developers and conservators.

In this example, it is interesting to note that it was the preparedness to compromise and seek *opportunities* on both sides that led to the *choices* and the agreed solution.

Example 3

The following can be used as an example or an exercise. The trainer can ask learners to create a list of job demands and constraints (or provide list), and then ask learners to list their choices (or provide them). The demands and imposed constraints should all be questioned, but in particular it is the discovery of choices and the freeing of self-imposed constraints that will change attitudes and situations. Coupled with the identification or creation of opportunities, the choices may find a way of being quickly exploited.

Demands

I must:
- manage sales;
- manage budget;
- manage customer service;
- manage the routine tasks;
- prepare reports;
- set realistic standards;
- manage delegation;
- manage crises;
- manage visitors, telephone, travelling, meetings, information, reading, socializing, administration, procrastination;
- manage organization;
- manage job roles;
- manage team;

– manage the 'out of hours' activities;
– manage stock levels.

Constraints self-imposed

I must not:
– learn;
– take risks;
– delegate;
– review my performance;
– change.

Constraints imposed

I cannot have more of anything;
I must not:
– exceed budget;
– exceed staffing levels;
– disobey company policy;
– disrupt company culture;
– do things illegally;
– ignore competitors;
– ignore technological limits.

Choices

I choose:
– how to do the work;
– to delegate, develop myself and acknowledge the work of good performers;
– to use my time more effectively;
– to negotiate away some Constraints and some Demands;
– to see problems as opportunities;
– to change my management style, role and power base;
– to develop a high profile for myself;
– my level of performance;
– to manage my boss.

Consider the following notes about this procedure:

- Easy to use.
- By creating Choices members may discover how Constraints can be overcome, and how Demands can be more easily achieved.
- To consider opportunities requires that members take time to use their intuition, imagination, creative thinking and logical thinking.
- The method helps to distinguish between imposed and self-imposed constraints.
- In general, the approach has the merit of challenging fixed ideas and assumptions.

THE 'POST-IT' METHOD

This method is particularly suitable for senior management problem-solving. The sequence of events using the Post-it method involves:

- the leader preparing and briefing group members with regard to the problem;
- the members writing their replies on 'Post-it' pads and passing them to the leader;

- the leader sticking the 'Post-it' labels to, say, a white board;
- the leader, with the help of members, grouping the replies to make meaning of all the contributions.

This method lends itself well to working on problems or issues where there is no absolute answer. For example: working out direction for company strategy; identifying ways to retain staff; identifying novel ways to acknowledge good worker performance and identifying ways to re-structure an organization and maintain high levels of communication. The important and exciting aspect of the process involves the stage of making sense of the (thirty-plus) 'Post-it' contributions. To determine how to group the replies, use may be made of content analysis, which involves grouping replies by 'like' content.

When using this method, the leader can develop a number of grouped replies: one perhaps about production matters, another about customers and another about finance. By standing back and studying these isolated groups, the next stage might be to see connections between them. The look of the final diagram may be described as a system of integrated contributions, which requires either a multi-solution or single-solution approach.

As before, further investigation may be required to solve the individual problems and detailed training needs.

Other comments about this method are:

- It is a user-friendly method, but the leader must have the confidence to 'discover' groupings, meanings and connections.
- The leader must involve the members both with encouraging their contributions and using their ability to interpret meanings and patterns.
- As the results unfold, everyone present will have had the opportunity to take part and witness the whole process. If it is handled well, members should feel satisfied and confident about their shared pooling of ideas. The detail may need to be gathered later.
- The method tries to avoid the 'group think' phenomenon, Janis (1971). Contributions, however, will reflect group member persuasions, and so the leader will need to consider the make-up of, say, the five to nine group members.

THE 'FORCE FIELD' METHOD

As discussed in Chapter 7, an organization is held steady by dynamic tensions that are the result of driving and resisting forces. This method is credited to Lewin (1951 and 1969) and examples can be seen in Woodcock (1979). The parallel of the force field analysis is the pushing and resisting of a rugby scrum. The resulting forces are shown in Figure 8.4. There are forces 'with you' and there are forces 'against you'. In the case of the rugby scrum, brute strength might be the determinant factor. In other situations, however, it may be possible to strengthen the forces that are with you, and weaken the forces against you.

Example

Senior management wanted to improve customer service throughout all departments within its store. They wished, however, that the drive to improve customer service emanate from within each department, rather than from pressure from head office. So when considering this change, the following analysis emerged.

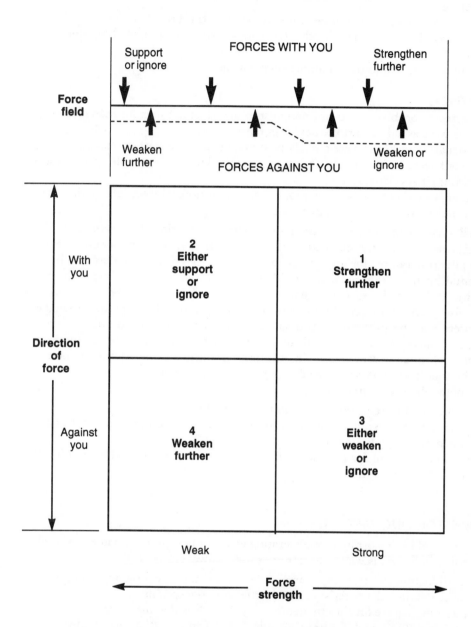

FIGURE 8.4 The Force Field Diagram

Driving forces
- Senior management wished to see improvements in this area.
- Of the thirty-five department heads, five were known to be prepared to pilot such a change.
- The training staff could fully support such change.

Resisting forces
- The aggregate problem of co-ordinating so much change by senior management, if everyone were asked to start the new programme.
- Many department heads were already busy with managing staff shortages.
- Many staff were likely to resist becoming multi-skilled salespeople, preferring to stay with their specialist role.
- Customers would need to be given more quality attention, which might, at first, work against the aim of providing a fast service.

As this analysis is now described, it displays a 'stalemate' situation. To create movement, the strengths need to be strengthened further. This was done by announcing to everyone that a pilot programme for improving customer service was to be undertaken by five departmental heads. Training was provided for everyone concerned, and the programme was duly developed over a period of time so that it could be implemented smoothly elsewhere. Through the process of piloting, other departmental managers showed interest in the programme and saw for themselves the benefits that accrued. This, in effect, was equivalent to 'weakening the resistance against the programme'. By the time all departments were 'phased in', the programme had gathered its own momentum and the training initiatives were taking on a life of their own.

A few notes about this procedure:
- Easy to prepare but requires tactical and strategic thinking.
- This example demonstrated how 'pilot programmes' can be useful for 'debugging' and for generating wider interest.
- This method is useful for describing the major forces at work, and examining the strength and nature of these forces.

THE 'BRAINSTORMING' METHOD
The application of brainstorming for generating ideas for new product names, as used in the advertising industry, is well known. Other uses, however, include:
- as an introduction to a training course to determine: the level of knowledge; level of experience; learner characteristics and learner misconceptions;
- after a training course finishes to identify, say, key ideas that have been learnt;
- as a problem-solving tool, for brainstorming causes and solutions to problems.

Example
The example below focuses on a possible solution for improving productivity.

Stage 1: State the problem and discuss for ten minutes
'We want to improve production staff productivity which currently makes use of traditional line methods.'

Stage 2: Restate the problem (perhaps ten to 100 ways)
How do we. . .
1 increase productivity?
2 reduce costs?
3 improve job satisfaction?
4 improve quality?
5 reduce waste?
6 reduce 'searching time' for parts?
7 improve wages?
8 improve working conditions?
9 get more business?
10 improve working arrangements?
11 . . .

Stage 3: Select one or two restatements
Either leader does this or it is done democratically.

Stage 4: Brainstorm the restatements (twenty minutes to three hours)
Brainstorm:
'In how many ways can we: item (10) improve working arrangements and item (1) get higher productivity?'
    The result of the brainstorm list was thus:
a Ask staff to make suggestions.
b Get sub-contractors.
c Create a new company.
d Train staff.
e Replace management.
f Work longer hours.
g Work weekends.
h Work shifts.
i Redesign floor area.
j Sack management and create autonomous teams.
k Pay by results.
l Make teams compete.
m Improve assembly equipment.
n . . .

Stage 5: Select wildest idea and brainstorm
The wildest idea selected was item (j) 'Sack management and create autonomous teams.'
The result of the brainstorm included:
A Select ten team leaders.
B Select ten teams.
C Train all staff.
D Go for total job versatility.
E Give targets to each team.
F Encourage teams to compete.
G Pay on results.
H Sack anybody not meeting targets.

I Make team leaders responsible to quality control leaders.

J ...

Stage 6: Evaluate

Evaluation as suggested by Rawlinson (1989) can take place as follows:

- individual members select 10 per cent of items as good ideas, and each distributes a list to the others;
- a final 10 per cent of good ideas is forwarded to the evaluation team;
- the evaluation team then makes a final selection.

What criteria are used by the evaluation team to make a final selection can vary. Selection may be based on:

- a projected cost-benefit analysis;
- what seems directly useful in the short/long term;
- the outcome of further detailed investigations.

In this example, items A, B, C, D, E, F and I all made a contribution to the final solution.

Other comments

- The method can take time to complete. Before starting the brainstorm it would be usual to include a ten-minute warm up session.
- Suitable for between twelve and twenty members who will remain committed to the brainstorming process.
- The group leader must be well versed in the method, flexible and quick at recording suggestions.
- The method has the merit of expanding the lateral thinking process, and pursuing ideas from a different viewpoint.
- The principles of brainstorming as indicated above can be modified in many ways.

THE 'INPUT/PROCESS/RESULT' METHOD

The Input/Process/Result method can assist with analysing problems in terms of the *Means* (inputs and processes) and *Ends* (products, immediate results; outputs, inter-mediate results; outcomes, ultimate results). This method is useful when a total view of the situation is required and when there is confusion about means and ends.

As shown in Figure 4.1, analysis can be focused on each part of a problem or issue. If we consider, say, a training issue this could be analyzed as follows:

Inputs (What resources are available/needed?)

- What is the training need/gap?
- Who are the learners?
- What resources will be required? (Facilities? Materials? Monetary? To pay trainers, trainees, etc?)
- What training methods are available, and which shall we use?

Processes (How will the inputs/resources be managed?)

- How will the training method help the learner?
- Will there be sufficient interaction between learners, trainers and others?
- How will we assess whether learners like the training experience? (During training.)

Product (The first or immediate result)

- What immediate results do we expect? (To pass examination? To be fully trained?)
- How will we measure what learning has taken place?

Output (The intermediate result or the sum of all the Product results)

- Will the trainee be able to apply his/her learning to the job?
- Will the trainee demonstrate that she/he has reached the experienced worker standard in the workplace?
- Will the trainee improve his/her performance on-job, and if so, how will we measure the increase in performance?

Outcome (The ultimate result or the sum of all the outputs)

- Will the performance of all staff increase, as a direct result of training (as measured by an increase in organizational net profit or an overall increase in productivity)?
- Will labour turnover, for the whole organization, decrease, as a result of the training?
- Will accident frequency, for the whole organization, decrease as a result of training?
- Will the quality of life improve for all employees, as a direct result of training?

As we examine how training can be undertaken, and as we examine the likely impact of a person's enhanced performance as a result of training, we can see how it is possible to ask some very searching questions prior to a training event taking place. If we extend this strategic thinking process, we can take an even wider view. We can, for example, look at the system in terms of the broad 'means' and the 'ends'. For example:

Looking at 'Means'

Why don't we train staff to the required standard which reflects the example above?

Looking at 'Ends'

Why don't we recruit staff with the necessary skills, rather then train staff? Why don't we 'sub-contract' this work rather than train our staff to do it?

Looking at 'Means' and 'Ends'

Why don't we direct department heads to decide whether to train staff or recruit staff, rather than involve central training?

Other comments

- The procedure is quick to use, once the initial ideas have been mastered.
- It has the merit of promoting both operational, tactical and strategic thinking.
- In particular, it is useful for examining 'levels' of results.

THE 'BENCHMARKING' METHOD

As an investigative tool, Benchmarking makes use of the 'Where are we now? Where do we want to be?' method and the 'Input/Process/Result' approach. (The 'Where are we. . .' process, in turn, draws on the ideas of the 'Performance Gap Curve' shown in Chapter 2.)

According to Leibfried (1994) 'Benchmarking is an external focus on internal activities, functions or operations in order to achieve continuous improvement.' Benchmarking, which can be used at any level, has the aim of 'measuring' others' performance, with a view then to questioning how one is achieving one's own performance. Benchmarking can be used to compare performance against:

- individuals;
- competitor organizations;
- non-competitor organizations (related/unrelated to industry);
- world class organizations.

While Benchmarking is about making performance comparisons against others, the focus of the comparison is on how it is possible to make better use of one's own inputs and processes in order to improve results. Thus, Benchmarking is not about imitating others. As an organization tool, Benchmarking is currently being integrated alongside 'quality' and 'problem-solving' initiatives.

When using Benchmarking as an individual development tool, performance comparisons can be made against others and performance discrepancies can be prepared. From here, the aim is to identify how it is possible to better clarify one's own resources/inputs and to better handle one's resources/processes. Such individual Benchmarking is best done with a more experienced person and preferably with a trainer, coach or mentor. As to what can be Benchmarked, the list encompasses all human behaviour. It can, for example, reflect: making presentations; interpersonal skills; telephone manner; handling meetings; writing reports; dealing with complaints; handling the press and displaying political acumen.

Other comments

- While the mechanics of comparison may rely a lot on subjective analysis, it will be the 'How to make better use of one's own inputs/processes' which will be the more difficult part of the process.
- Once mastered, however, there is no reason why this technique should not be part of one's continuous development mechanism.

SUMMARY

This list of problem-solving approaches is only indicative of what can be used. As the reader examines other models and figures in this book and other sources, she/he may find that many can be used as simple mechanisms for examining problems. On this basis, the reader is encouraged to 'collect' these problem-solving mechanisms from the widest variety of sources possible, for his/her proverbial trainer's 'tool kit'.

It is the author's experience that in order to focus the main points of, say, a conversation, meeting or training session, easy-to-use models, to pin ideas and comments to, are often much appreciated.

REFERENCES AND FURTHER READING

The 'Discussion Leading Group Problem Solving' Method

Andrews, D. J. W. (1980) 'The Verbal Structure of Teacher Questions: Its Impact on Class Discussions'. *Professional and Organizational Development Quarterly, Nos 2, 3 and 4*, 129–163.

Davis, R. H., Fry, J. P. and Alexander, L. T. (1977) *The Discussion Method. Guides for the Improvement of Instruction in Higher Education No. 6*. East Lansing: Michigan State University.

Debenham, A. I. S. (1976) *A Trainer's Guide to Discussion Leading*. London: British Association for Commercial and Industrial Education (BACIE).

Gillespie, R. J. (1972) *Developing Creative Problem Solving Talent*. London: InComTec.

Hyman, R. T. (1980) *Improving Discussion Technique*. Teachers College Press.

Jackson, K. F. (1975) *The Art of Problem Solving*. London: Heinemann.

Rickards, T. (1975) *Problem Solving Through Creativity Analysis*. Aldershot: Gower.

Tarr, G. (1973) *The Management of Problem Solving*. London: Macmillan.

Tuma, D. T. and Reif, F. (1980) *Problem Solving and Education: Issues in Teaching and Research*. New Jersey: Lawrence Erlbaum Associates.

Varieties of Group Discussion in University Teaching (1972). London University Institute of Education, University Teaching Methods Unit.

The 'Where Are We Now/Where Do We Want To Be?' Method

Price, C. and Murphy, E. (1987) 'Organization Development' British Telecom. *Training and Development Journal*, July, 45–8.

The 'Cause/Effect Fishbone' Method

Ferrari, S. (1986) 'Training for Quality – The Italian Experience of Quality Circles'. *Journal of European Industrial Training 10, 3*, 12–16.

Gryna, F. M. (1989) *Quality Circles*. New York: Ancona.

Robson, M. (1982) *Quality Circles: A Practical Guide*. Aldershot: Gower.

The 'Demands/Constraints/Choices' Method

Kakabada, A., Ludlow, R. and Vinnicombe, S. (1988) *Working in Organizations*. London: Penguin Books.

Stewart, R. (1982) *Choices for the Manager: A Guide to Managerial Work*. Maidenhead: McGraw-Hill.

The 'Post-it' Method

Janis, I. L. (1971) 'Groupthink'. *Psychology Today*, November, *44*.

The 'Force Field' Method

Lewin, K. (1951) *Field Theory in Social Science*. New York: Harper & Row.

Lewin, K. (1969) 'Quasi-Stationary Social Equilibria and the Problem of Permanent Change' in Bennis, W. G., Benne, K. D. and Chin, R. *The Planning of Change* (2nd Ed.). New York: Holt, Rienhart and Winston.

Lippett, R., Watson, J. and Westley, B. (1958) *Dynamics of Planned Change*. New York: Brace & World.

Pfeiffer, J. W. and Jones, J. E. (Eds) (1974) *A Handbook of Structured Experiences for Human Relations Training*. Volume II (Revised). La Jolla, California: University Associates Inc.

Woodcock, M. and Francis, D. (1979) *Unblocking Your Organization*. La Jolla, California: University Associates Inc.

The 'Brainstorming' Method

A tape/slide training programme, *Creative Thinking and Brainstorming*. Marketed by Guild Sound and Vision Ltd, Peterborough.

Bouchard, T. J. (1969) 'Personality, Problem Solving Procedure and Performance in Small Groups'. *Journal of Applied Psychology*, Monograph, *53*.

Bouchard, T. J. (1972) 'Training, Motivation and Personality as Determinants of the Effectiveness of Brainstorming Groups and Individuals'. *Journal of Applied Psychology 56, 4*.

Buzan, T. (1974) *Use Your Head*. Rugby: BBC Publications.

Creative Thinking and Brainstorming (1980). British Institute of Management.

de Bono, E. (1977) *Lateral Thinking: A Textbook of Creativity*. Middlesex, England: Pelican Books.

Osborn, A. F. (1957) *Applied Imagination*. New York: Charles Scribner and Sons.

Parris, S. J. and Harding, H. F. (1962) *A Source Book for Creative Problem Solving*. New York: Charles Scribner and Sons.

Pfeiffer, J. W. and Jones, J. E. (Eds) (1974) *A Handbook of Structured Experiences for Human Relations Training*. Volume III (Revised). La Jolla, California: University Associates Inc.

Rawlinson, J. G. (1981) *Introduction to Creative Thinking and Brainstorming*. Aldershot: Gower.

Rawlinson, J. G. (1981) *Creative Thinking and Brainstorming*. British Institute of Management.

Rawlinson, J. G. (1989) *Creative Thinking and Brainstorming*. Aldershot: Gower.

Rickards, T. (1974) *Problem Solving Through Creative Analysis*. Aldershot: Gower.

Rickards, T. and Freedman, B. L. (1978) 'Procedures for Managers in Idea Deficient Situations: An Examination of Brainstorming Approaches'. *Journal of Management Studies 15, 1*, February.

Smith, J. N. (1973) *Understanding Creativity: A Lightning Course for Executives*. Rugby: Mantec Publications.

The 'Input/Process/Result' Method

Carter, R. (1984) *Systems for Management of Change*. UK: Open University.

Cavallo, R. E. (1979) *Systems Methodology*. Boston, Massachusetts: M Nijhoff.

Checkland, P. (1981) *Systems Thinking, Systems Practice*. Bath, Avon: John Wiley.

Clarke, D. D. (1985) *Action Systems, Analysis of Complex Behaviour*. London: Methuen.

Dobrov, G. M. (1978) *Systems Assessment of New Technology*. International Institute for Applied Systems Analysis (IIASA).

Emery, F. E. (1981) *Systems Thinking Selected Readings*. Penguin.

Kramer, J. T. A. (1977) *Systems Thinking*. Boston, Massachusetts: M Nijhoff.

Open Systems Group (1981) *Systems Behaviour*. London: Harper & Row.

Warmington, A. (1977) *Organizational Behaviour and Performance: an Open Systems Approach to Change*. London: Macmillan.

Wilson, B. (1984) *Systems Concepts Methodologies & Applications*. Bath, Avon: John Wiley.

The 'Benchmarking' Method

Camp, R. C. (1989) *Benchmarking: The Search for Industry Best Practices That Lead to Superior Performance*. American Society for Quality Control (ASQC): Quality Press.

Codling, S. (1992) *Best Practice Benchmarking*. Aldershot: Gower Publishing Ltd.

Fauld, L. M. (1985) *Competitor Intelligence: How to Get to Use It*. New York: John Wiley & Sons.

Fauld, L. M. (1988) *Monitoring the Competition*. New York: John Wiley & Sons.

'First Find Your Bench'. *The Economist*, 11 May 1991.

Karloff, B. and Ostblom, S. (1993) *Benchmarking: A Signpost to Excellence in Quality and Productivity*. UK: John Wiley & Sons Ltd.

Lascelles, D. M. and Dale, D. M. (1993) *The Road to Quality*. UK: IFS Publications.

Leibfried, K. H. J. and McNair, C. J. (1994) *Benchmarking: A Tool For Continuous Improvement*. London: Harper Collins.

Walleck, A. *et al* (1991) *Benchmarking World Class Performance*, the McKinsey Quarterly No. 1. London: McKinsey & Co. Inc.

Watson, G. H. (1993) *Strategic Benchmarking: How to Rate Your Company's Performance Against the World's Best*. New York: John Wiley & Sons.

Zaire, M. (1992) *Practical Benchmarking: An Executive Guide*. UK: Technical Communications (Publishing) Ltd.

Zaire, M. and Leonard, P. (1994) *Practical Benchmarking: A Complete Guide*. UK: Chapman & Hall.

Other

Best Practice Benchmarking. London: Department of the Trade and Industry. Tel: 0171-510 0144.

An Introductory Guide to Benchmarking. ICI Chemicals & Polymers Ltd. Quality Library.

9

Training Needs Analysis techniques

INTRODUCTION

As we saw in Chapter 3, the approach and scale of a TNA can vary. When analysing the complete organization (*Glossary of Training Terms* (1981)), the TNA is described as: an examination of the organization's:

- present operations;
- expected operations;
- manpower requirements;

in order to identify:

- the number of staff and
- manpower categories needing to be trained and retrained;
- individual training needs which will enable a person to reach the required standard of performance in the current job or the future job.

We might also add to this definition, that some analysts may also be required to locate and acquire the human skills required, in addition to the development of them.

The analyst may need to consider both present and future requirements and, to achieve this, may often be called upon to analyse organizational problems to first locate training needs (Chapter 3), and then in some detail analyse the training need using a suitable TNA technique.

The reason for using TNA techniques is to describe the training need as clearly as possible. In some cases the analyst can be objective by making use of statistical techniques and validated tests. In many cases, the analyst will use techniques to 'get close' to the identification of training needs, and by definition 'get close' to the training objectives. To do this, the analyst:

- makes use of comparisons, for example, between effective and ineffective behaviour;
- makes use of 'benchmarks' of desired, ideal, other people's or other organizations' performance in order to provide a comparison by which to examine how one is handling one's own development;
- makes use of both quantitative and qualitative data in order to obtain a rounded impression;
- makes use of more than one TNA technique to determine if the 'cluster' of results is significant;
- uses the 'content analysis' technique, coupled with a systems approach, for unravelling the meaning of unstructured interview responses (as shown in Chapter 8: The Post-it method).

The difference between 'investigative or problem-solving techniques' and TNA techniques, is that the former are used prior to using TNA techniques. In other words, *investigative techniques locate, and TNA techniques define the training need* in readiness for a training intervention to be actioned. The reader may be aware that there is little literature on the subject of 'investigative' and 'TNA' techniques, and that some analysts do not make the distinctions indicated here.

TNA TECHNIQUES AND EXAMPLES OF THEIR APPLICATION

The following examples indicate the range of TNA techniques that can be used under different circumstances.

Example 1: Organizational rationalization

Guided by the corporate strategy, the TNA may be required to identify which staff will be required to perform differently as a result of an organization rationalization, for example. Perhaps an analysis of senior and middle management positions will be required.

Likely range of TNA tools (the number shown here relates to the numbered section later in this chapter):

- check list/1
- structured and unstructured interviews/2
- survey technique/3
- using appraisal techniques/4
- using assessment centre techniques for senior management/16
- management audit/8
- using repertory grid analysis on group and individual basis/13
- self- and peer assessment/4
- task/job analysis/6
- role analysis/7.

Example 2: Skills shortage

From manpower or succession plans, a TNA may be required to:

- identify the skills which are in short supply and which will be relevant for future requirements;
- identify from where skills can be found, perhaps somewhere else in the organization or perhaps 'bought-in'.

Likely range of TNA tools:

- check list/1
- collating appraisal data/4
- management audit/8
- survey for skills audit/3
- self-appraisal/4
- structured interviews/2
- self- and peer assessment/4
- task/job analysis/6
- role analysis/7.

Example 3: Technological change

When there is technological change, the TNA may need to discover:

- the skills required to cope with new technology;
- people's responses and their perceived or actual difficulties.

Likely range of TNA tools:

- check list/1
- survey of attitude/technical skills/3
- management audit/8
- performance testing/12
- self-appraisal against questionnaire/4
- structured interview/2
- task/job analysis/6
- role analysis/7.

Example 4: Change due to organizational growth

A TNA may be called for when an organization is experiencing rapid growth. At this level, the analyst will need to work alongside senior management and may be required to work with organization development specialists. In this situation, rapid promotion of staff may identify new skills and job roles to be acquired at speed.

Likely range of TNA tools:

- check list/1
- structured/unstructured interviewing/2
- psychological testing/15
- self- and peer assessment/4
- task/job analysis/6
- role analysis/7
- simulated exercises, if time permits, to examine behaviour under perhaps demanding circumstances/14.

Example 5: Matrix management

In this example, the TNA may need to focus on the skills required for setting up a project management team, and how to handle temporary reporting relationships. A similar situation emerges when analysing the needs of task force or steering committee members who need to work across functional boundaries.

Likely range of TNA tools:

- check list/1
- self- and peer assessment/4
- structural interviews/2
- structured observation/11
- surveys to determine project management skills/3
- task/job analysis/6
- role analysis/7
- critical incident technique/9.

Example 6: Training audit

When the focus is on individuals' rather than organizational demands, the TNA can focus on skills required for possible future demands. Some organizations even allow for individuals to focus on non-work activities, as part of developing a climate for learning. In both cases, much will depend on the culture and values of the organization.

Likely range of TNA tools:

- check list/1
- structured/unstructured interviews/2
- self-appraisal against questionnaires or open appraisal/4
- task/job analysis/6
- role analysis/7
- management audit/8.

Example 7: Improving fault-finding skills

The objective here is to enhance the skills of highly technical fault-finding specialists.

Likely range of TNA tools:

- check list/1
- protocol analysis technique/10.

Example 8: Improving work performance

A TNA may be useful for identifying why some workers can achieve results faster than others.

Likely range of TNA tools:

- check list/1
- critical incident technique/9
- structured/unstructured interviewing/2
- task/job analysis/6
- role analysis/7
- self-appraisal against performance criteria or upward appraisal/4
- performance testing/12.

1 CHECK LIST

Description

The use of the 'check list' is perhaps the most straightforward of all the techniques. The two forms described here include the Versatility Chart, Figure 9.1 (also see Chapter 3) and the General Checklist Approach. The idea in both cases is to identify a person's skills and their lack of them, in order to identify training needs and prepare training plans.

Training need: Using the Versatility Chart: Figure 9.1

This can be carried out on a team or an individual. The names(s) are listed along the top of, say, an A4 page in vertical columns. Along the left side of the page are listed the tasks which need to be carried out. By drawing horizontal lines to separate the tasks, a matrix (or array of boxes) of name(s) and tasks is now available. Through interviewing each person, through self-assessment or through observation about the possession of skills and knowledge, the person's competences can be broadly assessed as follows:

Method 1

If the task can be carried out, a tick can be placed in the appropriate box. If the task cannot be carried out, the box can be left blank.

Method 2

Instead of 'ticking' and 'blanking', as above, the level of competence can be rated out of 10, for example (where 10 is fully competent).

This done, the assessor is left with a matrix of tasks where some can be undertaken and some cannot. The potential training needs are those with 'blanks' or 'low scores'. The next step is to decide which tasks need to be learnt. For full versatility, for example, all team members will need to be trained to cover all tasks.

Training need: the General Checklist Approach

The General Checklist Approach has long been used as a 'list of things to do', a 'reminder of the sequence of some procedure or operation', and as a rough and ready 'yardstick by which to compare actual and required performance'. It is for the last of these uses that the general checklist can be used as a TNA technique. If, for example, we look at job performance, a checklist can be prepared of all the tasks to be done (perhaps using the job description to prepare the check list). What job tasks can be undertaken and what job tasks need to be learnt can be established by comparing individual worker performance against the list of tasks to be carried out.

Other comments

- It is very quick to use and can be done on a single sheet of A4.
- For both the Versatility Chart and the Matrix Management Chart (Example 5 above), outline training plans can be quickly constructed.
- Further analysis may be required to determine the exact nature of some training needs.

2 INTERVIEWING

Description

This can take different forms:

- structured interview with questionnaire and a choice of structured answers;
- structured interview with questionnaire and no structured answers;
- partially structured interview;
- open questioning and listening exercise.

For the first three types, the analyst will need to balance the requirement for quantitative and qualitative information. In the fourth example, the analyst will ask open and probing questions. With regard to listening, the analyst will listen to what is said, how it is said, why it is said, and importantly, what is not said.

Training need

In the first three cases, one approach is to gather factual data about the need for training, and the other approach is to compare answers against what the organization believes constitutes good organizational practice.

	JOBS				
NAMES	Preparing for painting	Painting	Preparing surfaces for wallpaper	Hanging wallpaper	Costing jobs
Tom	✔	✔	✔	✘	✘
Derek	✘	✘	✘	✔	✔
Mike	✔	✔	✘	✘	✘
David	✔	✔	✘	✘	✘
Harry	✔	✔	✘	✘	✘
Philip	✔	✔	✘	✘	✘
Ben	✔	✔	✘	✘	✘
Ideal cover	6	6	4	4	3
Number needing to be trained or recruited	0	0	(3)	(3)	(2)

Key: ✔ = Have skill   ✘ = Lack skill

By matching each person against each of the tasks, a table emerges of who has acquired the skill and who has not.

Where no or little skill has been gained, this represents a potential training need.

If a multi-skilled workforce was required, this TNA method would be well suited to identifying the potential training needs.

FIGURE 9.1 The Versatility Chart – examining a painting and decorating team

In the fourth case, the process is far more demanding for both the analyst and learner. For example: to ask a person 'Tell me what you did under those circumstances?' is one thing. To also ask the person 'Tell me what you did not do?' is to prompt the person about choices she/he did or did not make. If the person was unaware of the choices, this may indicate a need for development. If the person knowingly made a choice, why was that decision made? Again, such questioning and listening may reveal 'performance gaps'.

Example

A researcher wanted to better understand the cause of staff turnover. Rather than just examine leaver data, the researcher analysed the turnover figures (quantitative) and analysed exit interviews (qualitative) of 'leavers'; and also asked the 'stayers' why they remained in the organization (largely qualitative). By comparing both the leaver and the stayer information, the researcher was able to establish some important connections about retention and maintenance of staff.

By questioning the leavers and the stayers, this brings home the notion that to ask 'Tell me what you did' and 'Tell me what you did not do', contributed to finding a more comprehensive solution.

Other comments

- Time-consuming if undertaken *en masse*.
- Useful for discovering the qualitative information as well as covering key points.
- Can be undertaken on the telephone.
- For internal trainers, it has the major benefit of getting to know people and forming lasting relationships.
- 'Quantitative' is concerned with collecting factual information. By contrast, the 'qualitative' approach is focused on collecting information about people's responses, experiences, feelings and emotions. When both methods are adopted the result usually provides a well-rounded picture.

3 SURVEY TECHNIQUE

Description

The survey technique can be used to:

- determine attitudes in medium-to-large organizations;
- gather views about staff development needs;
- gather information for a skills audit;
- gather views about health and safety and quality issues.

This technique can comprise both interview and questionnaire. The interviewer usually seeks information about attitudes, beliefs, procedures etc., during a one-to-one interview, guided by a structured questionnaire. The survey can also be undertaken by telephone, in a group situation or by teleconferencing.

The technique is often used to carry out an attitude survey to determine training needs. In addition, the survey technique can be used to identify views and gather information for staff development or a skills audit.

Training need

Survey results can be compared against previous survey results, thus allowing for 'gaps' to be closed by a training intervention. In addition, the results of the survey can be compared with what is required, by senior management, in terms of good practice. The gap will thus be indicative of the training need.

Other comments

- To be successful, the analyst must be able to plan the survey, design and pilot the questionnaire, de-bug, administer, interpret results using statistical analysis and review results against the objectives of the survey.
- Yields large quantities of data.
- Can be expensive to design and administer.
- Is useful for indicating direction of attitudes or broad state of skill base, for example.
- May need to be followed up with more detailed TNA method, such as detailed skills audit, skills analysis, critical incidents and protocol analysis.
- If only questionnaires are used, the qualitative dimension may need to be sampled via interviewing.

4 APPRAISAL/PERFORMANCE REVIEW

Description

This can take the form of:

- boss appraising manager;
- manager appraising boss (upward appraisal);
- self-appraisal against operational requirements or checklist of skills;
- self-appraisal by questionnaire;
- open self-reporting with counselling.

Training needs

In all cases, the idea is to either identify training needs directly, or to discover clues about training requirements, in which case further investigation will be required. The range of approaches listed above can involve the analyst weighing up aggregate training needs as can typically emerge from a boss/manager appraisal, to interpretation of open self-reporting requiring perhaps careful interpretation and counselling.

Other comments

- Self-appraisals can vary. Sometimes individuals can be very hard on themselves which in turn requires correcting by the appraiser. Sometimes the appraisee may over-focus on one or two key points at the expense of the whole.
- Self-appraisal with questionnaire can be useful prior to a meeting with the appraiser.
- Self-appraisal against checklist of skills requires to be tailored.
- Self-appraisal, in general, may be imprecise and may require follow-up to determine the individual point of view or training needs.
- Upward appraisal must be congruent with organizational culture and managers must be sufficiently skilled to handle the process. If undertaken well, it does provide true two-way communication. In the words of Berne (1977) it does induce an adult-to-adult communication.
- Downward (or joint) appraisal has the merit that it does fit in with the more usual patterns of authority and responsibility. It is not therefore imposing different cultural mindsets. By itself it cannot correct any bias or prejudice of either party when relationships are not good, save only through appeal procedures.

- The downward (or joint) appraisal with a more senior manager (grandfather) or specialist attending the review, is an attempt to focus both parties on the needs of the job rather than the needs of the personalities.

5 DIARY ANALYSIS

Description

The diary method can be structured or unstructured. Typically, for time management analysis, a structured approach is used. When unstructured, it can be used as a journal, for examining thoughts, feelings, hopes and fears about role difficulties, for example.

Training need

In the first case, factual data about time spent in meetings or on the telephone may reveal training needs or changes in work procedures. For analysis of the unstructured diary, the learner would need to talk through situations in context, to add meaning and to provide useful interpretation.

In both cases, the diary or journal, when interpreted, will reveal patterns of activity, thoughts or emotions which will form the basis of the training need. In the case of time spent at meetings, for example, the judgement as to whether this is too much or not, may need to be discussed with the individual's boss, team members and peers and assessed against other work priorities.

When dealing with unstructured journal entries about personal feelings about handling the job role, for example, the analyst may need to assist the job holder to create benchmarks. This can be done by comparing actual performance against an ideal performance suggested by the job holder. A benchmark could also be derived from 'live organization role models', and the training gap could be closed with the help of a coach or mentor. More deep-seated emotions may require specialist attention.

Other comments

- Structured diary keeping can provide the factual data that a person needs to reflect upon how time and energy is being spent.
- The structured approach can take weeks to complete.
- Action on training needs can be monitored by the learner, if used for self-development, or jointly monitored by the learner and his/her boss.
- The unstructured journal can take time to complete, and may reveal personal data and hidden issues which can require careful de-briefing.

6 TASK ANALYSIS

Description

Task analysis includes within its methodology:

- topic analysis, analysis of intellectual tasks;
- skills analysis, analysis of psychomotor tasks;
- job analysis, which leads to:
  - preparing job descriptions;
  - preparing job specifications;
  - preparing person specifications;
  - preparing training materials;

– equipment design and ergonomics;
– vocational guidance.

Topic analysis involves identifying the tasks and concepts associated with, say, learning the principal of Ohm's Law.

Skills analysis involves examining hand movements, vision and other senses as used by glassblowers, for example.

Job analysis involves examining a job in detail in order to identify its component tasks. The detail and approach may vary according to the purpose for which the job is being analysed.

Training need

Task analysis involves preparing instruments by which to compare actual performance against required performance or 'experienced worker standard'. The training need will emerge from the comparison.

Because task analysis is reductionist, i.e. it breaks down the whole into manageable learning chunks, the learner can sometimes lose sight of the whole. To remind the learner of the eventual benefits of training, trainers should find opportunities for learners to feel the worth of their efforts. This can be done through working alongside skilled employees or in some way being close to the reality of the desired performance.

Other comments

• Topic and skills analysis can take time to complete and validate. Once prepared, however, the instruments can be used by the population of people they are designed for.
• Topic and skills analysis is, by definition, objective.
• Job analysis can also take time to complete and is also objective, but is a lot broader in its scope.
• Coupled with role analysis, task analysis is a very useful skill for the analyst to deploy.
• Task analysis may also employ techniques to:
  – use work observation, questioning techniques and video;
  – adopt a do-it-yourself approach;
  – use activity sampling: recording at pre-determined intervals what a person is doing;
  – interview job holder, manager, team members, instructors, new employees, suppliers, customers, advertisers, wholesalers, retailers, directors, and maybe even shareholders and competitors;
  – examine work records/samples at prescribed intervals produced by job holder to examine quality of work;
  – ask job holder to relate incidents which have adverse and positive effects on the job.
• The Position Analysis Questionnaire (PAQ), McCormick (1972 and 1976), is used to analyse skills in terms of human behaviour rather than tasks.
• British versions of the PAQ technique include:
  – the Job Component Inventory (JCI), Banks (1982 and 1983);
  – the Job Structure Profile (JSP), Patrick (1983 and 1985) and Rohmert (1983).
• PAQ can be used to prepare a profile of required abilities. For TNA purposes, the profile of abilities that are required for some positions, can then be compared against actual abilities. The deviation would thus outline the training need.

7 ROLE ANALYSIS

Description

If the job analysis focuses on job content (what is done), role analysis focuses on job context (how it is done). Too often it is 'assumed' that a person either knows what the invisible job role is, or will soon discover it. Unlike the job description, the job role is seldom discussed.

The job role can present difficulties for some, because it can mean, for example:

- working across unfamiliar departmental boundaries;
- setting up new lines of communication;
- informing, supporting and influencing a wider circle of colleagues;
- exercising wider social behaviour;
- using a great deal more initiative;
- being proactive in many more directions;
- having contingency plans in place.

When examining roles, the analyst helps the individual to adopt a multi-comparison approach between:

- what others observe and what the role holder experiences;
- what the role is or should be and what others observe;
- what the role should be and what the role holder experiences.

From each level of comparison, the differences would be identified and it would be the differences that would begin to identify training needs.

Training need

The object of role analysis is to assist the role holder to fit or match the demands of the many roles associated with the job. Such a match can happen quickly, or it may take time for the role holder to acquire the necessary skills, know-how and confidence. Sometimes project assignments can enable the person to study how things work from inside and outside, and thus provide an insight into the role required. Sometimes a coach or mentor can help with the facilitation process.

If it is to do with how a person uses his/her influence or power base, this can provide another area of study for the analyst. In this case the seven bases of power based on the work of French (1959), Raven (1975) and Hersey (1982) will prove useful. For example, analysis may reveal discrepancies in: coercive power; legitimate power; expert power; reward power; referent power; information and connection power.

Other comments

- As organizations become flatter, the need for role analysis, at all levels, may increase.
- Generally, the need for role definition is much underrated within organizations. The fact that it is the role that guides job performance indicates the importance of the job role.
- Role analysis can be more multi-faceted to undertake than job analysis because it deals with relationships, work boundaries and the need to use personal qualities such as good rapport, initiative and a range of empowering skills. Analysis of job roles can, for example, be from the point of view of 'other players' in the field. This may include looking at the job role from the point of view of the customer, supplier, wholesaler, advertisers, functional directors, and so on.

8 MANAGEMENT AUDIT

Description

The individual manager and his/her boss complete the audit and compare and discuss their answers together. The audit will comprise a checklist of statements which will constitute agreed good organizational practice. For example, both parties may respond to the question 'You review work progress regularly', by ticking 'daily/weekly/monthly' or by entering a figure for 'other'.

Training need

Although differences between the manager's and boss's answers will be indicative of training needs, they may also indicate the need for better internal procedures. Sometimes, as in all boss/manager examinations of training needs, both parties can be joined by a more senior manager or a management specialist. The purpose here is to assist both parties to maintain the overview as well as examine detail.

Other comments

- Can be undertaken at the same time as performance appraisal, or at any other time.
- The benefit of the approach lies in the process of jointly examining working practice differences and behaviour either in perception or practice. That differences can exist is one thing, but it is the differences which create performance difficulties that matter.
- When undertaken well, the technique can be relatively quick to administer.

9 CRITICAL INCIDENT TECHNIQUE

Description

The aim is to get from skilled practitioners, behaviours of people that are critical to the outcome of the skilled task. Such incidents can include effective and less effective behaviours, and can be obtained by face-to-face interview, group workshop, diaries or using a questionnaire.

Having established the effective and less effective behaviours that are critical for success, the information can be used as a benchmark. For example:

To assist less skilled job holders: Questions can be asked or observation made, and compared against the 'skilled response'. For example: 'When resolving a query for the ABC customer successfully, you must know how to search, within one hour, the international and national directories using product codes and translations of product names in various languages.' 'When actioning telephone orders above X,000 successfully, you must consult stock records/work in progress/the production controller and agree delivery with the transport manager.'

For interviewing new job holders: The interviewee can be asked 'What would you do if . . ?' and 'What skills do you regard important when . . . ?' In addition to this, trainability tests can be used to determine skill needs.

To generate training material: By examining the behaviour required, training material can be prepared, such as role plays and case studies.

Training need

Training needs will be indicated by the difference between the learner's response (actual behaviour) and the skilled response (required behaviour). When using new processes and equipment, skills critical for successful operation can be benchmarked and used by trainers.

Other comments

- The technique has a practical orientation, as it focuses on actual job behaviours which are critical for successful performance.
- Incidents can be time consuming to prepare.

10 PROTOCOL ANALYSIS TECHNIQUE

Description

This is a method of recording (using sound recorder, video or interview) how a person undertakes some task. The transcript is divided into protocols for analysis, and used to discover critical performance elements.

If undertaken verbally, the learner is encouraged to talk through the task.

Protocol analysis can be used to identify how a skilled person multiplies 29 x 410 in his/her head. As the skilled person describes the steps or protocols involved, a strategy will emerge through a series of protocols. A less skilled person could learn the sequence or pattern of protocols and, by so doing, improve their own performance. Such improvement is made possible because the person has learnt how to achieve a higher standard of performance. The person has, in effect, eliminated the constraints that held him/her to a lower standard. Put another way, access to the sequence of protocols has enabled use of a more effective strategy for performing the task.

The technique can be used to record fault-finding processes, analyse operator strategy and record interpersonal events in critical situations.

By comparison, the critical incident technique (9 above) is used to describe skill in terms of effective and less effective behaviour which is procedural rather than strategic in nature. Protocol analysis is useful for helping skilled workers to enhance their performance to a higher level. Whereas critical incidence is about identifying and learning behaviours that prove critical for performing the job around the 'experienced worker standard' (EWS), protocol analysis is aimed at securing the EWS and can lead to achieving superior performance.

For example, critical incidence identifies that a good standard of numeracy, along with other procedural tasks, is required; protocol analysis identifies the strategy and protocols for multiplying 29 x 410.

Training need

Training needs can be determined from comparison of how, for example, skilled and less skilled workers perform. For the skilled negotiator, analysis would identify the critical protocols used. The less skilled person could either consider whether to use these 'skilled protocols' or decide to devise his/her own. The idea of the technique for training is to provide a way for improving performance either by imitation of the protocol process or by development of new protocols.

Other comments

- Can take time to prepare.
- May need to consult more than one skilled person to identify a range of protocols and strategies that signal a way forward for high performance.
- Is very helpful for 'unblocking' the less skilled performer.

11 STRUCTURED OBSERVATION/BEHAVIOUR ANALYSIS

Description

Structured observation can be used to:

- analyse verbal behaviour at meetings;
- provide information about interpersonal communication;
- investigate level of participation in interviews;
- analyse effectiveness of verbal instructional methods.

This technique makes use of observing verbal behaviour in a structured way. Behaviour analysis made popular by Rackham (1977) is an example of this approach.

To determine the level of a person's responses within a meeting for example, as many as eleven behaviour contributions can be recorded. Such behaviour can include seeking information, supporting, disagreeing and summarizing.

When aware of the effect of behaviour on each other, users will recognize the very real power of the stimulus–response nature of verbal human interplay. The extent that other people's behaviour can be modified through such techniques, is the potential power of this approach.

Training need

Identification of training needs emerges when the analyst and parties involved examine the effectiveness of the verbal behaviours for specific or general situations. While comparisons with ideal profiles may be useful for reflecting against actual behaviour, it is more to do with the qualitative nature of the behaviours than the quantitative. For example, for the learner to be told that she/he 'disagreed' seven times may not mean much. To be aware of the effect on others when disagreeing takes place, will likely have more impact. To realize how certain behaviours empower others to effectively contribute, to achieve the required objectives, will have even more impact.

Other comments

- Requires some expertise to administer well, and takes time to practise effectively.
- Will empower users to consider how the stimulus and response mode of human interaction can be modified to achieve desired results.
- If not used to modify other people's behaviour directly, then indirectly benefits will accrue from the empathy and sensitivity that will be displayed when 'tuned in' to verbal behaviours.
- The limitation of behaviour analysis is in its objectivity. It can count behaviours but it cannot reveal underlying tensions and resentments.

12 PERFORMANCE/TRAINABILITY TESTS

Description

The idea of performance tests is to assess speed, level of skill and accuracy in carrying out some task or procedure. A performance discrepancy may indicate a training need.

Care needs to be taken in design to ensure the test is valid in assessing what it is intended to test. If the job is wide ranging, the test needs to reflect this. It is possible that such tests do not actually reflect the 'on-job' situation.

The fact that results are quantifiable and comparable focuses quickly on areas that need improvement.

When used for selection purposes it is called a trainability test. The idea here is to assess those with the right skills or those who can learn quickly.

Tests may also be used to sample the current state of learning.

Where performance must be kept to a high standard, performance tests are used, for example, with flight crews, air traffic controllers and some legal professions.

When used to discover an individual's potential or current level of skill, such tests may provide useful indicators of ability and competence.

Training need

Having identified the performance discrepancy, the analyst should examine the full implications of the shortfall, and design a training programme to suit.

Because we can forget how to carry out tasks which have once been learned, testing is a valuable tool. For pilots who need to land an aircraft during an emergency situation, which may never occur, the risk and ethics of the situation are such that frequent training and testing must be undertaken.

The idea of fire drills is based on the same premise. When undertaken regularly, the drill soon becomes routine.

Other comments

- Requires expertise to prepare and validate tests.
- Useful for identifying training needs objectively for a population of learners.
- May fail to recognize individual factors that cause poor performance, in which case interviewing and protocol analysis may be useful additions to the test.

13 REPERTORY GRID TECHNIQUE

Description

The fundamental idea of the repertory grid is to enable individuals to gain an understanding of how they make sense or meaning of the world around them. By taking three elements, or triads, of activities (objects, people, products, television programmes, training activities, ideas etc.), the individual is asked to decide what have two of them in common and what is different about the third. So for a triad of 'boss', 'wife' and 'best friend', the 'boss' is seen as *rigid* and the 'wife' and 'best friend' are described as *open*. Through the development of a number of 'constructs' (like rigid/open), the grid is prepared. From the comparison between elements and constructs and from analysis of the completed matrix, a person reveals how she/he makes meaning of the subject studied, and perhaps discovers insights into how she/he views the wider world. For the constructs rigid/open, for example, is this the way the grid user labels everyone? The advantages of the grid include:

- it allows interviewees to use their own words;
- it elicits personal perceptions;
- it can be used to structure subjective information;
- it enables personal meanings to be explored in detail.

Difficulties are that it can be time-consuming to 'learn' and prepare, and it may not be suitable for all company cultures.

In short, the grid can be used for anything for which it would prove useful to obtain a person's qualitative response. Although it may be possible for some individuals to 'teach themselves' the grid technique, it is felt that initial expert guidance is required.

Training need

The grid technique can be used by an individual or a group. For the individual, the realization that thinking patterns lead to fixed or inappropriate attitudes, may require training to check or alter the mindset. If, for example, the grid revealed negative attitudes toward contributing at team meetings, a training intervention may enable the person to practise more positive responses at meetings.

Within a training context, a group may use the grid to identify the characteristics of effective and less effective sales performers for example. By comparing actual performance with the 'ideal role model', an individual may discover training needs (see Chapter 8: Benchmarking).

The Board of Directors may likewise discover that through the grid, their collective mindset could be sending messages to the workforce which are not entirely encouraging. To bring home the impact of their attitudes, a director could be charged with identifying and reporting what effect management attitude is having on workforce behaviour.

Other comments

- Requires skilled facilitation and preferably computer support.
- Can deal with complex and inter-related issues.
- Can work with individuals and groups to provide real insight.
- Can take time for individual/group to learn and interpret.

14 SIMULATION

Description

Simulation involves representing the characteristics of a real physical system or actual set of human relationships, by means of simpler operating systems or circumstances. In the case of the physical system, this can include computer models and flight simulators. For human relationships and decision-making, this could involve role playing and using in-tray exercises. The idea in all cases is to get close to the factors that define the reality, both safely and cost-effectively.

Training need

Training needs using physical simulation will be indicated from the comparison between actual and required performance. In the case of the role play and in-tray exercise, the debriefing process may involve the learners and qualified observer(s) comparing actual behaviour against required behaviour. Observers, in turn, may use instruments such as checklists of key points, grids for analysing behaviour, sound or visual recording techniques and practical criteria for prioritizing successful behaviour.

Other comments

- For hi-tech use, it can be very expensive to design, manufacture and validate, e.g. aerospace industry, piloting ocean-going vessels.
- Results are likely to be predictive, i.e. right or wrong rather than many shades of grey.
- Useful technique when performance is determined by a known string of physical moves, verbal behaviours or list of priorities.
- Can be used with individuals and groups.

15 PSYCHOMETRIC INVENTORIES

Description

Although psychometric testing requires qualified testers to administer, some tests can be rated by self, boss, peers, team members or customers. In this field we have *psychometric tests*, testing: attainment, general intelligence, special ability or aptitude; and *psychometric questionnaires*, which profile: personality, interest, values, and other aspects of personality such as assertiveness; flexibility; stress tolerance; attitudes; motivations; physiological measures; handwriting; astrology; palmistry and phrenology.

Training need

As well as using such instruments for job selection, it is also possible to identify training needs, from comparison between actual results and industry standards.

Other comments

- Requires skilled design and staffing.
- Can take time to administer.
- Can be used with individuals and groups.

16 ASSESSMENT CENTRES

Description

This is regarded as the ultimate combination of measures, making use of, for example:

- psychometric inventories;
- interviews;
- observed performance on simulated tasks;
- written tests;
- exercises;
- peer rating;
- presentations.

Training need

To identify training needs will require qualified tester feedback, and an organizational specialist to match test results against organizational requirements.

Other comments

- Requires skilled design and staffing.
- Is expensive to administer.
- Tends to be used for senior management positions.

REFERENCES AND FURTHER READING
General References

Clover, V. T. and Balsley, H. L. (1984) *Business Research Methods*. Ohio: Grid Publishing.

Sanders, W. B. (1980) *The Sociologist as Detective*. Praefar University Press.

Questioning Technique

Brenner, M . (Ed.) (1985) *The Research Interview*. London: Academic Press.

Briggs, C. L. (1980) *Learning How to Ask*. Cambridge: Cambridge University Press.

Henry, T. (1982) *Effective Questioning: a Teaching Skills Workbook*. London: Macmillan.

Hiz, H. (1978) *Questions*. Dordrecht: Reidel.

Kissock, C. (1982) *A Guide to Questioning Classroom Procedures*. London: Macmillan.

Kissock, C. and Lyortsuun, P. T. (1982) *A Guide to Questioning Classroom Procedures for Teachers*. London: Macmillan.

MacKay, I. (1980) *A Guide to Asking Questions*. London: BACIE.

Sudman, S. (1982) *Asking Questions*. San Francisco: Jossey Bass.

Survey Technique

Alwin, F. (1978) *Survey Design Analysis*. London: Sage.

Dillman, D. A. (1978) *Mail and Telephone Surveys*. New York: John Wiley.

Fowler, F. J. (1984) *Survey Research Methods*. London: Sage.

Frey, J. H. (1983) *Survey Research by Telephone*. London: Sage.

Groves, R. M. (1979) *Surveys by Telephone*. London: Academic Press.

Higham, M. *The ABC of Interviewing*. London: Institute of Personnel Management.

Hoinville, G. (1985) *Survey Research Practice*. Aldershot: Gower.

Krishnan Namboodiri, N. (1978) *Survey Sampling and Measurement*. London: Academic Press.

Labaw, P. J. (1980) *Advances in Questionnaire Design*. Cambridge, Massachusetts: Abt Books.

Reeves, T. K. and Harper, D. (1981) *Surveys at Work*. London: McGraw-Hill.

Schuman, H. (1981) *Questions and Answers in Attitude Surveys*. London: Academic Press.

Youngman, M. B. (1978) *Designing and Analyzing Questionnaires*. UK: University of Nottingham.

Appraisal/Performance Review

Adams, R. (1973) 'Performance Appraisal and Counselling' in Torrington, D. P. and Sutton, D. F. (eds) *Handbook of Management Development*, 219–60. Aldershot: Gower.

Randall, G. A., Packard, P. M. A., Shaw, R. L. and Slater, A. J. (1972) *Staff Appraisal*. London: Institute of Personnel Management.

Stewart, V. and Stewart, A. (1978) *Managing the Manager's Growth*. Aldershot: Gower.

Stewart, V. and Stewart, A. (1978) *Practical Performance Appraisal*. Aldershot: Gower.

Taylor, D. S. (1976) *Performance Reviews*. London: Institute of Personnel Management.

Thomas, A., Wells, M. and Willard, J. (1992) 'A Novel Approach to Developing Managers and Their Teams: BPX Uses Upward Feedback'. *Management Education and Development 23, 1*, 30–2.

Transactional Analysis

Berne, E. (1977) *Games People Play*. London: Andre Deutsch.

Diary Analysis

Lane, C. (1980) 'Beating Time to Meet Objectives'. *Personnel Management 12, 3*, 36–9.
Mumford, A. (1980) *Making Experience Pay*. London: McGraw-Hill.
Stewart, R. (1970) *Managers and Their Jobs*. London: Pan.
Stewart, V. and Stewart, A. (1978) *Managing the Manager's Growth*. Aldershot: Gower.

Task Analysis

Annett, J. and Ducan, K. (1968) 'Task Analysis and Training Design'. *Bulletin of British Psychology 21, 72*, 181.
Annett, J. *et al.* (1971) 'Task Analysis Training'. Information Paper No. 6. London: HMSO.
Boydell, T. H. (1970) *A Guide to Job Analysis*. London: BACIE.
Piso, E. (1981) 'Task Analysis for Process-Controlled Tasks. The method of Annett *et al* applied'. *Journal of Occupational Psychology 54, 4*.
Seymour, W. T. (ed.) (1978) *The Analysis of Practical Skills*. Lancaster: MPT Press.
Shepherd, A. (1976) 'An Improved Tabular Format for Task Analysis'. *Journal of Occupational Psychology 49, 2*.

Role Analysis

Harrison, R. (1972) 'Role Negotiation: A Tough Minded Approach to Team Development' in Berger, M. L. and Berger, P. J. (eds) *Group Training Techniques*. Aldershot: Gower.
Mant, A. (1976) 'How to Analyze Management'. *Management Today*, October.
McGivering, I. (1980) 'Facilitating Re-Entry Through Role Analysis' in Beck, J. and Cox, C. (eds) *Advances in Management Education*. Chichester: John Wiley and Sons.
Reed, B. (1976) 'Organizational Role Analysis' in Cooper, C. L. (ed.) *Developing Social Skills in Managers: Advances in Group Training*. London: Macmillan.

Power

French, J. R. P. and Raven, B. (1959) 'The Bases of Social Power' in Cartwright, D. *Studies in Social Power*. Ann Arbor: University of Michigan, Institute for Social Research.
Hersey, P. and Blanchard, K. (1982) *Management of Organizational Behaviour*. Englewood Cliffs, NJ: Prentice-Hall, Inc.
Raven, B. H. and Kruglanski, W. (1975) 'Conflict and Power' in Swingle, P. G. (ed.) *The Structure of Conflict*. New York: Academic Press.

Management Audit

Dale, A. G. (1973) 'Management Audit'. *British Hospital Journal and Social Service Review*, 26 September.

Leonard, W. P. (1962) *The Management Audit: An Appraisal of Management Methods and Performance*. Englewood Cliffs, NJ: Prentice-Hall.

Rose, T. G. (1961) *The Management Audit*. Clwyd, Wales: Gee.

Santocki, J. (1974) 'Management Audit – Chance, Challenge, or Lost Opportunity'. *The Accountant*, 3 January.

Critical Incident Technique

AIR (1979) *Bibliography of 700 CIT Studies*. Palo Alto: American Institute for Research.

Bridges, F. J. (1977) *Critical Incidents in Organizational Behaviour and Administration*. Englewood Cliffs, NJ: Prentice Hall.

Flanagan, J. C. (1954) 'The Critical Incident Technique'. *The Psychological Bulletin 51, 4.*

Ronan, W. W. and Latham, G. P. (1974) 'The Reliability and Validity of the CIT'. *Personnel Psychology 5,* 53–64.

For training

Heron, J. (1973) *Experimental Training Techniques*. Guildford: Department of Adult Education, University of Surrey.

Lacey, J. D. and Licht, N. C. (1980) 'Culminating Experience: A Tool for Management Training'. *Training and Development Journal 34, 3,* 88–90.

Protocol Analysis Technique

Ericsson, K. A. and Simon, H. A. (1980) 'Verbal Reports as Data'. *Psychological Review 87,* 215–51.

Ericsson, K. A. and Simon, H. A. (1984) *Protocol Analysis*. Cambridge. Massachusetts: MIT Press.

Klaus, B. J. (1992) *Protocols Handbook for Nurse Practitioners*. Chichester: John Wiley.

Structured Observation/Behaviour Analysis

Clover, V. T. and Balsley, H. L. (1984) *Business Research Methods*. Ohio: Grid Publishing.

Fassnacht, G. (1982) *Theory and Practice of Observing Behaviour*. London: Academic Press.

Johnson, J. M. (1978) *Doing Field Research*. London: Collier Macmillan.

Simon, A. and Boyer, E. G. (1974) *Mirrors for Behaviour III: An Anthology of Observation Instruments*. Wyncote, Pa: Communications Material Centre.

Transactional Analysis

ITA Journal of the Institute of Transaction Analysis.

Barker, D. (1980) *TA and Training: The Theory and Uses of Transactional Analysis in Organizations*. Aldershot: Gower Press.

Berne, E. (1977). *Games People Play*. London: Andre Deutsch.

Jongeward, D. (1978) *Choosing Success – Transactional Analysis On-the-Job*. New York: John Wiley.

Morrison, J. H. and O'Hearne, J. (1977) *Practical Transactional Analysis in Management*. Wokingham: Addison Wesley.
Novey, T .B. (1976) *TA for Management: Making Life Work*. Enfield: Jalmar Press.
Villere, M. F. (1981) *Transactional Analysis at Work: A Guide for Business and Professional People*. Englewood Cliffs, NJ: Prentice Hall.
Woollams, S. (1979) *TA: The Total Handbook of Transactional Analysis*. Englewood Cliffs, NJ: Prentice Hall.

Behaviour Analysis

Bales, R. F. (1970) *Personality and Interpersonal Behaviour*. Project of Instructor Style Effectiveness, P.O.I.S.E. (1980). Cambridge: ITRU.
Bales, R. F. (1979) *SYMLOG A System of the Multiple Level Observation of Groups*. London: Collier Macmillan.
Flanders, N. A. (1963) 'Interaction and Feedback'. *Journal of Teacher Education 14*, 251–60.
Huthwaite Research Group Ltd (1983) *Spin(R) Project: The Motoroller Case; An Independent Evaluation of a Huthwaite Spin(R) Coaching Project by Silliman, M.A.*
McCredie, H. (1979) 'Behaviour Analysis Revisited: Some New Perspectives'. *Management Education and Development Journal 22, Part 4*, 315–22.
Rackham, N. and Morgan, T. (1977) *Behaviour Analysis in Training*. Maidenhead, Berkshire: McGraw-Hill.

Behaviour Modification

Bry, A. (1975) *A Primer of Behavioural psychology*. Dublin: Mentor.
Honey, P. (1976) *Face to Face*. London: Institute of Personnel Management.
Honey, P. (1980) *Solving People Problems*. Maidenhead, Berkshire: McGraw-Hill.
Luthans, F. and Kreitner, R. (1975) *Organisational Behaviour Modification*. Glenview, Ill.: Scott, Foresman & Co.

Repertory Grid Technique

Adams-Webber, J. R. (1979) *Personal Construct Theory: Concepts and Applications*. London: John Wiley and Sons.
Bannister, D. and Mair, J. M. M. (1968) *The Evaluation of Personal Constructs*. London: Academic Press.
Beail, N. (1985) *Repertory Grid Technique and Personal Constructs*. London: Routledge.
Brunel University. Centre For The Study Of Human Learning. Kingstone Lane, Uxbridge, Middlesex, UB8 3PH.
Candy, P. C. (1987) *Mirrors in the Mind – Personal Construct Theory in the Training of Adult Educators*. Department of Adult & Higher Education, University of Manchester.
Easterby-Smith, M. (1980) 'How To Use Repertory Grids In HRD'. *Journal of European Training 4, 2*.
Fransella, F. and Bannister, D. (1977) *A Manual for Repertory Grid Technique*. London: Academic Press.
Industrial and Commercial Training (1979). Vol 11, Nos 9 & 10.
Kelly, G. A. (1955) *The Psychology of Personal Constructs* (2 volumes). New York: Norton.

Smith, M. (1980) 'An Analysis of Three Managerial Jobs Using Repertory Grids'. *Journal of Management Studies*, 205–13.

Stewart, V. (1981) *Business Applications of Repertory Grid*. Maidenhead, Berkshire: McGraw-Hill.

Simulation

Atthill, C. R. A. and Dewdeswell, W. H. (1978) 'Simulation in Decision-Making: An Experiment in Industrial Education'. *British Journal of Educational Technology 9, 3*, 217–26.

Gibb, G. I. (1974) *Handbook of Games and Simulation Exercises*. London: E. and F. N. Spon Ltd.

Industrial Training International (1976) *Simulation in Training. Vol 11, Nos 3, 5, 6, 7, 9, 10 and 11*.

Jones, K. (1980) *Simulations: A Handbook for Teachers*. London: Kogan Page Ltd.

McCormick, J. (1972) 'Simulation and Gaming as a Teaching Method'. *Programmed Learning and Educational Technology 9, 4*, 198–205.

Parry, S. B. (1980) 'The Name of the Game is Simulation'. *Training and Development Journal 34, 6*, 99–105.

Stammers, R. B. (1981) 'Theory and Practice in the Design of Training Simulations'. *Programmed Learning and Educational Technology 18, 2*, 67–71.

Taylor, J. L. and Walford, R. (1978) *Learning and the Simulation Game*. Milton Keynes: Open University Press.

Walter, H. (1975) 'Organizational Simulation in Management Training'. *Industrial and Commercial Training 7, 3*, 118–20.

Zuckerman, D. W. and Horn, R. F. (1978) *The Guide to Simulation for Education and Training*, 2nd Ed. New York: Western Publishing Company.

Psychometric Inventories

Anastasi, A. (1982) *Psychological Testing*, 5th edn. New York: Macmillan.

Cronbach, L. J. (1984) *Essentials of Psychological Testing*, 4th edn. New York: Harper and Row.

Pern, M. (1979) *The Fair Use of Tests*. Windsor: NFER/Nelson.

Roberts, I. T. and Makin, R. J. (1986) 'Management Selection in Britain: A Survey and Critique'. *Journal of Occupational Psychology 59, 1*, 45–58.

Toplis, J., Dulewicz, V. and Fletcher, C. (1989) *Psychological Testing: A Practical Guide for Employers*. London: Institute of Personnel Management.

Assessment centres

Dulewicz, S. V. (1982) 'Assessment Centres: Practical Issues and Research Findings'. *Human Industrial Relations Supplement 17*.

Griffiths, P. and Goodge, P. (1984) 'Assessment Centres: Have We Got Them Wrong?' *Training Officer 20, 9*, 260–63.

Povah, N. (1986) 'Using Assessment Centres as a Means for Self-Development'. *Industrial Commercial Training*, March/April, 22–5.

Steel, V. and Howard, B. (1980) 'Self Insight Assessment Centres: An exciting new approach to the problem of identification of individual management training and development needs'. *Industrial & Commercial Training, 12, 9*.

Thornton, C. G. and Byham, W. C. (1982) *Assessment Centres and Managerial Performance*. New York: Academic Press.

10

Training methods and learning situations

INTRODUCTION

The main idea of this chapter is to prompt the trainer to ask questions about the nature of a training intervention so that suitable methods can be selected or modified to suit the training need and the context of training.

With regard to the design of a programme of training, this chapter will support Chapter 5: Design and evaluation of training.

CLASSIFICATION OF TRAINING METHODS AND LEARNING SITUATIONS

To use the following classification the trainer may ask a number of questions to locate a suitable training method or learning situation. For example:

A What are the training objectives? (See Appendix 8)

- Level 1: To acquire 'knowledge'.
- Level 2: To gain 'understanding'.
- Level 3: To seek 'application' of some skill in the correct way.
- Level 4: To enable learner to 'transfer' the skill to situations where there are no right answers.

B How much feedback will be necessary to fix the learning?

- Little or no feedback.
- A gradual development of feedback will be required.
- Feedback will be crucial to learning.
- Feedback will be equal to the learning.

C What role should the trainer play?

- As information provider.
- As learning facilitator.

D Where will training take place?

Off-job:
In the organization (e.g. training room/another work area).
Outside the organization (e.g. public or company specific training course).

On-job

This usually means training in the job holder's area. For some jobs, on-job can involve a wide variety of circumstances, e.g. a travelling salesperson's position.

E What area of learning is being considered? (See Appendix 8)

- Mainly knowledge (cognitive).
- Mainly affective (attitudes and feelings).
- Mainly manual skills (psychomotor).
- Mainly person-to-person skills (interpersonal).
- Mainly personal growth (self-knowledge).

F How well does the training method match the organizational culture's attitude and assumptions about learning? (See Chapter 7)

Can the training method be used within a:

- Power culture organization (action focused)?
- Role culture organization (systems driven)?
- Achievement culture organization (team orientated)?
- Support culture organization (individualistic)?

G What is the focus of the training?

- Individual focus.
- Relationship focus.
- Group focus.
- Inter-group focus.
- Organizational focus.

Appendix 11 provides an alternative classification of training methods for the reader based on 'G' above, the focus of the training. Both classifications can be cross-referenced.

The classification in Table 10.1 is in terms of levels of:

- knowledge acquisition;
- understanding;
- application;
- transfer

and is a reminder that certain training methods serve the purposes of certain training objectives more than others.

That some methods combine both off- and on-job training elements, and that some methods have been designed more for on-job use, adds to the make-up of the classification. Important in the classification is how learning changes from teacher-centred to learner-centred. How this affects the role of the training is critical. For some trainers, switching from information provider to learning facilitator, can prove a difficult transition.

There is a match between training method and organizational culture, reminding us that inherent in both are attitudes and assumptions that must be considered, and in most cases reconciled. When training methods are being used to deliberately change the emphasis of the prevailing culture, this will require the examination of likely consequences and preparation of contingency plans. Such a high profile and high risk manoeuvre will usually be driven by senior management.

TABLE 10.1 Showing relationship between criteria for determining appropriate training method

(A) Training objectives	(B) Feedback for learning	(C) Role of trainer	(D) Location of training
Level 1: To acquire knowledge	Little	Information provider	On-job Off-job
Level 2: To gain understanding	Gradual	Information provider	On-job Off-job
Level 3: To seek application	Crucial to learning	Learning facilitator	On-job Off-job
Level 4: To enable transfer	Equal to learning	Learning facilitator	On-job Off-job

Superimposed on the four criteria above are another three criteria, which the trainer will need to investigate, and they include:

(E) **What area of learning is being considered?**
   Mainly knowledge (cognitive)
   Mainly affective (attitude and feelings)
   Mainly manual (psychomotor)
   Mainly person-to-person skills (interpersonal)
   Mainly personal growth (self-knowledge)

(F) **How well does the training method match the organizational culture's attitude and assumptions about learning?**
   Can the training method be used within a:
   Power culture organization?
   Role culture organization?
   Achievement culture organization?
   Support culture organization?

(G) **What is the focus of the training?**
   Individual focus?
   Relationship focus?
   Group focus?
   Inter-group focus?
   Organizational focus?

This classification can only be used as a very rough guide for the selection and design of learning programmes. As can be seen, projects and case studies, for example, can be designed to satisfy more than one learning domain. The classification, in this sense, is fluid. More than this, such a classification simply invites trainers to turn it upside down by creating ever new learning methods and by modifying existing ones.

LEVEL 1: TRAINER AS INFORMATION PROVIDER

Objective: These teaching methods will aid acquisition of 'knowledge'. The teaching method enables the learner to recall facts, definitions, procedures, actions and behaviours. The learner will be able to identify, define and describe.

Feedback: The teaching methods provide little feedback.

Trainer role: Learning tends to be teacher- or expert-centred rather than learner-centred.

Off-job methods

1 Lecture/lecturette/talk methods.
2 Programmed learning method.

Off- and on-job methods

3 Reading assignment method.
4 Note-taking method.
5 Question/answer sessions.
6 Demonstration.
7 Case examples.
8 Using printed word such as: book/handout/pamphlet/journal/newspaper/bulletin/instruction sheet/checklist/recipe/rule/mnemonic.
9 Using non-projected visual aids such as: line drawing/photograph/mock up/cutaway/model/sample/exhibit/poster/cartoon/chart/illustration/diagram/algorithm/information map/label/code.

Off-job methods

10 Using projected visual aids such as: overhead projector/slide projector/epidiascope/epivisor/episcope/film without sound.
11 Using audio aids such as: radio/record player/CD/tape recorder.
12 Using audio-visual aids such as: films (35mm/8mm)/video tapes/film strips.

LEVEL 2: TRAINER AS INFORMATION PROVIDER

Objective: These teaching methods aid 'understanding'. The teaching method enables the learner to grasp concepts, ideas, procedures and techniques. The learner will be able to explain, compare and justify.

Feedback: The teaching method provides some feedback.

Training role: Learning tends to be teacher-centred rather than learner-centred.

Off-job methods

1 Lecture/lecturette/talk methods.
2 Programmed learning method.

13 Technology-based learning method.
14 Controlled/leader-centred discussion methods.
15 Panel discussion method.*
16 Symposium method.
17 Seminar method.
18 Syndicate method.
19 Buzz group method.
20 Tutorial method.*
21 Traditional management education.
22 Traditional management training.
23 Action maze method.
24 Test/quiz method.
25 Game method.
26 Open discussion method.
27 In-tray exercise method.
28 Case study method.
29 Incident process case study method.
30 Critical incident process.
31 Feedback meetings (with diagnostic instruments).
32 Structured instruments.

On-job methods

33 Traditional induction training method.
34 Field visit method.
35 Project/assignment methods.
36 Follow-through meetings.
37 Organizational mirroring.
38 Scenario training.
39 Role-set analysis.

On- and off-job methods

40 Exercise method.
41 Drill method.
42 Traditional instruction method: show/do/think (or lesson demonstration method).
42 Traditional instruction method: show/think/do.

LEVEL 3: TRAINER AS LEARNING FACILITATOR

Objective: These learning situations (rather than teaching methods) aid 'application'. These learning situations enable the learner to match expectations, and apply knowledge, skills and attitudes in the 'correct way'.

Feedback: Feedback at this level is crucial for learning.

Trainer role: Learning is learner-centred rather than teacher-centred.

Off-job methods

13 Technology-based learning method.
26 Open/group-centred discussion.
27 Tailored in-tray exercise method.*

28 Tailored case study method.*
31 Self-diagnostic instrument.*
43 Language-laboratory method.*
44 Role playing method.
45 Role reversal method.
46 Intimacy exercises.
47 Meetings for two.
48 Transactional analysis.
49 Gestalt therapy method.
50 Encounter groups.
51 Synectics.
52 Outward Bound training method.

On-job methods

35 Project/assignment methods.
39 Role-set analysis.
40 Exercise method.
41 Drill method.
42 Instruction discovery method: do/show/think.
42 Instruction discovery method: do/think/show.
53 Role negotiation.
54 Shadowing method.
55 Coaching method. (See helping relationships.)
56 Job restructuring methods:
   • Job rotation method;
   • Job enlargement method.
57 Behaviour/role modelling method.
58 Behaviour modification method.

Management style

59 Action-centred leadership.
60 Managerial grid.
61 McGregor's Theory Y/Theory X.
62 Reddin 3-D Theory.
63 Likert.

LEVEL 4: TRAINER AS LEARNING FACILITATOR

Objective: These learning situations (rather than teaching methods) aid 'transfer'. The learning situation enables the learner to modify or create new theories, ideas or tools to cope with ever new situations. At this level there are no correct answers.

Feedback: Feedback and learning at this level are one. Feedback equals learning. Without feedback, transfer of learning to the work situation will, in essence, fail.

Trainer role: Learning is learner-centred rather than teacher-centred. The learner is very much in control of his/her learning.

Off-job methods
64 Group development method.
65 Team building method.
66 Inter-group meeting method.
67 Sensitivity training/T-Group training method.
68 Coverdale training method.*

On-job methods
35 Project methods.
55 Job restructuring methods:
  • Job enrichment;
  • Semi-autonomous groups;
  • Autonomous groups.
55 Mentoring method. (See helping relationships.)
69 Action learning methods.
70 Process consultation method.

On- and off-job methods
42 Instruction discovery method: think/show/do.
42 Instruction discovery method: think/do/show.
55 Counselling method. (See helping relationships.)
71 Problem-solving method.
72 Kepner Tregoe.
73 Management development method.
74 Organizational development method.
75 Socio-technical programme.

* Description not given.

DESCRIPTIONS OF TRAINING METHODS AND LEARNING SITUATIONS

1 LECTURE (Level 1: Knowledge, and Level 2: Understanding)
Structured planned talk usually making use of visual aids, and/or without group participation other than through questions at the conclusion.

Points to consider
- For large audience, good planning and lively delivery is required to hold people's attention.
- Useful for passing on knowledge, or 'painting' a broad picture in words and visuals as a guide to later study.
- Also note *lecturette,* a short lecture, normally interposed into a particular training activity, covering one specific aspect of work being undertaken.
- See also the 'Talk' method.
- Suitable for *Role culture.*

Readings

Lecture/lecturette/talk methods

Borrell, P. (1977) *Lecturing*. Keele: Keele University Library.

Brown, G. (1978) *Lecturing and Explaining*. London: Methuen.

Gregory, I. D. (1975) 'A New Look at the Lecture Method'. *British Journal of Educational Technology 6, 1,* 55–62.

McLennan, R. (1975) 'Lectures, Learning and Information Transmission'. *Journal of European Training 4, 1,* 56–66.

Talk method

Abell, D. (1970) 'On Lecturing Without Really Lecturing, Part 1'. *CUEBS News 6, 3,* 7–10. Council on Undergraduate Education in the Biological Sciences, USA.

Carl, J. and O'Brien, N. (1970) 'Classroom Debate'. *Journal of Geological Education 18,* 122.

2 PROGRAMMED LEARNING METHOD (Level 1: Knowledge, and Level 2: Understanding)

Programmed learning is used to learn facts, principles and ideas. The method is designed for self-learning and self-pacing. The focus is usually on the acquisition of knowledge. The programme is designed to provide immediate knowledge of results, and successful learning can be judged by the number of errors made. One form of the programming involves learning a set sequence, and another allows for 'branching'. Programmed learning is suitable for quick and less able learners. In addition to the book format, materials can also be computerized.

Points to consider

- Compared to lectures and courses, the material is presented in a uniform manner.
- The method of presentation provides a great deal of flexibility for its use.
- The method is well suited for imparting factual information.
- May suit *Role culture.*

Readings

Dodd, B. (1967) *Programmed Instruction for Industrial Training*. London: Heinemann.

Hudson, H. (1976) *The Resurgence of Programmed Instruction.*
BACIE Journal.

Markle, S. (1969) *Good Frames and Bad*. Chichester: John Wiley and Sons.

Shirley-Smith, K. (1973) *Guide to Programmed Techniques in Industrial Training*. Aldershot: Gower.

3 READING ASSIGNMENT METHOD (Level 1: Knowledge)

For many people, reading remains the core method for obtaining information. When discussed, reading assignments are usually commented on within an educational context. The idea, however, can be applied to a work off-job context. By itself as knowledge acquisition, it will remain knowledge, but when linked with a tutor or coach, discussion and debriefing can elevate it to 'understanding' in readiness for 'application'.

Points to consider

- Reading by itself does not ensure comprehension. When feedback is added via a coach, meaning and understanding can be achieved.
- Learners often need help with distinguishing between core reading and supplementary material.
- May suit *Role, Achievement and Support cultures.*

Readings

Egger, R. (1959) 'The Administrative Novel'. *American Political Science Review, Vol. 53.*

Forster, G. C. F. (1968) 'Books in University Teaching' in Layton, D. (ed.) *University Teaching in Transition.* Edinburgh: Oliver and Boyd.

Guillet de Monthoux, P. (1979/80) 'A "Novel" Approach to Management'. *Journal of General Management 5, 2,* 42–52.

Kroll, M. (1965) 'Administrative Fiction and Credibility'. *Public Administration Review, Vol. 25.*

Mann, P. (1973) *Books and Students.* National Book League.

Perry, W. (1959) 'Students' Use and Misuse of Reading Skills'. *Harvard Educational Review, Vol. 29.* Also included in Gibbs, G. (1977) *Learning to Study: A Guide to Running Group Sessions.* UK: Open University.

4 NOTE-TAKING METHOD (Level 1: Knowledge)

This involves asking learners to take notes, at meetings or when listening to a recorded message, in order to develop listening, observation and writing skills. Like reading, the learner needs feedback to evaluate progress and standards.

Points to consider

- A coach is needed to facilitate progress.
- It is a useful and inexpensive technique for developing said skills.
- The method can be expanded to observe behaviour, management style and a host of influencing factors which may be missed if the learner were participating.
- The method can be used to consider the learner's own strengths and weaknesses when compared to effective and less effective role models. Used well, learners can thus enhance their reflective and self-assessment skills.
- May suit *Role, Achievement and Support cultures.*

Reading

Buzan, T. (1974) *Use Your Head.* London: BBC Publications.

5 QUESTION/ANSWER SESSIONS (Level 1: Knowledge)

This can be run as a separate activity or be used to follow other training techniques. Most useful in checking whether or not the information presented by other means has been clearly understood and absorbed.

6 DEMONSTRATION (Level 1: Knowledge)

An illustrated lecture or explanation to show how something works or is done. A demonstration can stand alone or can be part of the 'Instruction' method, item 42.

7 CASE EXAMPLES (Level 1: Knowledge)

These illustrate how principles and ideas can be applied practically by describing situations which have taken place.

Reading

Hague, H. (1974) *Executive Self-development*. London: Macmillan.

8 ALGORITHM (Level 1: Knowledge)

Information presented by means of a series of simple steps in the form of a logical tree or flow chart. Most useful in providing the learner with a way of understanding and handling a variety of different conditions in the right way. A series of such charts can thus be built up to form a useful reference document.

Readings

Lewis, B. N. and Woolfenden, P. J. (1969) *Algorithms and Logical Trees: A Self Instruction Course*. Cambridge: Algorithm Press.
Wheatley, D. M. and Unwin, A. W. (1972) *The Algorithm Writer's Guide*. London: Longman.

9 MNEMONICS (Level 1: Knowledge)

This involves the use of 'key' letters or rhymes to act as memory aids, e.g.: TULRA (Trade Union and Labour Relations Act); ACAS (Advisory, Conciliation and Arbitration Service); TUC (Trade Union Congress).

Reading

Mednick, S. A., Pollio, H. R. and Loftus, E. F. (1973) *Learning* (2nd edn). Englewood Cliffs, NJ: Prentice-Hall.

10 FILM/VIDEO TAPE (Level 1: Knowledge)

Similar in principle to 'Lecture' but the message is usually presented dramatically.

Points to consider

- The value of the learning is in the discussion of the ideas presented. Hence, this method requires good preparation in terms of discussing 'key points'.
- In this sense, the film or video should always be regarded as an 'idea jogger' to discussion, and it must be relevant to the task in hand.
- It can be used to facilitate exploration of feelings and emotions on some topic, it can help underline 'best practice' and can be used for 'benchmarking'.
- It is a popular learning method and a useful device which can 'get close to the reality' in a short period of time.
- May suit *Role and Achievement cultures*.

13 TECHNOLOGY-BASED LEARNING METHOD (Level 2: Understanding, and Level 3: Application)

This technology is well suited for learning complex programmable material. The main applications are:

- *Computer-based training (CBT)*. The computer is programmed to provide instructions, ask questions and respond to answers given by the learner. Such systems can test understanding and assess which elements have been mastered or avoided.
- *Interactive video (IV)*. Audio-visual instruction can be added to CBT – providing video, still photographs, animation, graphics and sound.
- *Interactive audio (IA)*. This adds speech and sound effects to CBT. IA is halfway between CBT and IV. This is useful for developing language skills and for assisting users of computer systems.
- *Simulation*. The computer simulates the work environment on the screen. Simulators can involve touch, sight, hearing and movement. Simulation can be used:
  - for problem solving;
  - to 'practise' where there are dangerous situations;
  - to 'practise' when making a mistake can be expensive; for example to train pilots or train financial managers.

Readings

Aronson, M. (1986) 'Computer-Based Business Simulations: Purchase Considerations'. *Training and Development Journal 40,* April, 53–5.

Curry, B. and Moutinho, L. (1992) 'Using Computer Simulations in Management Evaluation'. *Management Education and Development 23, 2,* Summer, 155–67.

Dean, C. and Whitlock Q. (1988) *A Handbook of Computer Based Training.* London: Kogan Page.

ESRC (1989) *Authoring of Computer Based Training Materials.* UK: Training Agency OL63.

Kearsley, G. (1989) *Computer Based Training.* Reading, Mass.: Addison-Wesley.

Laurillard, D. and Lefrere, P. (1985) *An Introduction to Computer Based Learning.* UK: Open University Press.

Madlin, N. (1987) 'Computer Assisted Training'. *Management Review 76,* June, 56–7.

National Computing Centre (1989) *A Review of the Cost Benefits of Computer Based Training (CBT).* UK: Training Agency.

Strawford G. (1988) *Authoring Packages, A Comparative Report.* USA: National Interactive Video Centre.

Vallely, I. (1992) 'Tap Into A Powerful Source of Learning (TBT)'. *Works Management 45, 6,* 29–35.

14 CONTROLLED/LEADER CENTRED DISCUSSION METHODS (Level 2: Understanding)

This will follow a planned path which is set by the leader's agenda. In this case information is imparted. With 'Open discussion' (item 26), information is shared.

Points to consider

- Suitable when members lack the skill for a more open discussion.
- Can be useful when required for tight briefing purposes.
- The 'telling' attitude that is displayed may distort the communication.
- May be suitable for *Power and Role cultures*.

Readings

David, R. H., Fry, J. P. and Alexander, L. T. (1977) *The Discussion Method. Guides for the Improvement of Instruction in Higher Education No. 6.* East Lansing: Michigan State University.

Debenham, A. I. S. (1976) *A Trainer's Guide to Discussion Leading.* London: BACIE.

Hyman, R. T. (1980) *Improving Discussion Leadership.* USA: Teachers College Press.

16 SYMPOSIUM METHOD (Level 2: Understanding)

A process for presenting all possible aspects of a subject to an audience (up to 500 people). Speakers, usually authorities on the topic, are asked to make speeches lasting no more than twenty minutes. For large groups there is usually no audience participation.

Points to consider

- Speakers need to be well briefed and competent presenters, if members are to maintain interest and be informed in a short period.
- The 'talking head' video can also be seen as a form of symposium, where a variety of ideas is presented to a small non-participating group. In this case, and in the case of the small-group symposium, a period can be devoted to examining the various points of view in more detail, after the symposium/video.
- May be suitable for *Role and Achievement cultures*.

17 SEMINAR METHOD (Level 2: Understanding)

A short course or conference making extensive use of participative methods and devoted to the exclusive study of one subject.

Points to consider

- Group sizes can vary between eight and twelve members.
- Guest experts who might introduce or lead the discussion, must be very well prepared and very skilled at handling all types of questions and observations.
- May suit *Achievement and Support cultures*.

Readings

Abercrombie, M. L. J. (1979) *Aims and Techniques for Group Teaching,* 4th edn. Guildford, Surrey: Society for Research into Higher Education.

Abercrombie, M. L. J. and Terry, P. M. (1978) *Talking to Learn: Improving Learning and Teaching in Small Groups.* Guildford, Surrey: Society for Research into Higher Education.

Ruddock, J. (1978) *Learning Through Small Group Discussion: A Study of Seminar Work in Higher Education.* Guildford, Surrey: Society for Research into Higher Education.

Wilson, A. (1980) 'Structuring Seminars: A Technique to Allow Students to Participate in the Structuring of Small Group Discussions'. *Studies in Higher Education 5, 1,* 81–4.

18 SYNDICATE METHOD (Level 2: Understanding)

A small group of learners (six to eight) forms to consider and report on a question, problem or exercise as part of a training course. The object is to promote learning by means of intra-group and inter-group analysis and discussion.

The syndicate sometimes nominates a secretary to write a report, a speaker to present findings and a chairman to co-ordinate the whole process.

Points to consider

- Activities need to be well co-ordinated and resourced.
- Results of analysis and discussion need to be shared.
- Organizers need to make sure that they do not just create 'an exchange of ignorance'.
- Although some participants find this method very stimulating, there is the danger that some members will contribute much more than others.
- May suit *Achievement culture*.

Readings

Adams, J. (1975) 'The Use of Syndicates in Management Training' in Taylor, B. and Lippitt, G. L. (eds) *Management Development and Training Handbook*. London: McGraw-Hill.

Bertcher, H. J. and Maple, F. F. (1977) *Creating Groups. Sage Human Services Guide.* London: Sage.

Collier, K. (1968–69) 'Syndicate Methods: Further Evidence and Comment'. *Universities Quarterly 23, 4,* 431–6.

Lawrence, G. (1972) 'The Syndicate Method in Varieties of Group Discussion. University Teaching.' University of London Institute of Education.

19 BUZZ GROUP METHOD (Level 2: Understanding)

The buzz group method can greatly enrich the traditional lesson or lecture format. Members of the audience form small groups (between two and six) to 'buzz' a particular issue. The buzz usually takes place for a short period of time with the objects of exploring options to a problem, providing feedback to lecturer, encouraging learners to explore and put forward their ideas, and providing lecturer with a breathing space.

Points to consider

- The method generally does create interest and involvement.
- The lecturer must be well prepared to respond to the feedback.
- A spokesperson can be appointed from each buzz group to report back to the entire group during and/or at the end of the session.
- May suit *Achievement cultures*.

Readings

Bligh, D. A. (1972) *What's the Use of Lectures?* Harmondsworth: Penguin.

Bligh, D. A. (1976) *Improving Teaching in Higher Education*. University Teaching Methods Unit, University of London.

21 TRADITIONAL MANAGEMENT EDUCATION (ME) (Level 2: Understanding)

Management Education can be described at level 1 as an activity which aims at developing the manager's knowledge, skills, attitudes, moral values and understanding of:

- the major managerial disciplines faced in most organizations (e.g. finance, production, marketing and human resourcing) and

- the influences which impinge on individual companies and countries throughout the world.

At level 2 Management Education can be described as providing an important 'real-location' function concerning 'mismatch' between individual managers and their jobs; and at level 3 as awarding highly valued qualifications, such as the Diploma in Management Studies (DMS), Master of Business Administration (MBA) and the stages provided by the Management Charter Initiative (MCI).

As listed above, ME can be valued on one, two or three levels, and the relative weights given to each by the manager may change during the learning experience.

Points to consider

- Both Management Education (ME) and Management Training (MT):
  - usually have little direct impact on real problems;
  - learning is usually off-the-job;
  - learning is manager-centred and predominantly task-orientated;
  - learning is usually knowledge- and course-based;
  - emphasis is on managerial effectiveness (in MT) and managerial competence (in ME).
- May suit *Role and Achievement cultures.*

Readings

AMBA (1992) *The MBA Experience – The Reality Behind the Myth.* London: Association of MBAs.

Hales, C. (1986) 'What Do Managers Do? – A Critical Review of the Evidence'. *Journal of Management Studies 23, 1,* 88–115.

Hall, K. (1984) 'Wither Business Schools? Some International Comparisons in Management Education'. *Journal of Management Development 3, 1,* 42–5.

Naymark, J. (1983) 'Training, Education and Culture: Observations on the Theory and Practice of Training in Developing Countries' in Blacker, F. (ed.) *Social Psychology and Developing Countries.* Chichester: John Wiley and Sons.

Pedlar, M. (1978) 'Learning in Management Education'. *Journal of European Training 3, 3,* 182–94.

22 TRADITIONAL MANAGEMENT TRAINING (MT) (Level 2: Understanding)

Management Training (MT) is usually the province of the company trainer which means it is usually conducted in-house, and could be called company-specific. MT involves any attempt to improve managerial effectiveness, in the short-term, through a planned and deliberate learning process. MT is best integrated with job requirements and organizational demands. The extremes of MT can be described as mainly knowledge-based, using the structured course method; and knowledge- and skills-based where use is made of pre-course preparation, on-job projects and the candidate's autonomy to introduce change.

As far as the learner is concerned, best results (e.g. changed behaviour, skills learnt, knowledge used) will be achieved when MT is integrated with Management Education (ME) and Management Development (MD) activity.

Points to consider

- See comments under 'Management Education'.
- May suit *Role and Achievement cultures*.

Readings

Analoui, F. (1993) *Training and Transfer of Learning*. Aldershot: Avebury.

Anderson, A. H. (1991) *Successful Training Practice: A Manager's Guide to Personal Development*. London: Blackwell. (Human resource management in action.)

Ballin, M. (1993) 'Forging a New Breed of Supervisor'. *Personnel Management 25, 4*, 34–7.

Banfield, J. (1992) 'Education and Training for the 21st Century'. *Modern Management 6, 2*, 30–2.

Bates, J. (1993) 'New Approaches to Training the Manager'. *CBI News*, March, 46–52.

Bunning, C. (1992) 'Turning Experience into Learning: The Strategic Challenge for Individuals and Organizations'. *Journal of European Industrial Training 16, 6*, 7–12.

Burgoyne, J. and Stuart, R. (1991) 'Teaching and Learning Methods in Management Development'. *Personnel Review 20, 3*, 27–33.

Casey, D. (1993) *Managing Learning in Organizations*. Buckingham: Open University Press. (*Managing Work and Organization* series).

Coulson-Thomas, C. J. (1992) 'Integrating Learning and Working'. *Education and Training 34, 1*, 25–9.

Honey, P. (1992) 'Learning from Experience: The Key to Management Development'. *Training Officer 28, 1*, 8–11.

Payne, J. (1989) *A Manual of Management Training Exercises*. Aldershot: Gower.

Peter Chadwick Limited (1993) *Supervisory Roles, Responsibilities and Training in Britain Today*. Richmond, Surrey: Peter Chadwick.

23 ACTION MAZE METHOD (Level 2: Understanding)

The action maze starts with a description of an incident for analysis (e.g. disciplining staff) and is followed by a list of alternative actions. The maze is usually in book format, and as each decision is made, the learner is provided with information at each stage to indicate if the learner is on the right 'path'. There are alternative approaches to handling progress through the maze but, in essence, learning comes from comparing the decision made with the preferred solution, through group discussion and through feedback by the programme leader.

Points to consider

- Learners generally find this approach stimulating.
- Mazes take time to prepare and need to be validated.
- The maze is suitable where decisions do require consideration of recognized procedural responses, either supported in law or supported by good organizational practice.
- The information supplied in the maze booklet or provided by the maze leader will need to justify decisions made.
- Although the maze is focused on cognitive subjects, discussion can embrace social issues and attitudes; and at suitable points, role playing and case studies can be added or linked in.

- Although different from it, action mazes have their roots in programmed learning.
- May suit *Power, Role and Achievement cultures*. For Power, it would suit the trial and error ethos. For Role, it might just suit the controlled risk situation. For Achievement, it will suit the drive to acquire skills.

Readings

Elgood, C. (1980) 'The Use of Business Games in Management Training'. *The Training Officer 16, 12,* 332–4.

Zoll, A. A. (1969) *Dynamic Management Education,* Chapters 11–12. Reading, Massachusetts: Addison-Wesley.

24 TESTS/QUIZZES (Level 2: Understanding)

Tests and quizzes can be given to prompt observation, generate interest in a subject and check past learning. Such mechanisms can be used as a pre-test and compared later with post-test results, to demonstrate the gain in learning.

Points to consider

- Tests and quizzes need to properly reflect the objectives of the course.
- Used well, they should motivate and encourage.
- May suit *Role and Achievement cultures*.

Readings

Griffin, H. and Houston, A. (1980) 'Self-Development for Managers in Making the Most of Existing Resources'. *Personnel Management 12, 9,* 46–8.

Lieberman, M. A. and Borman, L. D. (1979) *Self Help Groups.* San Francisco: Jossey Bass.

Smith, P. B. (1980) *Group Processes and Personal Change,* Chapter 9. London: Harper and Row.

25 GAME METHOD (Level 2: Understanding)

Games are usually competitive events, whereby learners play a role with a mission to win or survive. Learners are presented with a scenario and at certain times are required to make decisions. When a number of small groups (two-plus) are competing against each other, the data is often processed using computer facilities.

Points to consider

- The method is useful for examining business ideas and models.
- Learners usually obtain a high level of involvement, and can generate high levels of friendly competitiveness.
- Course leaders sometimes need to allow participants to 'cool off' when the game is over, before providing feedback and seeking reflective comments.
- As the game dramatically compresses time and events, this simplification will form part of course feedback, in terms of its application to real life.
- May suit *Role and Achievement cultures*.

Readings

Elgood, C. (1975) 'Designing a Business Game'. *Journal of European Training 4, 1,* 15–24.

Elgood, C. (1976) *Handbook of Management Games.* Aldershot: Gower.

Kibbee, J. M. *et al.* (1961) *Management Games.* New York: Holt Rinehart.

Lloyd, D. C. F. (1978) 'An Introduction to Business Games'. *Industrial and Commercial Training 10, 1,* 11–18.

Lovelock, C. (1975) 'The Construction, Operation and Evaluation of Management Games' in Taylor, B. and Lippitt, G. L. (eds) *Management Development and Training Handbook.* London: McGraw-Hill.

Meurs, F. and Choffray, J. M. (1975) 'Business Games: Their Role in Training and Development'. *Journal of European Training 4, 2,* 81–112.

26 OPEN DISCUSSION METHOD (Level 2: Understanding)

This allows participants to learn freely from each other through the sharing and clarification of ideas and their meanings. The agenda is determined by the members' priorities.

Points to consider

- Used to develop and adjust attitudes and opinions.
- Depending on maturity of group, a chairperson or leader may be required to skilfully handle interplay, without closing down genuinely held opinions and ideas.
- There can become a point, if members are not skilled, where attitudes may harden rather than remain open.
- May be time-consuming.
- May suit *Achievement and Support cultures.*

27 IN-TRAY EXERCISE METHOD (Level 2: Understanding)

In-tray exercises vary in their degree of difficulty. The learner is presented with samples of administrative work in the form of a manager's in-tray, to be completed within a short period (up to one-and-a-half hours). The learner is given a situation such as, 'You have just returned to work from holiday, and your first job is to action your in-tray.' How the learner copes with the information and what priorities are decided upon, form part of later discussion and feedback from course leaders.

Points to consider

- The exercise is conducted in real time and so is a simulation of a work situation.
- Course leaders need to provide convincing reasons for recommending a particular sequence of activity.
- Course leaders must not be too clever in discussing 'hidden agendas' and 'political considerations' out of all recognition to the situation in-hand and the learner's experience. In this sense, the initial brief and the 'context' of the situation need to be clear.
- When there are differences between the recommended and the learner's approach, the learner can be encouraged to explain why the recommended solution is given.
- This method is well suited to a *Role culture.*

Readings:

Meyer, H. H. (1970) 'The Validity of the In-basket Exercise as a Measure of Manager-ial Performance'. *Personnel Psychology 23,* 297–307.

Stewart, A. and Stewart, V. (1976) *Tomorrow's Men Today,* Chapter 5. London: Insti-tute of Personnel Management.

Stewart, V. (1981) 'Training for Managerial Effectiveness, Core Skills 2'. *Journal of European Industrial Training 5, 1,* 5–8.

28 CASE STUDY METHOD (Level 2: Understanding)

A method for using problem-solving or investigative approaches to analyse either a real or fictional situation, and to compare solutions to actual or best practice results.

Points to consider

- Works well when analysing financial and statistical data, and for examining discipli-nary or grievance procedures.
- It may not be easy to replicate the political tensions, the frustrations, the irrational actions, and the loves and hates of the situation.
- Very useful for 'practising' with problem-solving and investigative tools.
- People must have the necessary pre-knowledge to deal with the case, and it needs to be relevant to the learner's situation.
- Case studies are useful for developing:
  – analytical skills, such as classifying;
  – application skills, such as using techniques and rules;
  – interpersonal skills, such as building on other people's ideas during discussion;
  – self-analysis skills, such as realizing that marketing skills need to be improved;
  – presentation skills, such as making an oral presentation to small or large groups;
  – problem-solving skills, which require creative and logical thinking.
- May suit *Role and Achievement cultures.*

Readings

Case study method

Easton, G. (1982) *Learning from Case Studies.* London: Prentice-Hall International Inc.

Reynolds, J. I. (1980) *Case Method in Management Development.* Geneva: International Labour Office.

Ronstadt, R. (1977) *The Art of Case Analysis: A Student Guide.* Needham, Massachu-setts: Lord Publishing Company.

Case study sources

Source of Case Studies. European Case Clearing House, Cranfield Institute of Technol-ogy, Cranfield, Bedford MK43 0AL.

Employee Relations (a group within Arthur Young), Compass House, 80 Newmarket Road, Cambridge CB5 8DZ. Tel 01223 315944.

Intercollegiate Case Clearing House (ICCH), Soldiers Field Post Office, Boston, Massachusetts 02163, USA.

29 INCIDENT PROCESS CASE STUDY METHOD (Level 2: Understanding)

Compared to the case study method with its strong emphasis on data processing, problem-solving and implementation, the incident method focuses on problem definition. It aims to promote analytical thinking and reasoned judgement. The method is built around a six-stage structure, namely:

- the members are briefed;
- learners ask questions of the facilitator and the person whose real case it is;
- each person is required to note down their views;
- syndicates are made up of like-minded learners;
- each syndicate presents its views;
- the facilitator summarizes all comments and draws attention to the strengths and weaknesses of each syndicate's conclusions.

Points to consider

- Requires careful preparation and skilled handling.
- Has the merit of examining causes of problems and the context of situations, which in turn promotes a problem-prevention attitude.
- The process makes learners aware of the many viewpoints that can be generated.
- The process brings home the ease with which we hold to beliefs and assumptions which cannot be justified.
- May suit *Role and Achievement cultures*.

Readings

Binsted, D., Stuart, R. and Long, G. (1980) 'Promoting Useful Management Learning: Problems of Transition and Transfer' in Beck, J. and Cox, C. (eds) *Advances in Management Education*. Chichester: John Wiley and Sons.

Boyd, B. B. (1980) 'Developing Case Studies'. *Training and Development Journal 34, 6.*

Pigors, P. and Pigors, F. (1955) *The Incident Process: Case Studies in Management Development*. Washington DC: The Bureau of National Affairs Inc.

30 CRITICAL INCIDENT PROCESS (Level 2: Understanding)

This technique identifies and analyses those incidents based on a person's own experience (or provided by the trainer). Incidents which have become critical for the individual may include, for example, decision-making or a human relations situation. Such incidents are then discussed by group members with a view to seeking new perspectives. The process can be extended to involve the use of 'Role Play' and the 'Problem-solving Cycle'. As well as clarifying the *demands* (the things I feel I *must do*) and the *constraints* (the things I feel I *must not do*), the process has the merit of focusing on the often forgotten *choices* (the things I *can or may do*). See Chapter 8.

If the incidents are provided by the trainer, members can be asked to work alone or in small groups to examine a situation and to explain what their response would be. To provide a comparison, the trainer may in turn be able to describe what the actual response was, or may suggest or seek a best practice solution.

Readings

Schroder, H. M., Driver, M. J. and Streufert, S. (1967) *Human Information Processing: Individuals and Groups Functioning in Complex Social Situations.* Orlando: Holt, Rinehart and Winston.
Also Chapter 9, item 9.

31 FEEDBACK MEETINGS (Level 2: Understanding)

The process by which information about the results of certain actions is fed back to the learner with or without diagnostic instruments. This enables the individual or the group to modify their immediate and subsequent actions to achieve more closely any set of objectives. The feedback sessions can then be used as a 'trigger' for further training activities.

Readings

Annett, J. (1969) *Feedback and Human Behaviour.* Penguin.
Lawrence, P. R. and Lorsch, J. W. (1969) *The Developing Organization: Diagnosis and Action.* London: Addison-Wesley.
Also note: Diagnostic instruments. Carefully prepared materials in the form of questionnaires, surveys, etc. designed to produce an assessment of intangibles such as ideology, and the supportive nature of an organization's culture.

32 STRUCTURED INSTRUMENTS (Level 2: Understanding)

Training techniques which are designed to encourage a group to discuss and work through information which it has generated itself. This method normally takes the form of questionnaires or checklists on a particular subject, and are completed by learners. The information is then collated and coded for further analysis, discussion and assessment.

Readings

Berger, M. L. and Berger, P. J. (eds) (1972) *Group Training Techniques: Cases, Applications and Research.* Aldershot: Gower Press.
Pfeiffer, J. W. and Jones, J. E. (1975) *A Handbook of Structured Experiences for Human Relations Training, Vols 1–5.* Iowa: University Associates.

33 TRADITIONAL INDUCTION TRAINING METHOD: (Level 2: Understanding)

Induction training has the aim of orientating a new employee as quickly as possible to the organization culture and work situation. Depending on the circumstances, induction can take place over days, weeks or months. Done well, the process will help reduce anxiety, speed up job orientation, assist employee retention, promote goodwill and provide opportunity to develop effective relationships. If induction is done badly or not done at all, this can signal to employees, at an early stage, that the organization is not prepared to invest in people. Whether this is true or not, the lack of initial training may convey a non-supportive attitude which, in turn, may take time to redress. Today, most large- and medium-size companies implement induction procedures.

Points to consider

- Make induction relevant to new starters.
- Where possible, tailor induction programmes to suit the needs of individuals.
- View induction as an opportunity for both parties to constructively determine their suitability for each other.
- *Role and Achievement cultures* will welcome fully.

Readings

Fowler, A. (1990) *Getting Off to a Good Start: Successful Employee Induction.* London: Institute of Personnel Management.

Fowler, A. (1990) *A Good Start.* London: Institute of Personnel Management.

Meighan, M. (1991) *How to Design and Deliver Induction Training Programmes.* London: Kogan Page.

Skeats, J. (1991) *Successful Induction: How To Get The Most From Your New Employees.* London: Kogan Page.

34 FIELD TRIP (Level 2: Understanding)

A field trip can last more than one day and involve first-hand study of some process. Such a study can be used by members for improving their own systems, for benchmarking or for later purchase.

Points to consider

- It can sometimes take time to find suitable 'comparisons'.
- Field study can be applied to managerial activities like planning, quality and training systems, as well as manufacturing and technical processes.
- Members need to be well disciplined for collecting reference data during the study.
- May suit *Role and Achievement cultures.*

35 PROJECT METHOD/ASSIGNMENT (Level 2: Understanding)

Project work may be undertaken as part of an integrated in-house or educational programme. Project work allows learners to work at their own pace and study a particular issue or problem at some depth. Projects can be undertaken both within a work or non-work situation. There is usually an opportunity for the learner to display initiative and originality, and to combine knowledge from different disciplines. In essence there are four basic modes of project work:

(a) Tackling familiar task in familiar organization

(The company setting and project are familiar.) This in effect becomes an extension of the person's own job. This could involve the preparation of marketing strategy for a new market by, say, a young marketing manager. The level of difficulty here is both technical (the new task) and social (dealing with a number of new contacts).

A variation of this method is the *'Study assignment' method,* which can also be undertaken in a department not familiar to the learner. In this case the learner is asked to study and report on some specified procedure or operation. This method can be made use of by new recruits or established personnel.

(b) Tackling unfamiliar task in familiar organization

(The company setting is familiar but the project is unfamiliar.) This type of project work is often used to broaden junior and senior managers. Take the case of a project manager studying a sales problem. The level of difficulty will be threefold: one, tackling an unfamiliar problem; two, working with different colleagues; and three, working within a different sub-culture.

This method is sometimes called *'Consultant assignment'* or *'Development assignment'*, and variations of this type of project work include:

- *Acting assignment* – the manager, for example, takes on a different job for a short period to study and report on a particular problem.
- *Committee assignment* – in this case, managers are requested to serve on an in-house committee to study some problem and report on it. In addition to technical skills, a variety of interpersonal and committee handling skills would be developed.
- *Evaluation assignment* – a sales manager, for example, is required to evaluate new production technology or a new system and present a report. The sales manager would in this case be trained to undertake the task. The task itself would require judgemental skills to be developed, and working with different colleagues would broaden the sales manager's skill base.

(c) Tackling familiar task but in unfamiliar organization

(The company setting is unfamiliar but the project is familiar.) In this example, the production manager studies a production problem in another organization. This method may also be referred to as a 'Consultant assignment'.

For the production manager to be successful, she/he must be able to handle the technical difficulties, work effectively with new colleagues and work within a similar but different organization culture.

Other variations at this level include:

- *Assignment to government body study group* – managers with particular expertise can sometimes be asked to serve on government committees to investigate a particular issue, for which they have the requisite depth and/or breadth of experience.
- *Assignment to community organization* – this involves, say, a specialist marketing manager being seconded from a commercial organization for about one year to, say, develop a new marketing strategy for a civic, community, voluntary or social organization.
- *Task force assignment* – this would involve a task force taking on a specific role such as planning and implementing a production control system for an organization, of which task force members are not familiar. The task force may be made up of internal members or they may be specialist outsiders.
- *Field project/attachment* – in this case, a student of finance, for example, will spend time attached to the finance department of an organization, of which she/he is not an employee, to carry out a finance project.

(d) Tackling unfamiliar task in unfamiliar organization

(Both the organizational setting and project are unfamiliar.) As an example, a personnel director might investigate what business strategy is required by an organization she/he is not familiar with. Not only are the task and organization unfamiliar, so is everything connected with it. This is close to the highest level of difficulty that a manager could face.

Perhaps working in a different country might add an extra dimension of complexity. When working under these circumstances, the manager will need to be very resourceful, quick to learn new skills, and remain sensitive and responsive to the nuances of national and organizational cultural influence and social intercourse.

Points to consider

- Be it desk research or working within a work situation, project work can be very liberating and stimulating for learners.
- Project work does require the learner to adopt effective project self-management skills.
- To avoid over-reaching themselves, which some learners can be tempted to do, to prevent organizational misunderstandings about the purpose and value of project work and to assist the learner throughout, the process does require managing by a more senior member of staff.
- Project work is time-consuming and intellectually challenging, both for the learner, his/her supervisor and for those to whom he/she comes into contact.
- Also see 'Action learning', item 69.
- May suit *Achievement and some Power cultures.*

Readings

Daley, P. and McGivern, C. (1972) 'The On-Going Management Situation as a Training Vehicle'. *Industrial and Commercial Training 4, 3,* 137–41.

Honey, P. (1976) 'On-The-Job Management Training'. *Industrial and Commercial Training 8, 6,* June, 229–35.

Zeira, Y. (1973) 'Introduction of On-The-Job Management Development'. *Personnel Journal 52,* December, 1049–55.

36 FOLLOW-THROUGH MEETINGS (Level 2: Understanding)

Meetings which can be used to revive enthusiasm and commitment after a previous learning period and so restore good intentions and ensure that longer-term action plans are carried through. Especially appropriate for team development exercises. Suitable for *Role and Achievement cultures.*

37 ORGANIZATIONAL MIRRORING (Level 2: Understanding)

A meeting that allows a unit or group to collect feedback from a number of key people with whom it relates (e.g. customers, users of services). See also Benchmarking, Chapter 8.

Readings

Francis, D. and Woodcock, M. (1975) *People at Work.* Iowa: University Associates.

Walton, R. E. (1969) *Interpersonal Peacemaking: Confrontation and Third-party Consultation.* London: Addison-Wesley.

38 SCENARIO TRAINING (Level 2: Understanding)

An exercise where those involved with top-level planning and policy-making try to build up a total picture (scenario) of what the organization will look like at some point in the future. This image of the future is then used to clarify objectives and plans. Scenario training can be regarded as a form of Benchmarking. See Chapter 8 for references.

Readings

Greaves, W. (1973) *Technological Forecasting in Practice*. London: Industrial and Commercial Techniques Limited.

Wills, G. and others (1972) *Technological Forecasting: the Act and its Managerial Implications*. London: Penguin.

39 ROLE-SET ANALYSIS (Level 2: Understanding)

An individual identifies the significant people within (or outside) the organization with whom he has to relate. These people will have expectations of him and will be involved in his work. He then writes down what these expectations are. These expectations can then be tested through discussion and changed through 'Role negotiations' (item 53). Suitable for *Role and Achievement cultures*.

Readings

Gross, H. *et al.* (1958) *Explorations in role analysis*. New York: John Wiley.

Kahn, R. L. *et al.* (1964) *Organizational Stress: Studies in Role Conflict and Ambiguity*. New York: John Wiley.

Katz, D. and Kahn, R. L. (1966) *The Social Psychology of Groups*. New York: John Wiley.

40 EXERCISE METHOD (Level 2: Understanding)

The trainer presents learner with a written description of a problem or task to be performed, and corrects any errors.

Points to consider

- This method is useful for reinforcing learning by giving practice and testing learning of procedures, principles or motor skills.
- With safety in mind, exercises can be carried out off-job or on-job.
- Such an approach would follow on well from the 'Instruction' method, item 42.
- May suit *all* cultures.

41 DRILL AND PRACTICE METHOD (Level 2: Understanding)

This involves teaching and learning through repetition. The trainer sets up sequences and exercises to be practised, and corrects any errors made.

Points to consider

- It can be useful for developing motor skills or where sequence of procedure is vital.
- Checklists, algorithms and other performance aids may be used to assist memory, understanding and application.
- May suit *Power and Role cultures*.

42 INSTRUCTION METHOD (Level 2: Understanding)

Sometimes called 'Lesson demonstration', 'Tell-and-Show' or 'Sit-By-Nelly' approach. As shown in Chapter 6, instruction can take at least six forms, namely:

- 'Traditional'
  - Show/do/think;
  - Show/think/do;
- 'Discovery'
  - Do/show/think;
  - Do/think/show;
  - Think/show/do;
  - Think/do/show.

Points to consider

- Of all training methods, instruction must be the most widely practised of all. The author suspects, however, that because the 'traditional' strategy is mostly practised, many users fail to perceive the variety of discovery modes.
- When used effectively, instruction also requires that 'informing' and 'debriefing' should top and tail each stage in the process.
- This method has the reputation of being used to train average or below-average learners to learn cognitive and psychomotor tasks. Used to its full potential the method provides the basis for high-level coaching, mentoring and what is known as 'Discovery learning' or the 'Discovery' method.

Discovery method

- The 'Discovery' method can build confidence as learners master new skills for themselves.
- The 'Discovery' method has the merit of not relying on memorization but on making use of the learner's own learning patterns.
- To assist with 'application of learning' to the actual job situation, the tasks for 'Discovery' learning need to be realistic.
- The 'Discovery' method of learning is predesigned and safety considerations are paramount. The idea is that the learner discovers for him/herself how to best undertake some procedure. The facilitator is usually ready to debrief at the appropriate time.
- The 'Discovery' method does rely on judging when to allow the learner to continue with his/her 'trial and error' learning process, and when to intervene by prompting the learner to find a way forward.
- 'Traditional' instruction may suit *Power and Role cultures*.
- 'Discovery' instruction may suit *Power and Achievement cultures*.

Readings

Ayres, R. (1977) 'Strategies in Giving Group Instruction'. *BACIE Journal 31, 7,* 118–20.

Ayres, R. (1977) *A Trainer's Guide to Group Instruction.* London: British Association for Commercial and Industrial Training (BACIE).

Belbin, R. M. (1969) 'The Discovery Method in Training'. Training Information Paper No. 5. HMSO.

Clay, M. (1980) 'Discovery Learning'. *Training 6, 3,* 17–19.
Majer, R. F. (1984) *Preparing Instructional Objectives.* California: Fearon.
Rogers, J. (1977) *Adults Learning,* Chapter 9. Milton Keynes: Open University Press.

44 ROLE PLAY METHOD (Level 3: Application)

This method is used to rehearse cognitive skills, develop interactive skills and bring about changes in attitude. The method involves learners taking on a role which usually takes the form of a problem-solving scenario. Application of the method can be either highly structured or spontaneous. In this sense, role playing can be as much about engaging a person's feelings as it can their skills and knowledge.

Points to consider

- Not all learners are happy about 'playing themselves or roles' in what they regard as 'in public'.
- The method does require careful monitoring by the facilitator, to avoid embarrassing learners, to remind participants of the overall aims and to debrief members.
- The argument that lifelong learning involves risk and so does role playing is a useful parallel that needs qualifying. The difference between the two is that with role playing, the risk must be calculated not to offend the individual or damage the individual's self-esteem.
- The method has the merit of fully engaging the individual's mind, body and attitudes and so can be useful for:
  - imprinting cognitive, verbal, motor and social patterns;
  - challenging firmly held assumptions;
  - dissipating tension;
  - developing observational skills;
  - drawing conclusions about behaviour;
  - reinforcing learning;
  - drawing out new points;
  - deducing ways to improve behaviour;
  - linking to previous learning;
  - applying to other situations;
  - providing a plan for future learning.
- The method is typically used for sales training, handling complaints and dealing with a variety of interview situations.
- Review and debriefing of events can be undertaken by the facilitator, observers and those taking part.
- May suit *Achievement culture.* This would be too risky for Role, too soft for Power and too structured for Support cultures.

Readings

Aston, D. E. (1985) *Management Games for Building. Vol. 1 Case Studies and Role Playing.* Ascot: Chartered Institute of Building.
Milroy, E. (1982) *Role Play: A Practical Guide.* Aberdeen: Aberdeen University Press.
Towers, J. M. (1969) *Role-Playing for Supervisors.* Oxford: Pergamon.
van Ments, M. (1983) *The Effective Use of Role Play.* London: Kogan Page.
Wohlking, W. and Gill, P. J. (1980) *Role-Playing.* The Instructional Design Library, Englewood Cliffs, NJ: Educational Technology Publications.

45 ROLE REVERSAL METHOD (Level 3: Application)

This method is generally used to enable learners to experience different viewpoints. The method can be used to resolve conflict between, usually, two protagonists; or to enable learners to gain a deeper appreciation of another's position.

In both situations, the two learners will outline their differences to each other and then, as part of the symbolism, will switch chairs and become each other. The participants may switch back into their roles again, this time reflecting on their own and the other's insights.

Points to consider

- Requires skilful handling.
- Very useful for appreciating other viewpoints and challenging fixed assumptions.
- Review and debriefing can be provided by the facilitator, observers and participants.
- Also see 'Role play' method.
- May suit *Achievement culture*.

Readings

Heron, J. (1973) *Experiential Training Techniques*. Department of Adult Education, University of Surrey, Guildford.

Muney, B. F. and Deutsch, M. (1968) 'The Effects of Role Reversal During Discussion of Opposing Viewpoints'. *Journal of Conflict Resolution 12, 3,* 345–6.

46 INTIMACY EXERCISES (Level 3: Application)

Group exercises designed to increase the rate at which people get to know one another, to study the experience of self-disclosure and to develop authenticity in groups. Group members pair off and ask each other questions of varying degrees of intimacy. Rules for the exercise include that a person must be willing to answer any question. Later, pairs are formed into groups to discuss the experience and then the whole group hears reports from each of the smaller groups.

See also 'Sensitivity training' (item 67).

47 MEETINGS FOR TWO (Level 3: Application)

Two people meet for the specific purpose of improving the way they work together. A third party is normally involved to facilitate a free exchange of opinions and feelings about the relationship.

48 TRANSACTIONAL ANALYSIS (TA) (Level 3: Application)

This involves the analysis of conscious and unconscious behaviour in relationships so that individuals may understand and improve the way they relate to others.

Points to consider

- Like T-Groups (67) and Encounter Groups (50), sensitivity training is not so popular as it once was.

- When handled well, some people can experience real insight into personal and group behaviour. When handled badly some people have felt deeply threatened.
- The technique must be run by a specialist, the goals must be clearly stated and people must have an option of leaving the group if they so wish.
- May suit *Achievement culture*.

Readings

Berne, E. (1964) *Games People Play*. London: Penguin.

Franz, E. H. (1974) 'Transactional Analysis and the Trainer'. *Vocational Training Information Bulletin,* October, 2–5.

Harris, T. A. (1973) *I'm OK – You're OK*. London: Pan.

James, M. and Jongeward, D. (1971) *Born To Win*. Reading, Mass.: Addison-Wesley.

Jongeward, D. (1973) *Everybody Wins: Transactional Analysis Applied To Organizations*. Reading, Mass.: Addison-Wesley.

Jongeward, D. and James, M. (1973) *Winning With People: Group Exercises in Transactional Analysis*. Reading, Mass.: Addison-Wesley.

49 GESTALT THERAPY METHOD (Level 3: Application)

The Gestalt approach encourages the integration of experience into a meaningful whole. The end result of the Gestalt process is personal change, and this is achieved by becoming 'aware' and accepting 'how one is'. The process has been used for management training, organizational development, counselling and group development. In particular, the outcomes of the process can help create a higher sensitivity toward listening, observing and communicating. It can also help a person to use conflict constructively, and enhance influencing skills.

Points to consider

- Requires professional counsellor.
- The process can help individuals deal with unproductive behaviours and relationships.
- Learners must be willing to take part. It is a process that requires personal discovery, rather than one which is confronting.
- May suit *Achievement culture*.

Readings

Hatcher, C. and Himelstein, P. (eds) (1976) *The Handbook of Gestalt Therapy*, 809. New York: Jason Arunson.

Herman, S. M. and Korenich, M. (1977) *Authentic Management: A Gestalt Orientation to Organizations and their Development,* 236. Reading, Mass.: Addison-Wesley.

Passons, W. R. (1975) *Gestalt Approaches in Counselling*, 239. New York: Holt, Rinehart and Winston.

Perls, F. S. (1969) *Ego, Hunger and Aggression: the Beginning of Gestalt Therapy*, 273. New York: Vintage Books.

Zinker, J. (1978) *Creative Process in Gestalt Therapy,* 283. New York: Vintage Books.

50 ENCOUNTER GROUPS (Level 3: Application)

An approach to improving self-analysis, self-understanding and individual growth and development through exchanging personal experiences and exploring feelings in a group situation. See also 'Sensitivity training', item 67.

Readings

Lieberman, M. A. (1973) *Encounter Groups: First Facts*. Aylesbury, Bucks: Basic Books.
Rogers, S. R. (1973) *Encounter Groups*. London: Penguin.

51 SYNECTICS (Level 3: Application)

A unique set of skills and experience developed by Synectics Inc. (USA) since 1960. Starting from the pursuit of techniques to enhance creativity, Synectics have evolved a wide range of methods to increase the effectiveness of individuals and groups in developing new courses of action and working productively together. The team-building and personal interaction skills can provide a practical and acceptable approach to organizational development (OD) and industrial relations. May suit *Achievement culture*.

Readings

Nolan, V. (1972) 'Synectics: A Related Method of Improving Management Performance'. *Management by Objectives*, 2 (1).
Nolan, V. (1975) 'Creating the Atmosphere for Innovation: New Developments of Synectics'. *London Business School Journal*, Spring, *9–11*, 31.

52 OUTWARD BOUND METHOD (Level 3: Application)

Outward Bound owes much to military officer training. The method makes use of the outdoor environment and usually focuses on leadership and group work. Members are usually presented with a problem-solving or physical event to tackle, and like an experiential exercise, members are encouraged to examine 'how' they react to situations and other people. As well as reflecting on behaviour and thinking patterns, participants are encouraged to develop themselves throughout, by typically strengthening strengths and supporting weaknesses.

Points to consider

- The approach is based on the assumption that leadership is the key to effective management.
- Careful debriefing of this type of event is the key to interpreting the parallels between a work-related situation and a physical exercise. Debriefing may be twofold, first within the training context and again 'back home'.
- 'Back home' entry needs to be well co-ordinated. The organizational culture must be able to support the 'change' that is likely to occur.
- As the learner 'gets back in' she/he will likely benefit from a coaching relationship.
- This method will not suit everyone.
- May suit *Achievement and some Power cultures* (see page 98).

Readings

Kenton, L. (1976) 'Management's Toughest Course'. *Industrial Management*, November.

Keslake, P. S. and Radcliffe, P. J. (1980) 'Inward Bound – A New Direction for Outward Bound: Towards a Holistic Approach to Management Development' in Beck, J. and Cox, C. (eds) *Advances in Management Education*. Chichester: John Wiley and Sons.

Krouwell, B. (1980) 'Management Development Using the Outdoors'. *The Training Officer 16, 10*, 262–5.

Parsons, A. G. (1980) 'How to Train Managers to Lead the "Leadership Trust" Way'. *Training 6, 8*, 5–7.

Radcliffe, P. J. and Keslake, P. S. (1981) 'Outward Bound?' in Boydell, T. and Pedler, M. (Eds) *Management Self-Development: Concepts and Practices*. Aldershot: Gower.

Sewell, C. (1991) 'Learning from the Outdoors'. *Transition 91, 7*, 15–17.

Williams, D. H. (1980) 'Adventure With a Purpose'. *The Training Officer 16, 10*, 259–61.

53 ROLE NEGOTIATION (Level 3: Application)

A technique which involves changing, by means of negotiations with other interested parties, the role which an individual performs. The process of change for Harrison (1972) involves:

* not probing feelings;
* maintaining openness;
* full sharing of expectations;
* agreeing to 'exchange' desired behaviour with each party ;
* writing down the agreed changes in behaviour.

Points to consider

* The 'negotiation' will require the assistance of an experienced facilitator.
* The technique hinges on the honesty and trust of individuals, and it depends on the supportive nature of the organization culture.
* May suit *Role and Achievement cultures*.

Reading

Harrison, R. (1972) 'When Power Conflict Triggers Team Spirit'. *European Business,* Spring, 57–65.

54 SHADOWING METHOD (Level 3: Application)

The assumption here is that managerial practices can be learnt by observing a model manager at work. When the learner is asked to interpret events, and to explain what action they might take in a given situation, this type of learning can be very successful at providing insight, and provides a real 'hands-on feel' for the activity. Coupled with debriefing at each stage, this process can certainly support first-hand understanding, and it can act as a guide to application.

Points to consider

* Some dangers of using this method derive from not properly defining the shadow role. The learner should neither just become a caddy, nor take on responsibilities for which she/he has no contract.
* A more serious problem lies in the methodology. There is a danger that within the same organization, the learner may not distinguish bad practice from good and not distinguish bias from open examination.

- Done well, with informing, questioning and debriefing taking place at each stage, the method can be extremely rewarding.
- The role of the shadow and of the model need to be well defined.
- May suit *Role, Achievement and Support cultures.*

Reading

Taylor, C. (1977) 'Shadowing: The Creative Approach to Supervisory Training'. *Management 24, 8,* 14–15.

55 HELPING RELATIONSHIP METHODS (Level 2: Understanding, Level 3: Application, and Level 4: Transfer)
Instructing/Coaching/Counselling/Mentoring/Therapy

By examining a number of helping relationships, the reader may better determine differences between:

- Instructing (Level 2, 3 and 4)
- Coaching (Level 3)
- Counselling (Level 4)
- Mentoring (Level 4)
- Therapy (Level 4).

Instructing (See Chapter 6)

- Focus: Helping the person learn tasks.
- Role of instructor: Expert, using traditional or discovery instruction methods.
- Over a period of time: Minutes, hours or days.

Coaching

- Focus: Helping the person understand the requirements of the job.
- Role of coach: A questioner, reflector and joint problem-solver.
- Over a period of time: Weeks or months.

Counselling

- Focus: Empowering client to cope better with his/her work and home life.
- Role of counsellor: To help the client discover and explore for himself/herself possible solutions to the needs and feelings that the client expresses directly or indirectly.
- At one level the counsellor may need to supply factual information, as required for career counselling for example.
- At another level the counsellor may need to use empathetic skills, and by asking relevant questions encourage the client to face up to, and come to terms with, non-helpful opinions, attitudes and assumptions.
- Over a period of time: Hours, weeks or months.

Mentoring

- Focus: Helping the protégé to learn, cope with and master:
  - organizational subtleties;
  - social expectations/norms;
  - political skills;

- unwritten practices, techniques;
- interpersonal communications at the highest level;
- how and when to make and take opportunities.
- Role of mentor: To help the protégé:
  - survive (in the post);
  - adapt (to a new situation);
  - cope (with the environmental and cultural complexities);
  - develop (to new heights);
  - learn (new skills);
  - take opportunities (as they arise);
  - take over (the organization).
- Over a period of time: One to five years.

Developmental therapy

- Focus: Helping the client through psychotherapy practices to better cope with life.
- Role of therapist: Expert, guiding the client through a 'process of change' which involves the client:
  - growing;
  - developing;
  - maturing;
  - functioning better;
  - better coping with life.
- Over a period of time: Sometimes years.

Points to consider

- Each type of helping relationship has a different focus requiring different skills, roles and time spans.
- Each helping relationship is not just an extension of the previous one, but is separate and makes use of its own body of knowledge and skill.
- The trainer may take on the roles of training instructor, counsellor, coach and mentor directly or train others to do so.
- The training of therapists has its own professional trainers as do some aspects of counselling training.
- Although, by comparison, training of instructors presents few problems, the training of coaches and mentors can be problematic. In particular, managers as coaches and mentors are not all psychologically suited to these roles. When there is also job insecurity, there can be the added problem of drawing-up the drawbridge and looking after oneself.
- Instructing, coaching and mentoring are concerned with:
  - orientating people quickly and effectively to their work;
  - empowering people to succeed;
  - preventing the job holder from failing.

Coaching may suit *Achievement* culture. Coaching and mentoring may suit a *Support* culture. The 'macho' quality of Power cultures may tend to preclude coaching, mentoring and developmental therapy helping practices. Traditional and discovery instruction methods, however, will suit the *Power* culture. Counselling may suit *Achievement* and *Role* cultures.

Readings
Coaching method

Boydell, T. and Megginson, D. (1979) *A Manager's Guide to Coaching*. London: British Association of Commercial and Industrial Education.

Singer, E. J. (1974) *Effective Management Coaching*. London: Institute of Personnel Management.

Counselling method

Argyle, M. (1988) *Bodily Communication*, 2nd edn. London: Methuen.

Benjamin, A. (1974) *The Helping Interview*, 2nd edn. Boston, Massachusetts: Houghton Mifflin.

Bond, T. (1989) 'Towards Defining the Role of Counselling Skills'. *Counselling: The Journal of the British Association for Counselling 69*, 3–9.

Brammer, L. M. (1988) *The Helping Relationship: Processes and Skills,* 4th edn. Englewood Cliffs, NJ: Prentice-Hall.

British Association for Counselling (1984) *Code of Ethics and Practice for Counsellors, Form No. 14.*

Dainow, S. and Bailey, C. (1988) *Developing Skills with People: Training for Person to Person Client Contact*. Chichester: John Wiley.

Egan, G. (1985) *Exercises in Helping Skills*, 3rd edn. Monterey, California: Brooks/Cole.

Gilmore, S. K. (1973) *The Counsellor-in-Training*. Englewood Cliffs, NJ: Prentice-Hall.

Inskipp, F. (1985) *A Manual for Trainers: A Resource Book for Setting-up and Running Basic Counselling Courses*. USA: Alexia.

Mearns, D. and Dryden, W. (1989) *Experiences of Counselling in Action*. London: Sage.

Mearns, D. and Thorne, B. (1988) *Person-Centred Counselling in Action*. London: Sage.

Nelson-Jones, R. (1988) *Practical Counselling and Helping Skills*, 2nd edn. London: Cassell.

Oldfield, S. (1983) *The Counselling Relationship: A Study of the Client's Experience*. London: Routledge and Kegan Paul.

Reddy, M. (1987) *The Manager's Guide to Counselling at Work*. London: Methuen.

Mentoring method

Buckley, R. and Caple, J. (1991) *One-to-One Training and Coaching Skills*. London: Kogan Page.

Clutterbuck, D. (1985) *Everyone Needs A Mentor*. London: Institute of Personnel Management.

Murray, M. (1991) *Beyond the Myths and Magic of Mentoring*. San Francisco: Jossey-Bass.

Sergerman-Peck, L. M. D. (1991) *Networking and Mentoring, A Woman's Guide*. Avon: Platkus.

56 JOB RESTRUCTURING (Level 3: Application, and Level 4: Transfer)

- Job rotation (Level 3).
- Job enlargement (Level 3).
- Job enrichment (Level 4).
- Semi-autonomous work groups (Level 4).
- Autonomous work groups (Level 4).

Job rotation

(Involves job holder rotating on different jobs at same level. This requires a horizontal job change.) This enables the job holder to switch jobs to reduce monotony and broaden skills, knowledge and outlook. Job rotation can take place on the shop floor or at management level.

Points to consider

*   It does not follow that job interest, productivity, flexibility and quality of life will improve, but these can be gains.
*   Some people may resent moving jobs.
*   Output may decrease initially.
*   May suit *Power and Role cultures*.

Job enlargement

(Involves doing more of the same job. This requires a horizontal job change.) This enables the job holder to perform a larger or more complete part of the job, and thereby achieve increased job interest, job satisfaction and job output.

Points to consider

*   Job enlargement involves a 'horizontal' job change. The variety of tasks increases, but the level of skill remains the same.
*   Similar to job rotation. There may be many benefits but they are not guaranteed.
*   Like job rotation, there can be inefficiency during the start-up phase.
*   May suit *Power, Role and Achievement cultures*.

Job enrichment

(Increases responsibility and authority and involves a vertical job change.) This enables job holder to accept increased responsibility and authority, like preparing reports which was previously done by the supervisor.

Points to consider

*   The method provides opportunities for multi-skilling and satisfying Herzberg's (1974) Motivators.
*   The organizational culture must match the ethos of this initiative, which embodies McGregor's (1960) Theory Y attitude.
*   May suit *Achievement culture*.

Semi-autonomous work groups

(Increases group responsibility and authority, which involves a vertical job change.) This enables work groups to have a level of autonomy over their work, to reduce monotony, increase flexibility, increase job satisfaction, increase quality and increase productivity.

Points to consider

*   The work group may find better ways of undertaking their work simply because the group is prepared to be more open, more considerate and share ideas more fully.

- The supervisor may need coaching to cope with a new role.
- May suit the *Achievement culture*.

Autonomous work groups

(Group approaches self-management which involves a vertical job change.) The arrangement allows work groups to be largely independent of external control for substantial periods.

Points to consider

- Members may already be multi-skilled, and moving toward autonomy may be a natural result.
- Many benefits can be gained at this level, such as a readiness to cover for each other when members are absent.
- The style of control of the group by management will need to match the work group ethos, which will need to be participatory.
- May suit the *Achievement culture*.

Readings

Job rotation/enlargement methods

Guerrier, Y. and Philpot, N. (1978) *The British Manager: Careers and Mobility*. Management Survey Report No. 39, British Institute of Management Foundation.

Hague, H. (1976) 'Job Rotation Beats Stagnation'. *Industrial Management*, April, 11–12.

Hill, R. (1974) 'Exxon Plays Global Chess with its Managers'. *International Management 29*, September, 14–18.

Lord, D. (1972) 'Uniroyal Trains its Managers by Moving Them Around'. *International Management*, April, 59–62.

Wren, W. H. (1970) 'Management Development Through Planned Job Transfer'. *Factory Management 8, 10*, October, 4–6.

Zeira, Y. (1974) 'Job Rotation for Management Development'. *Personnel 51*, July, 25–35.

Job enrichment method

Buchanan, D. A. (1979) *The Development of Job Design Theories and Techniques*. Aldershot: Gower.

Buttriss, M. (1971) *Job Enrichment and Employee Participation: A Study*. London: Institute of Personnel Management.

Cooper, R. (1974) *Job Motivation and Job Design*. London: Institute of Personnel Management.

Mansfield, B. (1980) 'The Superior's Share of Job Enrichment'. *Personnel Management 12, 4*, 40–4.

Paul, W. J. and Robertson, K. B. (1970) *Job Enrichment and Employee Motivation*. Aldershot: Gower.

Taylor, L. K. (1980) *Not for Bread Alone: An Appreciation of Job Enrichment*, 3rd edn. London: Business Books.

Semi-autonomous/autonomous group methods

Grayson, D. (1990) *Self-Regulating Work Groups. An Aspect of Organizational Change*. WRU Occasional Paper, 46. London: ACAS Work Research Unit.

57 BEHAVIOUR/ROLE MODELLING METHOD (Level 3: Application)

This is a technique based on positive behaviour modification and acting as a role model to impart skills. The facilitator demonstrates and invites learners to practise using the desired skills. The facilitator will demonstrate how to give and receive feedback, ask questions and listen to what is said and not said.

Points to consider

- This is a powerful tool for enhancing skill levels and insight.
- Unlike the usual description of passive role models who are imitated from a distance, the 'role model' here is proactive and empowers, as a teacher and observer of his/her own as well as other people's behaviour.

Readings

Bandura, A. (1969) *Principles of Behaviour Modification*. New York: Holt, Rinehart and Winston.

'Behaviour Modelling: A New Approach to Supervisory Training'. *People and Profits* (1975) *2, 11*, 28–31.

Moses, J. L. and Ritchie, R. J. (1976) 'Supervisory Relationships Training: A Behaviourial Evaluation of a Behaviour Modelling Programme'. *Personnel Psychology 29, 3*, 337–43.

Smith, P. E. (1976) 'Management Modelling Training to Improve Morale and Customer Satisfaction'. *Personnel Psychology 29, 3*, 351–9.

Tosti, D. T. (1980) 'Behaviour Modelling: A Process'. *Training and Development 34, 8*, 70–4.

58 BEHAVIOUR MODIFICATION METHOD (BMod) (Level 3: Application)

The development of BMod is based on experiments by the Classical Conditioning School (Sechenev (1829–1904); Pavlov (1849–1936) and Watson (1878–1958)) and the Reinforcement Conditioning School (Thorndike (1874–1949) and Skinner (1904–)).

The Classical School emphasised an association between a Stimulus (cue) and a Response (behaviour). The Reinforcement School emphasised how the Reinforcing Stimulus can sustain the Response. The combination of these two conditioning associations has been called Behaviour Modification.

As a tool of training, the process recognizes that a Stimulus > induces a Response > and the Response if reinforced can be sustained. This is where the Stimulus is sometimes referred to as a Cue, Cause, Conditioning Stimulus or Input. The Response, which can be a feeling or behaviour in another person, is sometimes called Symptom, Conditioned Response or Process and Result. The Reinforcing Stimulus is sometimes called the Pay-Off or New Input.

Example

Suppose a manager wants to set and maintain a good standard of work:

- the manager sets the standard and trains job holder (Stimulus/Input);
- the job holder responds by achieving the standard (Response/Process and Result);
- the manager rewards (Reinforcing Stimulus/New Input) the job holder for achieving the standard through monetary payment and positive verbal comment or some other mechanism of recognition (and the job holder experiences a Pay-Off). As a

result of the Reinforcing Stimulus the desired job holder behaviour is maintained and repeated.

The above example demonstrates the process of *'positive reinforcement'* (nice when it happens). We note here that the positive reinforcer 'reward' is applied.

May suit *Achievement and Support cultures.*

In the author's view the above 'process of human exchange' is much under-rated as a highly effective mechanism for sustaining desired standards of work and for reinforcing good working relationships. Other reinforcement strategies include:

- *Negative reinforcement* (nice when it stops).

| Manager nags worker to achieve standard | > | worker achieves standard | > | manager stops nagging |

  - The negative reinforcer 'nagging' is removed.
  - Can be linked to *Power and Role culture* attitudes.

- *Punishment by application* (nasty when it happens).

| Manager sets standard | > | worker fails to achieve standard | > | worker is reprimanded |

  - The negative reinforcer 'reprimand' is applied.
  - Adopted by *Power and Role culture* attitudes.

- *Punishment by removal* (nasty when it happens).

| Manager sets standard | > | worker produces poor work | > | manager deducts money from wages |

  - The positive reinforcer 'money' is removed.
  - Adopted by *Power culture* attitudes.

Readings

Connellan, T. K. (1978) *How to Improve Human Performance: Behaviourism in Business and Industry.* USA: Harper and Row.

Gullett, C. R. and Reisen, R. (1975) 'Behaviour Modification, a Contingency Approach to Employee Performance'. *Personnel Journal 54, 4.*

Honey, P. (1980) *Solving People Problems.* Maidenhead: McGraw-Hill Book Co. (UK) Ltd.

Luthans, F. and Kreitner, R. (1975) *Organizational Behaviour Modification.* Glenview, Illinois: Scott, Foresman and Company.

Miller, K. L. (1975) *Principles of Everyday Behaviour Analysis.* Monterey, Cal.: Wadsworth Publishing Company.

Sherman, A. R. (1973) *Behaviour Modification: Theory and Practice.* Andover, Hants: Brooks/Cole Publishing Company.

59 ACTION-CENTRED LEADERSHIP (Level 4: Transfer)

Action-centred leadership is an approach to leadership training developed by John Adair from his research and training work at Sandhurst. In his functional approach he describes the interdependent needs which a leader must try to satisfy if he is to lead others to achieve an objective. These are:

- *Task* – the need to achieve the task objectives.
- *Group* – the need for members of the group to co-operate effectively with each other to achieve the objective.

- *Individual* – the satisfaction of the different highly personalized needs which each individual brings into a group, which may cause physical or psychological withdrawal if they are not met.

  Will suit an *Achievement culture.*

Readings

Adair, J. (1973) *Action-Centred Leadership*. Maidenhead: McGraw-Hill.
Adair, J. (1978) *Training for Leadership*. Farnborough: Gower.
Adair, J. (1983) *Effective Leadership*. Farnborough: Gower.
Industrial Society (1973) *Action-Centred Leadership*.
Wilce, H. (1971) 'Managers Learn How to Lead'. *International Management,* July, 42–5.

60 MANAGERIAL GRID (Level 3: Transfer)

An overall approach to management development using the theories of Blake and Mouton, which classifies management styles and resulting behaviour in terms of concern for production and concern for people. A managerial grid training programme can bring these into better balance.

Reading

Blake, R. R. and Mouton, J. S. (1964) *The Managerial Grid*. Houston, Texas: Gulf Publishing.

61 MCGREGOR'S THEORY X AND THEORY Y (Level 3: Transfer)

Based on the work of Douglas McGregor, this set of theories describes management styles in terms of being based on sets of assumptions which are either Theory X (i.e. man is lazy and needs driving) or Theory Y (i.e. man is self-motivating, achievement-directed and needs guiding).

Readings

Argyris, C. (1971) *Management and Organizational Development: The Path from XA to YB*. New York: McGraw-Hill.
McGregor, D. (1971) *The Human Aspect of Enterprise*. New York: McGraw-Hill.

62 REDDIN-3-D THEORY (Level 3: Transfer)

An extension of Blake's grid by adding, to the two dimensions of 'task-orientation' and 'people-orientation', a third dimension of 'effectiveness'.

Readings

Reddin, W. J. (1969) 'Is there an Ideal Management Style?' *Industrial Training International,* May, 224–66.
Reddin, W. J. (1969) 'Management in 3-D'. *Industrial Society,* July, 139–41.
Reddin, W. J. (1970) 'Managing Organizational Change'. *Industrial Training International 5, 3,* 132–4.
Reddin, W. J. (1970) 'What is Wrong with the Style Theories?' *Industrial Society,* August, 24.

Reddin, W. J. (1971) 'More Effective Managers – via 3-D'. *Business and Finance,* 19 March.

Reddin, W. J. (1971) 'Effective Management Teamwork and Team Modes'. *Works Management 24, 8, 7 and 15.*

Reddin, W. J. (1974) 'The Urgent Need For Supervisory Training'. *Electrical Supervisor 54, 1, 16.*

63 LIKERT (Level 3: Transfer)

Likert distinguishes between supervisors who are 'job-centred' in that 'they tend to concentrate on keeping their subordinates busily engaged in going through specific tasks at a satisfactory rate determined by time standards', and those who are 'employee-centred', concentrating on the human aspects of work, and allowing maximum participation in decision-making. He suggests four management types (labelled systems 1 to 4): 'exploitive authoritative', 'benevolent authoritative', 'consultative' and 'participative group', respectively. System 4 management produces high productivity, greater involvement of individuals and better labour–management relations.

In 1986 Likert extended the four system structure and added System 5.

Readings

Likert, R. (1961) *New Patterns of Management.* New York: McGraw-Hill.

Likert, R. (1967) *The Human Organization.* New York: McGraw-Hill.

Likert, J. G. and Araki, C. T. (1986) 'Managing Without a Boss: System 5'. *Leadership and Organization Development Journal ,Vol. 7, 3, 17–20.*

64 GROUP DEVELOPMENT (Level 4: Transfer)

An intervention which can be undertaken by 'trainers' as well as 'professional team builders'. The intervention enables group members to:

- undertake a mode of working where there is some need to share the uncertainty;
- deal with tasks of an 'operational' nature which at the extreme end can be called 'complex puzzles' as opposed to 'genuine problems', assuming that about 95 per cent of decision-making time is directed in this area;
- engage in situations where the task process predominates but where some feeling processes and team role activities are practised.

Points to consider

- A Group Development intervention may include similar sorts of task and feeling processes as does Team Building, item 65. The emphasis, however, may not be so penetrating and some feeling aspects may not be so relevant and important. Both types of development may include, for example:
  - setting goals and priorities;
  - analysing the ways the group does its work;
  - examining group characteristics and processes for communication and decision-making;
  - examining interpersonal relationships within the group;
  - examining team roles and taking appropriate rectifying action.
- Group Development could be seen as a preparatory phase to Team Building.
- May suit *Achievement culture.*

Readings

Belbin, R. M. (1981) *Management Teams: Why They Succeed or Fail*. London: Heine-mann.

Belbin, R. M. (1993) *Team Roles at Work*. London: Butterworth-Heinemann.

Berger, M. L. (1978) *Group Training Techniques*. Farnborough: Gower Press.

Burns, G. (1977) *Introduction to Group Theory with Applications*. London: Academic Press.

Cooper, C. L. (1972) *Group Training for Individual and Organizational Development*.

Jaques, D. (1984) *Learning in Groups*. Beckenham: Croom Helm.

Margerison, C. (1992) 'Margerison and McCann Discuss the Team Management Wheel'. *Industrial and Commercial Training 24, 1*.

Woodcock, M. (1979) *Team Development Manual*. London: Gower.

65 TEAM BUILDING (Level 4: Transfer)

An intervention undertaken by professional team builders, who are fully cognizant of organizational cultural influences, which can be critical when dealing with teams who usually comprise senior managers. The intervention enables senior managers to:

- undertake a mode of working where the uncertainty is shared;
- deal with 'genuine problems' such as strategic decision-making, assuming that about 5 per cent of decision-making is directed in this area;
- engage in task and feeling processes together;
- examine their compatibility as team members in terms of team roles, and enable them to take rectifying action as required.

Points to consider

- Must be facilitated by experienced practitioners.
- See comments under 'Group development'.
- May suit *Achievement culture*.

66 INTER-GROUP MEETING (Level 4: Transfer)

The purpose of the meeting is to reach the state of mutual understanding that fosters co-operation and cuts down competition and conflict between groups. The meeting usually follows a set procedure involving information exchange and discussion. The process is normally helped by the presence of a third party. The *inter-group laboratory* is a more structured variation of the above for use when relationships are critical, such as an industrial relations situation.

Readings

Argyle, M. (1967) *Psychology of Interpersonal Behaviour*. Penguin.

Argyle, M. (1969) *Social Interaction*. London: Tavistock.

67 SENSITIVITY/T-GROUP TRAINING METHOD (Level 4: Transfer)

A particular method of behaviourial skills training, based on highly participative learning methods, whose purpose is to improve skills in:

- appreciating how others are reacting to one's own behaviour;
- gauging the state of relationships between others;
- carrying out skilfully the behaviour required by the situation.

The approach is essentially unstructured. The terms 'Sensitivity training', 'Group dynamic training' and 'Group relations training' are sometimes used.

Points to consider

- When working well over a period of days or a week, members can find that the experience can provide a very rich insight into human behaviour.
- The facilitator must be highly experienced. There is a real danger of emotions running high and personalities clashing.
- The method may not suit everyone, given there is no agenda and it is left to the group to create its own norms and procedures.
- May suit *Achievement culture*.

Readings

Bradford, L. P., Gibb, J. R. and Berne, K. D. (1964) *T-Group Theory and Laboratory Method*. New York: John Wiley.

Lippitt, G. L. (1975) 'Guides for the Use of Sensitivity Training in Management Development' in Taylor, B. and Lippitt, G. L. (eds) *Management Development and Training Handbook*. London: McGraw-Hill.

Smith, P. B. (1969) *Improving Skills in Working with People, The T-group, T.I.P.4*. London: HMSO.

Whitaker, F. P. G. (1965) *T-Group Training*. Oxford: Blackwell.

68 COVERDALE TRAINING METHOD (Level 4: Transfer)

Based on the work of Ralph Coverdale, this is a package of techniques dealing with an individual, group and intergroup approach to problem solving.

Readings

Coverdale, R. (1968) *Thought – a Frame to Teamwork*. Coverdale Training Limited.

Roche, S. (1967) 'Coverdale Training – a Method for Developing Managers and the Organization'. *Manpower and Applied Psychology*. (Cork, Eire: Ergon Press.)

Roche, S. G. and Waterson, J. (1972) 'Coverdale Training – Building on Ability'. *Training Development Journal*, February, 44–8.

Smallwood, A. (1976) 'The Basic Philosophy of Coverdale Training'. *Industrial and Commercial Training 8, 1*, 12–16.

Taylor, M. (1979) *Coverdale on Management*. London: Heinemann.

Waterson, J. (1979) 'Coverdale Training' in Babington-Smith, B. and Farrell, B. A. (eds) *Training in Small Groups: A Study of Five Methods*. Oxford: Pergamon Press.

69 ACTION LEARNING METHOD (Level 4: Transfer)

Developed by Reg Revans, the method is based on 'learning by doing' rather than learning by teaching. Action learning makes use of all four project types described under 'Project Method', item 35. Rather than a professional educator, the group of four to six people (or set) make use of a professional set adviser whose job it is to develop the set into an effective learning group. Individual members take on projects and discuss their project aims, problems, progress and conclusions with their set members. To undertake projects within any company setting, managers are first equipped with all the necessary skills. In this sense, this is the only part of the programme that may follow a traditional teaching pattern. From here on, when tackling the project, the set member will mostly make use of other set members and the set adviser to challenge his/her approach to the task ahead.

Points to consider

* Successful outcomes depend on the set facilitator and the preparation of set members for their tasks.
* The method has been successfully applied at an international inter-organizational level, and forms the basis of learning for higher level management education programmes.
* At the highest level of difficulty, tackling an unfamiliar task in an unfamiliar organization, managers are sometimes 'swapped' between organizations.
* Action learning is based on specific assumptions about how people learn, such as:
  – Learning is deepest when it involves the whole person, mind, values, body and emotions.
  – We learn not so much as when we are motivated to learn, as when we are motivated to achieve something.
* Although it matches the *Power* culture's 'learning by doing' ethos, full organizational support will be required. It will work within an *Achievement* culture where learning from each other is practised.

Readings

Boddy, D. (1980) 'An Action Learning Programme for Supervisors'. *Journal of European Industrial Training 4, 3,* 10–13.

Boddy, D. (1981) 'Putting Action Learning into Action'. *Journal of European Industrial Training/MCB Monograph 5, 5.*

Casey, D. and Pearce, D. (eds) (1978) *More than Management Development.* Aldershot: Gower.

Elgin, R. (1977) 'Business Schools Come Under Fire from Action Man'. *Industrial Management,* May, 25–7.

Revans, R. W. (1972) 'Action Learning – A Management Development Programme'. *Personnel Review 1, 4.*

Revans, R. W. (1976) 'Management Education: Time for a Re-think'. *Personnel Management 8, 7,* 20–4.

Revans, R. W. (1980) *Action Learning.* London: Blond Briggs.

Revans, R. W. (1983) *The ABC of Action Learning.* London: Chartwell-Bratt.

See also 'Experience-based learning'.

Anderson, B., Boud, D. and McLeod, G. (1980) *Experience Based Learning – How and Why?* Australian Consortium on Experiential Education.

Keeton, M. T. and Tate, P. J. (eds) (1978) 'Learning by Experience – What, Why and How?' *New Directions in Experiential Education No. 1.* San Francisco: Jossey Bass.

Roskin, R. (1976) 'Learning by Experience'. *Journal of European Training 5, 4,* 181–212.

See also 'Action research'.

Foster, M. (1973) 'An Introduction to the Theory and Practice of Action Research in Work Organizations'. *Human Relations 25, 6,* 529–56.

Pedler, M. (1974) 'An Action Research to Training Interventions'. *Management Education and Development,* August, 54–67.

70 PROCESS CONSULTATION METHOD or Behaviour Analysis (Level 4: Transfer)

Process consultation is used to identify 'how' problems are being solved, 'how' a group interacts or 'how' a lecturer carries out a lecture, for example. In short, process analysis can be used on any activity which involves the interaction of people. The purpose of the analysis is to help participants examine how processes, or some behaviours, can stifle or limit effective functioning of a group. Such examination would then lead on to developing effective process skills. For example: the observation of the 'content' of a meeting might be, 'Members made a number of suggestions but none gained much acceptance.' The observation of the 'process' would show, 'All suggestions came from junior members, and senior members did not build on or discuss the suggestions made, and toward the end of the meeting, junior members appeared discouraged.' When analysing the process observations with the members, it was found that senior members had discussed and discounted the suggestions at a previous meeting but did not inform junior staff. Although not intended to snub junior staff, no one from management thought to explain this point. Junior members felt discouraged because it seemed no one was listening to them. Junior members also thought that it was not their place to question why their suggestions were not being considered.

Points to consider

- Analysis can be undertaken on-job.
- The awareness and training that result from the analysis is very much learner-centred and focused on the real consequences of human interaction.
- Benefits and time-savings as a result of improving processes can be felt very quickly.
- A high level of consultancy expertise is required.
- May suit *Achievement culture.*

Readings

Mumford, A. (1976) 'Management Development and the Powers of Observation'. *Personnel Management 8, 10,* 26–9.

Rackham, N. and Morgan, T. (1977) *Behaviour Analysis in Training.* London: McGraw-Hill.

Rackham, N., Honey, P. and Colbert, M. (1970) *Developing Interactive Skills.* Northampton: Wellens Publishing Company.

Schein, E. (1969) *Process Consultation: Its Role in Organizational Development.* Reading, Massachusetts: Addison-Wesley.

71 PROBLEM-SOLVING METHOD (Level 4: Transfer)

The problem-solving method can be used to develop groups or individuals. The method can be used to examine difficulties faced by the learner, or examine a particular issue or problem. Problems are studied by breaking down the analysis into manageable chunks such as: identify problem, consider solutions, decide on solution, implement and evaluate. The benefits to the learner, in addition to acquiring problem-solving skills, can include encouraging learners to widen and deepen their thinking processes; and enhancing creative, logical, tactical, strategic and reflective thinking. The method could also include looking at process skills, i.e. how people interact and influence each other.

Points to consider

- A good problem-solver with proven process skills would be most suited to the task of group leader.
- Analysis of the problem can be carried out at a number of levels, for example:
  - identifying causes and results;
  - examining the context of the problem;
  - identifying the demands, constraints and choices available;
  - seeking opportunities to apply solutions;
  - examining 'how' problems are tackled and solved.
- The pre-knowledge of learners must match the requirements of the task.
- The Problem-Solving Cycle Method is a similar method. That is where learners form groups to each study a stage of the analysis, and join at some point to collate findings.
- May suit *Achievement culture*.

Readings

Ackoff, R. L. (1980) *The Art of Problem Solving*. Chichester: John Wiley and Sons.
Gillespie, R. J. (1972) *Developing Creative Problem Solving Talent*. London: InComTec.
Jackson, K. F. (1975) *The Art of Solving Problems*. London: Heinemann.
Kaufman, R. (1979) *Identifying and Solving Problems: A Systems Approach,* 2nd edn. San Diego, Cal.: University Associates of Europe.
Rickards, T. (1975) *Problem Solving Through Creativity Analysis*. Aldershot: Gower.

72 KEPNER TREGOE (Level 4: Transfer)

A form of training which helps participants to identify the ideal working situation and by using a systematic approach to the processes of problem-analysis and decision-making identify deviations from the ideal. May suit *Achievement culture*.

Reading

Kepner, C. P. and Tregoe, B. B. (1965) *The Rational Manager: a Systematic Approach to Problem Solving and Decision Making*. New York: McGraw-Hill.

73 MANAGEMENT DEVELOPMENT METHOD (MD) (Level 4: Transfer)

Management Development (MD):

- Is about development, improvement and assessment of the individual manager and management group.
- Involves activities predominantly aimed at developing managers' abilities to cope with real situations. Managers may be given individual projects or join a task group to solve real company problems. It is experience-based and is very much the responsibility of the individual.
- Is flexible, risky and unpredictable.
- Involves the individual and organization changing together.
- Builds on managers' previous management training, education, values, attitudes, personality, skill, experience and judgement.

- Satisfies need for succession and promotion.
- Includes career planning, job rotation, appraisal/review, elements of planned study, training, coaching, counselling and mentoring.
- Is an integral aspect of organizational design and planning, it requires that a medium- to long-term view be taken (i.e. a strategic view) of MD outcomes, and top management support is essential.
- Requires company trainers to play more of an in-house consultative role and be clear about satisfying organizational goals.

To assist managers who feel that they may have lost their sense of direction in some way, Career Life Planning may be appropriate. The idea is based on individual goal setting, and can be linked to in-house career and management development programmes, or it can be undertaken externally to the organization.

Points to consider

- The strategic nature of the intervention is indicative of the importance and cost of the programme.
- The factors likely to disrupt progress are changes in management philosophy, style, culture and the marketplace.
- The programme must be realistic about promotion prospects, and managerial expectations should be matched before the programme starts.
- The results of the programme should yield more competent, confident and focused managers.
- May suit *Achievement culture*.

Readings

Butteriss, M. (1975) *Techniques and Development in Management*. London: Institute of Personnel Management.

Gold, J. (1990) 'Learning to Learn through Learning Contracts'. *Training and Management Development Methods 4, 4*. (Bradford: MCB University Press.)

Hammond, V. (1985) *Current Research in Management*. London: Frances Pinter (Publishers) Ltd.

Harrison, R. (1988) *Training and Development*. London: Institute of Personnel Management.

Honey, P. and Mumford, A. (1986) *Using Your Learning Styles*, 2nd edn. Maidenhead: Peter Honey.

Honey, P. and Mumford, A. (1992) *The Manual of Learning Styles*. Maidenhead: Peter Honey.

Jones, J. E. and Woodcock, M. (1985) *Manual of Management Development*. Aldershot: Gower.

Mumford, A. (1989) *Management Development: Strategies for Action*. London: Institute of Personnel Management.

Neale, F. (1991) *The Handbook of Performance Management*. London: Institute of Personnel Management.

Taylor, B. and Lippitt, G. (eds) (1983) *Management Development and Training Handbook*, 2nd edn. Maidenhead: McGraw-Hill.

Weelens, J. (1970) 'An Approach to Management Training'. *Journal of Industrial and Commercial Training 8, 7*.

74 ORGANIZATIONAL DEVELOPMENT METHOD (OD) (Level 4: Transfer)

Organizational development (OD) can embrace all forms of learning and all types of training interventions. The multi-dimensional nature of OD is reflected in the following description of it.

- *Organization mission.* OD is related to the organizational mission, is about profitability, organizational effectiveness and health.
- *Managed.* OD:
  - is organization-wide;
  - is planned and is adaptive;
  - takes a long-term/strategic view of the effort and results;
  - is not involved in 'conversion' type situations;
  - is managed from the top but aims to involve all levels of staff.
- *Improving.* OD is about improving a company's strategy, structure, systems, and developing staff skills, knowledge, attitudes and style, by working through the company's value systems. It is not about selling ready-made, pre-packaged and nicely wrapped OD value systems.
- *Power.* OD is not conducted in power-based entrepreneurial cultures which emphasise personal power and covert influence.
- *Politics.* OD uses political knowledge and skills and therefore is not politically neutral.
- *Pluralistic.* OD takes a pluralistic view rather than a unitary view. It takes a realistic rather than a theoretical stance.
- *Time.* OD takes account of a company's history as well as its future.
- *Organizational culture.* OD assesses the organization's culture very critically and does not implement OD programmes which cannot be supported and sustained by its formal and informal behaviour.
- *Complex.* OD views man and organizations as complex, and yet does not lose sight of the fact that people come together to do work in a satisfactory way. Perhaps OD can help bring about more satisfactory ways of doing work, as defined by the 'users'.
- *Experience-based.* OD is experience-based and action-orientated.
- *Skilled practitioners.* OD makes use of only the most skilled OD practitioners.
- *Groups.* OD works primarily through groups and may incorporate:
  - Management development.
  - Team building.
  - Management training.
  - Management education.
  - Group development.
  - Self-development.

Points to consider

- The ultimate in organizational change, OD's strategic (long-term) approach means it must be owned and managed by senior management.
- OD requires the highest level of interventionist skills, and by definition will be expensive in terms of time and cost.
- The benefits argue for a changed organization, working at a more effective level in the marketplace.
- Although the intervention induces a changed way of life, there is a danger it can be perceived as 'taking over' rather than supporting organization activities.

- The intervention may be influenced by changes in the marketplace, and by internal changes including changes of priority at top management level.
- May suit *Achievement culture and some Role cultures*.

Readings
Organization development/learning methods
Beckhard, R. (1969) *Organization Development: Strategy and Methods*. Reading, Massachusetts: Wesley.

Bennis, W. G. (1969) *Organization Development: Its Nature, Origins and Prospects*. Reading, Massachusetts: Addison-Wesley.

Child, J. (1982) *Organisation: A Guide to Problems and Practice*. London: Harper and Row.

Jones, A. M. and Hendry, C. (1992) *The Learning Organisation: A Review of Literature and Practice*. London: The HRD Partnership.

See also references for Re-engineering, Chapter 3.

Career life planning
Ford, G. A. and Lippitt, G. L. (1976) *Planning Your Future: A Workbook for Personal Goal Setting*. La Jolla, Cal.: University Associates of Europe Ltd.

Hopson, B. (1976) 'Personal Growth and Career Development' in Cooper, C. L. (ed.) *Developing Social Skills in Managers*. London: Macmillan.

Kirn, A. G. (1974) *Lifework Planning: Workbook and Trainer's Manual*, 3rd edn. La Jolla, California: University Associates Inc.

Swartz, D. H. (1975) 'Life Goals Planning for Managers' in Taylor, B. and Lippitt, G. L. (eds) *Management Development and Training Handbook*. London: McGraw-Hill.

75 SOCIO-TECHNICAL PROGRAMMES (Level 4: Transfer)

An organization development approach which has particular relevance to industrial relations. The socio-technical approach concentrates on the relationship between the technical and structural aspects of work organization and the social framework which relates to it. A specific development of this approach which looks at the relationship between systems within the total organization is the open-systems approach. May suit *Achievement culture*.

Reading

Argyle, M. (1969) *Social Interaction*. London: Tavistock.

OTHER FORMS OF LEARNING

In addition to the methods for learning listed above, there are other forms of learning which may be better described as an attitude or a sensitivity to learning. For the trainer, however, these forms of learning are very real and in some cases can underpin other learning interventions. These forms or attitudes to learning can be described as:

- Self-development and independent study.
- Accidental learning.
- Intuitive learning.

Self-development

One view about self-development is that we should all be lifelong self-developers. However, learning via self-development may not be an easy process for everyone. To assist self-developers, we note, first, the approach to effective self-development can be learnt; second, self-developers can be assisted by more able self-developers; and third, the organization can actively support self-developers. Boydell (1981), for example, identified twenty principles of self-development and among them are:

- Engage in learning conversations with life partner, family, friend, colleague and learning facilitators.
- Share information, ideas and feelings.
- Set up or join a group of like-minded people, and form a learning community.
- As a manager, use your management skills and power creatively to assist others.
- Recognize and overcome the many mental blockages that may be encountered.
- Engage in independent study.
- Seek formal qualifications as a way of obtaining job choice.
- Do something rather than nothing:
  – take a subject, read about it, write about it;
  – gradually develop learning skills;
  – gradually focus on what you want to do;
  – visit other places, countries;
  – widen your outlook.

When self-developers do learn via the sort of training opportunities presented here, they should be encouraged to continue their learning via their own self-development programme.

The danger for all self-developers is becoming stuck in mindsets and not using opportunities to practise their untried skills. In this sense self-developers must avoid deceiving themselves. In a situation where the learner relies so much on his/her own motivation to change, there is sometimes a danger of creating a more closed than open world of learning.

Independent study

This is self-development writ large when applied to following an education programme. Learners decide the pace, choice of study, help to decide objectives, participate in assessment and are involved in establishing success criteria.

Accidental learning

This refers to learning that happens at random whilst carrying out work and life tasks. When this happens, the learner who appreciates accidental learning happenings, is more conscious than unconscious when the learning occurs.

For some organizations and some people, the sad reflection is that this form of learning may be the only mechanism by which personal growth is possible.

Accidental learning is important because it happens in the real world and is owned by the learner. The drawback is that such learning lacks clear developmental objectives and follow-up.

For the trainer, she/he must be conscious that we are all products of this process; further, that we can become more sensitive to its occurrence, and lastly, that we need to find ways to evaluate and build on it. In addition, the trainer must realize that such learning will happen when learning more formally, and that this learning needs to be acknowledged and developed.

Intuitive learning

This is both accidental and unconscious. On the face of it, the merit of intuitive learning is that it seems to mirror our true feelings. It is often said that the best intuiters start with thought and feeling and then work outwards to rationalization. Perhaps the major difference between effective intuiters and ineffective ones is that the experienced intuiter explores his/her intuitive feelings for meaning and relevance. The fact is that our intuition can sometimes steer us clear of danger, and our intuition can also be incorrect.

The trainer can help learners to examine situations intuitively, and compare such results when using a more rational approach. When helping learners learn, via more formal approaches, trainers can seek intuitive responses as part of the learning process. By examining past learning habits with a learner, perhaps feelings and intuitions may reveal both strengths and weaknesses in the make-up of the learner.

In summary, the trainer has the choice of ignoring unplanned learning or using it. In practice, when the unplanned and planned learning are stacked, the understanding becomes richer and the meanings become deeper. Self-development is useful because it can be employed to help better structure all our learning modes and moods.

Continuous development

Linked to ideas about self-development, independent study and all other forms of learning, is the idea of Continuous Development (CD). What distinguishes CD is that:

- it perceives that learning activity is ongoing in all spheres of life;
- it can be about learning *with* work (What), and learning *through* work (How);
- it requires a strong element of self-management;
- it can embrace the practice of Continuous Professional Development (CPD) where development is a professional requirement of a said profession.

As a philosophy CD supports the idea of the learning organization, Garratt (1989), and even surpasses the emphasis on learning that embodies Total Quality Management (TQM), Collard (1989). What distinguishes CD from TQM is that it takes on board the notion of 'learning how to learn'. For example, a team supporting the CD ideal, would, in addition to all other forms of learning, be prepared to examine and improve the team's interactive processes and learning to learn skills. That is, it is prepared to examine 'how' people interact with each other and 'how' people learn to make these adjustments. Learning in this sense is total. It involves learning 'within' a work situation and learning 'through' a work situation. For more detail see Wood (1988), Jones (1992) and the Institute of Personnel Management *Continuous Development Code* (1986).

Readings
Self-development

Bardwick, J. (1986) *The Plateauing Trap*. New York: Amacom.

Boydell, T. H. and Pedler, M. (Eds) (1981) *Management Self Development*. Aldershot: Gower.

Pedler, M., Burgoyne, J. and Boydell, T. (1978) *A Manager's Guide to Self-Development*. Maidenhead, Berkshire: McGraw-Hill Book Company (UK) Limited.

Pemberton, C. and Herriot, P. (1993) *Managing Different Plateaux*. Paper presented at AMED 1993 Research Conference.

Independent development

Atherton, C. (1972) 'Lecture, Discussion and Independent Study: Instructional Methods Revisited'. *Journal of Experimental Education 40, 4,* 24–8.

Boud, D. (Ed.) (1981) *Developing Student Autonomy in Learning*. London: Kogan Page.

Cornwall, M. (1981) 'Putting It Into Practice: Promoting Independent Learning in a Traditional Institution' in Boud, D. (ed.) *Developing Student Autonomy in Learning*. London: Kogan Page.

Dressel, P. L. and Thompson, M. M. (1973) *Independent Study*. San Francisco: Jossey-Bass.

(1974) *Towards Independence in Learning*. Nuffield Foundation Group for Research and Innovation in Higher Education.

Continuous development

Garratt, B. (1989) *The Learning Organization*. London: Fontana.

Institute of Personnel Management (1986) *The Institute of Personnel Management Code: Continuous Development: People and Work*. London: Institute of Personnel Management.

Jones, A. M. and Hendry, C. (1992) *The Learning Organization: A Review of Literature and Practice*. London: The Human Resource Development Partnership.

Pedlar, M., Burgoyne, J. and Boydell, T. *The Learning Company Project*. Sheffield: Training Agency.

Wood, S. (ed.) (1988) *Continuous Development: The Path to Improved Performance*. London: Institute of Personnel Management.

Total quality management

Collard, R. (1989) *Total Quality: Success Through People*. London: Institute of Personnel Management.

SUMMARY

When selecting training methods we discovered that it was useful to ask:

- What are the training objectives?
- How much feedback will be necessary to fix the learning?
- What role should the trainer play?
- Where will training take place?
- What area of learning is being considered?
- How well does the training method match the organizational culture's attitudes and assumptions?
- What is the focus of the training?

It was stressed that the classification was not forwarded as a rigid structure. By asking such questions about organizational culture and the role of the trainer, the 'classification' becomes useful as a broad structure to aid training method comparison.

By modifying training methods, the trainer can experiment with matching training objectives to the appropriate level of learning. For example:

- To acquire *'knowledge'*, the learner can be asked to read a book.
- To test *understanding,* the learner may be given a test or quiz and this may be followed up with 'open discussion'.
- To reach a situation where the knowledge can be *applied* correctly, the learner may be 'coached' on-job, follow an on-job 'drill' or undertake a relevant 'project'.
- To actually *transfer* the learning to new situations where there are no correct answers, the learner may undertake an 'action learning project' which requires implementation.

To find other clues about the most appropriate selection of training methods, we can also look at how learners evaluate the effectiveness of training. If the trainer puts him/herself in the learner's position, the trainer can ask for example:

- Is the content of this programme matching my requirements?
- Am I interacting enough with other learners and facilitators to allow me to question and discuss what I am learning?
- Is this method of training matching the reality of my work situation?

REFERENCES AND FURTHER READING
Training method classification

Bloom, B. S., Engelhart, M. B., Furst, E. J., Hill, W. H. and Krathwohl, D. R. (1956) *Taxonomy of Educational Objectives. The Classification of Educational Goals Handbook 1: Cognitive Domain.* New York: Longmans Green.

Burgoyne, J. G. and Cooper, C. L. (1976) 'Research on Teaching Methods in Management Education: Bibliographical examination of the State of the Art and Management'. *Education Review 16, 4,* 95–102.

Burgoyne, J. G. and Stuart, R. (1978) 'Teaching and Learning Methods in Management Development'. *Personnel Review 7, 1,* 53–8.

Fyfe, T. W. and Richardson, R. (1974) *Educational Technology, Programmed Text.* Dundee College of Education.

Huczynski, A. (1983) *Encyclopedia of Management Development Methods.* Aldershot: Gower.

Krathwohl, D. R., Bloom, B. S. and Masia, B. B. (1964) *Taxonomy of Educational Objectives, Handbook 2: Affective Domain.* New York: David McKay Co. Inc.

Long, B. (1969) 'A Theoretical Model For Method Selection'. *Industrial Training International 4, 11,* 475–7.

McDonald-Ross, M. (1973) 'Behaviourial Objectives – a Critical Review'. *Instructional Science 2, 1,* 1–52.

Pedler, M. (1974) 'Learning in Management Education'. *Journal of European Training 3, 3,* 182–94.

Pedler, M. (1978) 'Negotiating Skills Training Part 4: Learning To Negotiate'. *Journal of European Industrial Training 2, 1,* 20–5.

Wallen, N. E. and Travers, R. M. W. (1963) 'Analysis and Investigation of Teaching Methods' in Gage, N. L. (ed.) *Handbook of Research on Teaching.* Chicago: Rand McNally.

Experiential learning

The learner makes use of substitute tasks (building a Lego bridge) where the focus is on 'how' something is done rather than what is done. The method makes use of process consultation skills. The experiential exercise differs from process consultation in that it attempts through structured exercises to put flesh onto theories via experience which is parallel to the one being studied. When examining decision-making, for example, a group will carry out a decision-making exercise, they will be sensitive to how they undertake the task and will reflect upon it when complete. In addition, observers will comment and debrief the participants. Prior to the event, the concepts and practices that support the exercise are explained.

Boydell, T. H. (1976) *Experiential Learning*. Manchester Monograph No. 5. Department of Adult Education, University of Manchester.

Bradford, D. and Eoyang, C. (1976) 'The Use and Misuse of Structured Exercises' in Cooper, C. L. (Ed.) *Developing Social Skills in Managers: Advances in Group Training*. London: Macmillan.

Finch, F. E., Jones, H. R. and Litterer, J. A. (1976) *Managing for Organizational Effectiveness: An Experiential Approach*. Maidenhead: McGraw-Hill.

Harvey, D. F. and Brown, D. R. (1976) *An Experiential Approach to Organizational Development*. Englewood Cliffs, NJ: Prentice-Hall.

Knudson, H. R., Woodworth, R. T. and Bell, C. H. (1973) *Management: An Experiential Approach*. Irwin Dorsey.

Lau, J. B. (1976) *Behaviour in Organizations: An Experiential Approach*. Irwin Dorsey.

Simulation

Simulation materials and activities attempt to recreate the job environment in a controlled way. The best-known of these is the flight simulator. The hallmark of a simulation is that it takes place in 'real time': that is, it takes place in a period of time that is commensurate with the time it takes to carry out the real job. A simulation involves the learner receiving direct feedback based on his/her responses. Simulation is concerned with application of the skill and knowledge. The complexity of the simulation will determine the extent of the pre-study materials. Examples of simulations can include: In-Tray Exercises; Role Plays and Communication/Interviewing Exercises. Although Games usually shrink real time, some may come close to simulation.

Gibb, G. I. (1974) *Handbook of Games and Simulation Exercises*. London: E. and F. N. Spon Ltd.

Industrial Training International (1976) *Simulation in Training* 11, 3, 5, 6, 7, 9, 10 and 11.

McCormick, J. (1972) 'Simulation and Gaming as a Teaching Method' in *Programmed Learning and Educational Technology 9, 4*, 198–205.

Parry, S. B. (1980) 'The Name of the Game is Simulation' in *Training and Development Journal 34, 6*, 99–105.

Stammers, R. B. (1981) 'Theory and Practice in the Design of Training Simulations'. *Programmed Learning and Educational Technology 18, 2*, 67–71.

Taylor, J. L and Walford, R. (1978) *Learning and the Simulation Game*. Milton Keynes: Open University Press.

Walter, H (1975) 'Organizational Simulation in Management Training'. *Industrial and Commercial Training 7, 3,* 118–20.

Zuckerman, D. W. and Horn, R. F. (1978) *The Guide to Simulation for Education and Training,* 2nd edn. New York: Western Publishing Company.

Appendix 1

NVQ/GNVQ/TDLB/Management levels of competence

NVQ/GNVQ LEVELS OF COMPETENCE

One of the objectives set for the National Council for Vocational Qualifications (NCVQ), is to create a framework which is clear and allows comparability of qualifications. So far, five levels have been defined in the framework. The following definitions of the NVQ levels provide a general guide and are not intended to be prescriptive. Source: *The NVQ Monitor,* Winter 1994–95.

Level 1

Competence in the performance of a range of varied work activities, most of which may be routine and predictable.

Level 2

Competence in a significant range of varied work activities, performed in a variety of contexts. Some of the activities are complex or non-routine, and there is some individual responsibility or autonomy. Collaboration with others, perhaps through membership of a work group or team, may often be a requirement.

Level 3

Competence in a broad range of varied work activities performed in a wide variety of contexts and most of which are complex and non-routine. There is considerable responsibility and autonomy, and control or guidance of others is often required.

Level 4

Competence in a broad range of complex, technical or professional work activities performed in a wide variety of contexts and with a substantial degree of personal responsibility and autonomy. Responsibility for the work of others and the allocation of resources is often present.

Level 5

Competence which involves the application of a significant range of fundamental principles and complex techniques across a wide and often unpredictable variety of contexts. Very substantial personal autonomy and often significant responsibility for the work of others and for the allocation of substantial resources feature strongly, as do personal accountabilities for analysis and diagnosis, design, planning, execution and evaluation.

APPENDIX 1

TRAINING AND DEVELOPMENT LEAD BODY (TDLB) NVQ/SVQ FRAMEWORK

The framework for NVQ/SVQs comprises two levels of qualification, NVQ/SVQ Level 3 and Level 4 as broadly described above. Level 3 is titled Training and Development. Level 4 has two titles: Learning Development and Human Resource Development.

Table A1.1 shows how NVQ and traditional management qualifications can be compared.

TABLE A1.1 Comparison of some NVQ and traditional management qualifications

Competence NVQ/SVQ Levels	Traditional college qualifications	National Examination Board of Supervisory Management (NEBSM)		Management Charter Initiative (MCI)
Level 3 NVQ/SVQ	Certificate in Management	NEBSM Certificate in Supervisory Management	NVQ Supervisory Management at Level 3	MCI Supervisory Management Standards
Level 4 NVQ/SVQ	Diploma in Management Studies (DMS)	NEBSM Diploma in Management	NVQ Management at Level 4	MCI First Line Management Standards
Level 5 NVQ/SVQ	Master of Business Administration (MBA)	—	Pending NVQ at Management Level 5	MCI Middle Management Standards

NOTE:
NEBSM also offer an Introductory Programme prior to the start of Level 3 at both entry points.
MCI also provide other programmes entitled Senior Management Standards and Management Development.

Appendix 2

Competence

BACKGROUND AND CONTEXT

The origins of the competence approach started in the USA (early 1970s) led by the American Management Association (AMA), a forum for leading American business. The idea of generic management competences was based on the study of 1,800 management jobs. The definition of competence was: 'a generic knowledge, motive, trait, social role or skill of a person linked to superior performance on the job' (Hayes 1980). This study drew attention to the idea that successful performance was a result of possessing a set of competences. Cave (1993) argues, however, that as well as possessing competences, it might be how they work together that is important. But the study did not examine this.

In the 1980s in the UK, the Training Agency and industry wanted to develop competent managers in both the public and private sectors. In 1982, Boyatzis was credited with developing a logical, integrated model of management competence, in his book *The Competent Manager: A Model for Effective Performance*. This work has been cited as another root of the competence movement (Lewis 1992).

The Handy and McCormick reports (1987) intensified the debate about the poor state of management training and development.

In 1988 the Management Charter Initiative (MCI, 50 per cent funded by the government) was launched, with its much narrower view of competences than Handy and McCormick had suggested.

In terms of its conception and birth, the competences movement was conceived when the classical view of management was still held, when for some the rationality of management prevailed, and when the government wanted a narrowly-defined value for money programme for training managers (Cave 1993).

At the same time as the competence movement was under way and in contrast to its approach, other researchers were observing complexity rather than simplicity when it came to the performance of managers. For example, Perrow (1979) described the complexity of organizations, and Stewart (1967, 1976, 1980, 1982), Mintzberg (1975) and Kotter (1982) provided empirical evidence of the significant differences between the behaviour of managers.

When addressing the dangers and limitations of going down the competence route, Lewis (1992) summarizes many of the concerns of those who feel the competence movement is too close to the wood to see the trees and above the trees. For Lewis the competence approach, apart from being too bureaucratic, mechanistic and reductionist, does not induce the adventurous spirit of management, which is what makes it different from other professions, such as accountancy.

Rather than say that the competence route is inappropriate, it would seem that those who have concerns about it are drawing attention to both the concept and the shortfalls, such as:

- Is competence an act or a process? Pye (1988), for example, contends that 'competence is a social construct . . . not to be possessed'.
- Do competences engage the emotions and soul of managers?
- Do competences address the chaos of the manager's world as well as its predictability?
- Do competences address the business of handling risks and uncertainties?
- Do competences explore the need for integrity and ethics?
- Do competences match the complexity of the subject matter and the variety of situations involved?

SOME VIEWS OF COMPETENCE

To date, there is still discussion about what competence means. When discussing managerial effectiveness, Cave (1993) found he had to abandon the concept of competence in order to develop a model of what contributes to effective management action. On the other hand, we have the five levels of competence developed by the National Council for Vocational Qualifications (NCVQ) shown in Appendix 1, and we have a full description of competence suggested by the Management Charter Initiative (MCI). To explore the meaning of competence we shall consider:

General views

- A dictionary definition.
- Generic, Specific and Threshold Competence.

Management views

- Burgoyne (1989).
- Constable (1987).
- The Management in Business Administration (MBA) Model.
- The Management Charter Initiative (MCI) Model of Competence.

The NVQ view

- The Competency Model.
- NVQ/TDLB Concept of Competence.

General views

A dictionary definition (Concise Oxford Dictionary, 6th Edition)

- *Competent* means adequately qualified, effective, appropriate and legitimate.
- *Competence* means sufficiency of means for living and ability to do.

This tells us that the term competent/competence can mean 'adequate, ability to do', and it can mean 'effective'.

The term 'effective' carries with it the idea of being able to 'do things right' rather than 'do the right things' adequately. The term 'effective' is more attractive than 'adequate', as an end state, but will demand more in terms of 'experience and personal qualities' to both achieve and measure. Binstead (1986) and Reddin (1989) also equate competence with effectiveness.

Generic, Specific and Threshold Competence

Here we have the situation that a person can be competent at driving a car with floor gear change, but is not competent at driving a car with steering column gear change or automatic gear change. This idea that a person is competent to drive a car because she/he has passed the driving test compounds the point. The fact is, using the driving analogy, that this level of competence is more like a 'threshold level of competence' (Hamlin 1994); that is, a level of competence below the required level or experienced standard (sometimes called experienced worker standard (EWS)). Practice suggests, using this example, that people become competent drivers (or not) 'after' they have passed the driving test! And some commentators would say that this is similar to what happens with those gaining NVQ qualifications.

As a model of competence, we get:

(Generic) Competence = Specific Competence (specific knowledge + specific skills)
+ Experience gained (or not) over some period of time.

Management views

Burgoyne (1989)

On the subject of management competence Burgoyne said 'Research and common sense show clearly that managing is not the sequential exercise of discrete competences . . . It follows that using divided-up lists of competences to manage by, to select managers by, or to develop managers against, creates the problem of how the list is reintegrated together again into a holistic management performance. Learning separate aspects of managerial competence one at a time does not guarantee integral managerial performance, nor can a manager who has been identified as having separate managerial competences be guaranteed to be able to use them effectively.' When describing competences, Burgoyne sees them as being able to learn, adapt, anticipate and create change.

In terms of a model, Burgoyne (1990) saw:

Management Competence = Knowledge + Skill + Understanding + Will.

Constable (1987)

For Constable, however, competences were described as: ability to make sound judgements, ability to be creative, ability to take risks and ability to act decisively. Compared to the MCI description of task-focused competences, Constable, Burgoyne and Handy viewed competences as sets of generic over-arching attributes and abilities.

Finding it difficult to separate out competence from skills and knowledge, Constable said 'It seems probable that a manager may have knowledge (and skills) but not be competent, but it is increasingly unlikely that a manager will be competent without having knowledge and skills.'

The Traditional Management in Business Administration (MBA) Model

The traditional MBA model which adopts an educational approach, embraces knowledge and skill on three broad areas, so that:

Management (Educational) Competence = Knowledge + Skills,

where knowledge and skill are made up of:

- management skills (management science, quantitative methods, interpersonal skills and organization theory and practice);
- functional management (finance, marketing, operations and personnel);
- strategy (strategic management, business policy and environment).

The Management Charter Initiative (MCI) Model of Competence

In the MCI literature, *For Managers and Supervisors* (April 1995), competence, or the ability to perform to standards expected in employment, is gained from:

- experience of actually doing the job;
- knowledge and understanding;
- personal qualities, such as judgement.

This view, when compared to the others, stresses that:

Management Competence = Knowledge + Skills + Experience + Personal Qualities
(e.g. judgement, self-confidence).

The NVQ view

The Competency Model

The National Council for Vocational Qualifications (NCVQ), and in Scotland SCOTVEC, was established in 1986. It had the purpose of developing and overseeing a national framework of 'National Vocational Qualifications' (NVQs). Standards are not defined by NCVQ, but by industry and occupation 'Lead bodies'.

The Management Charter Initiative (MCI) is the body that sets the standards for Management NVQs.

Set up in 1989, the Training and Development Lead Body's (TDLB) National Standards for Training and Development were prepared by 1992.

The competences movement claims that competences measure the 'outputs' of knowledge and skill that have been learnt. The competency model follows a tree-like structure. It starts with:

- the over-arching 'key purpose' (main trunk);
- a number of 'key purposes', or main branches, and this leads to:
- 'sub-areas' (smaller branches) and these branches develop into:
- 'units of competences' (further smaller branches) until finally we reach the:
- standards described as 'elements of competence', made up of 'performance criteria' and 'range statements' (or 'outputs').

NCVQ/TDLB Concept of Competence

The concept of competence adopted by the National Committee for Vocational Qualifications (NCVQ) is based on functional analysis, i.e. analysis of what job-holders do. It is therefore very specific and task-related. It involves the development of standards of competence which 'describe the job competence achieved by the individual under the demands of a particular workplace or training location' (Matthews 1985). It follows that as Erridge (1993) perceives, the competence-based standards 'are a definition of performance which is regarded as satisfactory'. This we note also supports the dictionary definition where 'competent' can be defined similarly as 'adequate'.

In the NCVQ (January 1995) *NVQ Criteria and Guidance* publication, competence is discussed in terms of 'to the standard expected in employment'. This, while meeting the needs of employers, also allows for a variety of interpretations. To determine that the 'standard' has been achieved, assessors require a portfolio of performance and knowledge evidence, with evidence preferably derived from the workplace. However, where this is not possible, it can be obtained from simulations or projects. Compared to the MCI description, the NVQ model of competence does not include Experience or Personal Qualities. In this sense, the NVQ competence model is about demonstrable knowledge and skills, within a particular workplace. In this case:

Competence (to the standard expected in employment) = Knowledge + Skills.

The two levels of competence used by the Training and Development Lead Body (TDLB) which set the National Standards for Training and Development (1995) have been set at Level 3 and 4. With an emphasis on knowledge and performance evidence, we can say that:

For the TDLB model:
Competence = Knowledge + Skills + some Experience (via performance).

SUMMARY

Simplicity, Generality, and Accuracy: The Impossible Design Criteria

Thorngate (1976) suggested that when analysing complex social situations, explanations *cannot be:*

- simple, general and accurate

but they *can be:*

- accurate, simple and specific;
- accurate, general and complex (of interest here);
- simple and general with a danger of being inaccurate;
- specific and complex with a danger of being inaccurate.

Thus, as discussed in Chapter 5, traditional management education courses (MBA/DMS), and the competency movement could be said to strive for accuracy and generality, but they lose full understanding because both designs fail to match the complexity involved in learning and mastering the subject matter. And this fact still needs to be addressed.

One Best Way

When examining the MBA and the competency approach, we find that the MBA approach is to view management reality from the overall functions of management (macro view); and the competence approach (adopted by TDLB and MCI) focuses on the individual task and the functional skills needed in their performance (micro view).

While there cannot be a single one best way to learn about management, the differences between a macro and micro view of management do perhaps indicate that both approaches cannot be correct. If taken together (as some MBA courses do and the second year of the Diploma in Management Studies course does), there may be joint advantages. The joint approach may mean that the macro view provides opportunity to experience development and appreciate the context and meaning of the situation; and the micro view may help focus on the detail of training and help appreciate the content and relevance of the situation.

Learning Curve and Effectiveness

In all cases, competence parallels the learning curve concept (Chapter 2), where required level of performance represents the experienced worker standard (EWS). Although competence is not seen as excellent or in high performance terms, some see it in terms of effectiveness. This view is also supported by Ronan (1993) who sees competence as a mid-point on his effectiveness and efficiency matrix.

Knowledge and Skills

All models also share the idea that Knowledge (body of information) + Skills (techniques, procedures, aptitudes acquired through training and practice) forms the basic trainable components. Paraphrasing Constable (1987) however, knowledge and skill do not guarantee competence, but a manager is unlikely to be competent without having knowledge and skill.

Experience

That Experience (MCI/driving car) is required stresses that 'knowledge' needs to be applied and that 'skills' need to be practised over 'a period of time', in order to move from 'threshold competence' to the 'Experienced Worker Standard' or the expected standard.

Personal Qualities and Integration

That Personal Qualities are involved (MCI) stresses an integration of human attributes must be at work, to bring together and cope with ever new circumstances. Burgoyne (1989) also stresses the recognition of integration within the model of competence. Burgoyne (1990) also uses the term 'Will', and again we can see the need to consider Personal Qualities within a model of competency.

Descriptions of Competence

Dictionary Competence = Adequate, ability to do or effective.

Threshold Competence:
Driving car = Specific Competence (Specific Knowledge and Skill) + Experience (Gathered later).

Burgoyne (1990) = Knowledge + Skill + Understanding + Will.

MBA Traditional Educational Model:
Model Management = Knowledge + Skills.

MCI Competence:
Ability to perform to standard expected = Knowledge + Skills + Experience + Personal Qualities. (1955)

NVQ/TDLB Competence:
Ability to perform to the standard expected in employment = Knowledge + Skills.

Of all of these descriptions it would seem that the MCI description of competence incorporates many of the ideas so far discussed. That is:

Management Competence = Knowledge + Skills
(which everyone agrees are the basic building blocks of performance)
+ Experience
(which enables repeated application of the Knowledge + Skills to be achieved)
+ Personal Qualities
(which provides the function for integrating personality and the factors above).

That this description is problematic is due to the fact that the term itself (like leadership) is a process in the fullest sense, rather than an act. Added to this, competence/effectiveness is a function of who defines it (Pye 1988).

SOME COMPARISONS

If we compare (see Note below) the various descriptions of competence against:

- the complexity of the situation;
- the means/ends (or results) model, Chapters 4 and 5 and
- the hierarchy of training objectives, Chapter 10 and Appendix 11

the pattern of results emerge, as shown in Figure A2.1. Looked at this way, we can see how Knowledge and Skills must be *gained* to learn the basics of a job (or to achieve immediate results). As a more demanding position is taken on, Experience is often judged as being necessary, because it demonstrates that a portfolio of Knowledge and Skills has been repeatedly *applied*. At the highest level, we see how Personal Qualities, which integrate performance at all stages, take on a more prominent role. At the highest level, Knowledge, Skill and Experience almost become 'givens', and it is the deployment of Personal Qualities that largely determine effective performance. And it is the Personal Qualities which enable the *transfer* of Knowledge, Skill and Experience to any situation.

Note. Comparison of any new model or concept against other known models, is a worthwhile discipline because it can induce questions about differences that might exist. Such differences can lead to insights into all the models under question, which in turn can lead to the creation of yet another model. In this example, there does appear to be a commonsense correlation between the formula for Competence, the hierarchy of Results, Training Objectives and the Complexity of the Situation.

SOME LEARNING POINTS

When applying the above model of competence, we observe that:

- *For NVQ Levels 1/2/3,* competence may equate with Knowledge + Skills. That is, threshold competence may be close to the 'Experienced (or expected) Worker Standard'.
- *For NVQ Levels 4/5,* competence would require not only Knowledge + Skills, but also a greater emphasis on Experience and Personal Qualities.
- *For senior management development,* proven Personal Qualities becomes paramount. At this level performance is focused on ability to interpret situations, display political acumen, display a balanced judgement and use intuition effectively.
- *For the trainer,* when developing and assessing competence in its fullest sense:
  – decide on (specific and generic) Knowledge and Skills requirements;

– give learners time to practise these skills within a wide variety of circumstances;
– encourage learners to recognize and develop their innate Personal Qualities which are used to integrate effective performance;
– consider how to facilitate an integrated overview, if a competency programme prevents the learner seeing the big picture, the connections, the context and what the subject is all about.

Showing the ends or results of the means/ends model
(*see* Chapters 4 & 5)

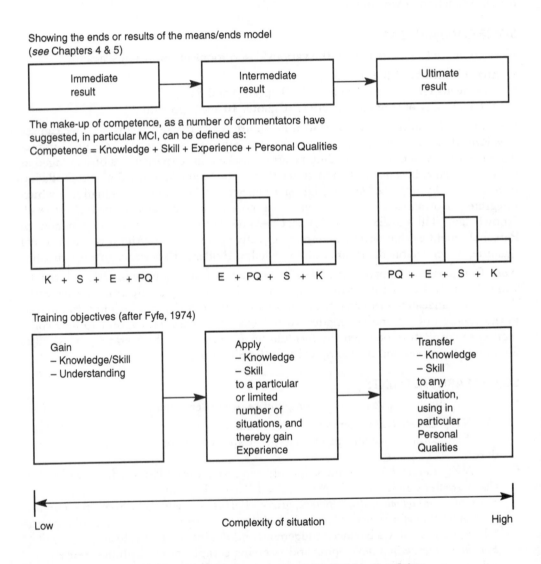

FIGURE A2.1 Comparing competence/results/objectives/jobs

REFERENCES AND FURTHER READING

Binstead, D. (1986) *Developments in Interpersonal Skills Training*. Aldershot: Gower.

Boyatzis, R. E. (1982) *The Competent Manager: A Model for Effective Performance*. Chichester: John Wiley.

Burgoyne, J. (1989) *Management Development: Context and Strategies*. Aldershot: Gower.

Burgoyne, J. (1990) *Doubts About Competency in the Photofit Manager*. Devine, M. (ed). London: Unwin Hyman.

Cave, E. and McKeown, P. (1993) 'Managerial Effectiveness: The Identification of Need'. *Management Education and Development 24*, 2, Summer.

Constable, J. and McCormick, R. (1987) *The Making of British Managers*. Corby: British Institute of Managers.

Everard, B. (1984) 'Competence in Education and Education Management'. *Management in Education 3, 2,* 10–14.

Fenell, E. (1993) 'GNVQ: A Case of Critical Assessment'. *Competence and Assessment, No. 22*. Employment Department.

Fyfe, T. W. and Richardson, R. (1974) *Educational Technology, Programmed Text*. Dundee College of Education.

Hamlin, B. and Stewart, J. (1994) 'Competence-Based Qualifications: Maintaining Forward Momentum'. *Competence and Assessment No. 24*, January.

Handy, C. (1987) *The Making of Managers*. MSC/NEDO/BIM.

Hayes, J. (1979) 'A New Look at Management Competence: The AMA Model of Worthy Performance'. *Management Review,* November, 20–21.

Jacobs, R. (1989) 'Getting the Measure of Management Competence'. *Personnel Management,* June, 32–37.

Lewis, A. (1992) 'Addressing the Dangers and Limitations of Going Down the Competence Route' in *Applying Competences: Competence-Based Approaches To Management Development*. London: AMED.

Management Charter Initiative (April 1995) *For Managers and Supervisors*. London: MCI.

Perrow, C. (1979) *Complex Organisations*. Illinois: Scott, Grienview.

Pye, A (1988) 'Management Competence in the Public Sector', *Public Money and Management, 8, 4, Winter,* 62–64.

Quinn, R. E., Fairman, S. R., Thompson, M. P. and McGrath, M. R. (1990) *Becoming a Master Manager – A Competency Framework*. Chichester: John Wiley and Sons.

Reddin, W. (1989) 'Expressing Effectiveness in Terms of Outputs'. *Personnel Management,* October, 86–91.

Ronan, N. J. (1993) 'Developing The African Manager – The Good, The Bad and The Competent'. *Management Education and Development 24, 4,* 388–94.

Stewart, J. and Page C. (1992) 'Competences – Are They Useful To Trainers?' *Industrial and Commercial Training 24, 7,* 32–35.

Stewart, R. (1976) *Contrasts in Management*. London: McGraw-Hill.

Stewart, R. (1980) *The District Administrator in the National Health Service*. London: King Edward's Hospital Fund for London.

Stewart, R. (1982) *Choices for the Managers: A Guide to Managerial Work and Behaviour*. London: McGraw-Hill.

The National Council for Vocational Qualifications (January 1995) *NVQ Criteria and Guidance*. Employment Department.

Thorngate, W. (1976) 'Possible Limits on a Science of Social Behaviour' in Strickland, L. H., Aboud, F. E. and Gergen, (eds) *Social Psychology in Transition*. New York: Plenum.

Training Agency (1988) 'The Definition of Competences and Performance Criteria'. *Development of Assessable Standards for National Certification, Guidance Note No. 3*. Employment Department.

Appendix 3

Change and what is valued today

	Previously Valued and Still Valued	Valued Today and Tomorrow
	At the INDIVIDUAL Level	
	Be led	Individual leadership
	Be aware of healthy living	Take action to achieve a healthy life – keep fit – eat healthy foods – give up destructive habits – recycle resources
Handy (1989) The Age of Unreason	Dependency and individual paternalism	Enrichment and enhancement of self plus support and encouragement of others
	Conformity	Individual differences plus fraternity valued
	9–5 working full-time work	Major swing to temporary/part-time self-employment
	Set male attitude	Gender-free attitude
	Work on-site	Work at home
	One job	Portfolio of jobs
	Employ	Hire

	Satisfy demands of job (must do) and job constraints (must not do)	Seek and exploit job choices and opportunities (can do)
General	Seek quantity/ material things of life	Seek quality of life

At the TRAINING AND DEVELOPMENT Level

General	Training and education is prescribed by organization	Be responsible for own development
Naisbitt (1984) Megatrends	Institutional help	Self-help
General	Structured learning – classroom/courses – instruct – tutor-centred – learn at tutor's pace	Flexible learning – distance/open learning – mentor/empower – learner-centred – learn at own pace

At the MANAGEMENT Level

Drucker (1977) Management	Seek efficiency (Do things right)	Seek effectiveness (Do the right things)
Drucker (1989) The New Realities General	Middle management Learning Communicate Motivate to work Seek conformity	Information specialist Unlearning Involve Work it out Seek initiative
Harrison Course handout (1990) Empowerment	Control Direct Get compliance Mechanize Set rules Build hierarchies	Share Inspire Obtain co-operation Organize Provide knowledge Develop communities
General	Solution-centred Deal with static situations	Problem-centred Deal with dynamic situations

At the ORGANIZATIONAL Level

	Production focus	Market focus
General	Production focus	Market focus
Bartlett (1989) Managing Across Borders	Managing within borders	Managing across borders
Handy (1989)	Rigid structure	Fluid teamworking
General	Organize around tall structures/pyramids	Organize around flat structures/pyramids
Naisbitt (1984)	Hierarchies Industrial society	Networking Information society
	Traditional technology	High technology
	National economy Short-term Centralization	World economy Long-term Decentralization. And from decentralization to federalism, Handy (1989)
	Democracy by representation Either/or	Democracy by participation Multiple option
Drucker (1968) Managing for Results	Minimizing risk	Maximizing opportunity
Handy (1989)	Rational thinking Respond to patterns of incremental change	Upside down thinking Respond to discontinuous change
	React to necessity	Encourage curiosity
Drucker (1989) The New Realities	Think local Respond	Think global Shape events
Kanter (1990) When Giants Learn To Dance	Work Do more with more resources	Think/work and enjoy it Do more with less resources

Appendix 4

Summary of government initiatives and actions

1964   # With the Industrial Training Act came the Industry Training Boards (ITBs).
- The ITBs set the scene for the 'standardized systematic approach' to training. However, the ITBs bureaucratic procedures, its levy system and its lack of flexibility did not endear it to industry.
- When the ITBs should have been updating and improving performance of industries' workforces, they focused instead on redressing skill shortages as a way back to economic growth. In the 1960s overmanning and wage rises may have had more to do with lack of competitiveness.
- The ITBs, however, paved the way for many of the training initiatives that followed, but by the 1980s most ITBs had been wound up.

1972   # Training Opportunities Scheme (TOPS) began. Ended in 1985.

1973   # The Youth Employment Service, renamed Careers Service, was a local education authority (LEA) run service.
          # The 1973 Employment and Training Act created a new national body, the Manpower Services Commission (MSC), and was funded by the Treasury. The MSC took control of the ITBs.

1975   # Job Creation Programme (JCP).
          # Recruitment Subsidy for School Leavers (RSSL).
          # Temporary Employment Subsidy (TES).

1976   # Work Experience Programme (WEP).
          # Youth Employment Subsidy (YES) – replaced RSSL.

1977   # Job Release Scheme.
          # Small Firms Employment Subsidy.
          # Job Introduction Scheme (JIS).

1978   # Youth Opportunities Programme (YOP) and
          # Special Temporary Employment Programme (STEP) together replaced JCP and WEP.

1979   # Temporary Short-Time Working Compensation Scheme (TSTWC).

1980   # Job Search Scheme (JSS).

1981   # The government introduced its White Paper entitled 'A New Training Initiative' aimed at
- developing skills training;
- providing education and planned work experience opportunities for young people under the age of 18;
- providing opportunities for adults to update their skills and knowledge.

Community Enterprise Programme (CEP).

1982   # Community Programme (CP) –replaced CEP.

Voluntary Projects Programme (VPP).

Open Tech.

1983   # Skills Training Agency (STA) formed.
- Part of Manpower Services Commission.
- The STA provided training in a range of technical and supervisory skills through a network of sixty Skillcentres, previously called Government Training Centres (GTCs). The Training Opportunities Scheme (TOPS) was largely undertaken within Skillcentres.

Business & Technical Education Council established (now BTEC).
- Promotes work-related studies and awards work-related qualifications for Business/Engineering/Science/ Computing/Hotel and Catering.
- Certificate and Diploma offered.
- Approved also as NVQs.

Enterprise Allowance Scheme (EAS).

Technical & Vocational Education Initiative (TVEI). Replaced by local schemes circa 1995.

Youth Training Scheme (YTS) – replaced YOP.

Young Workers Scheme (YWS).

The Manpower Services Commission (MSC), a semi-independent agency funded by government which managed the government's unemployment and training activities from the 1970s, was disbanded and replaced by the Training Agency (TA).

There was an upturn in the UK economy.

1984   # Local Collaborative Projects (LCP).

1985   # Training for Enterprise (TE).

Job Training Programme (JTP) and Wider Opportunities Training Programme (WOT).

1986   # Two-Year Youth Training Scheme (YTS).

Jobclubs.

Restart.

Career Development Loans.

Jobstart Allowance.

New Workers Scheme (NWS) – replaced YWS.

Action for Jobs.

The programme of work to create national standards for all occupations in the UK was launched by the government's White Paper 'Working Together: Education and Training'.

The National Council for Vocational Qualifications (NCVQ) set up as a result of the above White Paper. Scotland has the SVQ and the Scottish Vocational Education Council is known as SCOTVEC.
- The aims of the Councils were to design a new national database of qualifications, so that
  - qualifications reflected workplace needs;
  - qualifications would be valued by their respective industries;
  - employers' views would shape further education activities;
  - Europe would accept such qualifications.

- NVQs/SVQs were arranged in five levels, the highest being Level 5. See Appendix 1.

1987   # The Open College (OC) was made available.
- The OC primarily addressed vocational skill training needs.
- These qualifications required no entry qualifications, and provided 'open access'.

Two reports, one by Handy (1987) and another by Constable (1987), concerned the low priority given to management training.

Job Training Scheme (JTS).

The National Training Awards (NTA) scheme was launched to publicize examples of excellence in training.

The British Standard BS 5750 (ISO 9000) was introduced.

1988   # Employment Training (ET), an adult version of YTS, brought together several programmes including CP and JTS Compacts.

Both YTS and ET were accused of providing 'cheap labour' opportunities for unscrupulous employers.

Education Reform Act. It provided the main provisions for the establishment of the National Curriculum for pupils age 5 to 16.

The General Certificate of Secondary Education (GCSE) was introduced.
- This became the UK's single system of examining at 16+. There was an emphasis on knowledge and skills, and not just memory. Pass grades were A to G and below they were unclassified.

Guided by the Management Charter Group (MCG), the MCI set about identifying standards of performance, in terms of 'competences' to be achieved.
- The Management Charter Initiative is an independent body set up by employers and backed by the government with the aim of improving the performance of UK managers.
- MCI has two roles: to improve the provision of management development in the UK and to develop national Management Standards which are benchmarks of best practice used by managers to help them perform better.

1989   # Business Growth Training (BGT), launched by the TA but it lacked widespread industrial support. The idea was to help employers finance training activities linked to technical development.

Unemployment started to fall.

The government wanted employers to share much more in the costs of supporting YTS, but they baulked against it.

The National Curriculum for Schools was introduced.
- This required three core subjects (science, mathematics and English) along with seven Foundation subjects to be offered.

Local Further Education (FE) colleges became self-governing in 1993.

The National Training Task Force (NTTF). In operation until 1992. NACETT set up in 1993 (see 1993) replaced NTTF.
- NTTF was charged with overseeing the creation of TECs/LECs. The aims were to tailor schemes to match skill shortages, promote specific enterprise initiatives and shift funding onto employers.

The Training and Development Lead Body (TDLB) was set up to provide

National Standards for Training and Development. The government's 1986 White Paper 'Working Together: Education and Training' was the spur to this work.

1990   # The Training, Education and Enterprise Directorate (TEED) replaced the TA.

      # The TA replaced the MSC in 1988 which had been operating since 1974.

      # The Training and Enterprise Councils (TECs), (and Local Enterprise Councils (LECs) for Scotland) were set up. These bodies were deemed to be 'employer-led'.

- The TECs/LECs were managed by a Chief Executive and, not adding to their long-term vision of things, were subject to one-year financial contracts. (In 1996 some budgets are being set for three years.)
- To date such initiatives were 'managed' by the government.

      # Youth Training (YT).

      # Investors in People (IiP).

- Aimed at improving training activities and attitudes via a systematic approach, which in turn, forms a national standard.
- Assessment of the standard was undertaken by TECs/LECs.

1991   # The Confederation of British Industry (CBI) listed its 'World Class Targets' and was supported by the Employment Department (ED) and the Trade Union Congress (TUC).

- These targets (Appendix 9) were mostly expressed in NVQ/SVQ terms.

      # Training Credits.

- Enables school-leavers entering employment to purchase approved vocational courses, usually NVQs/SVQs.

      # Employment Action (EA).

      # Job Review Workshops.

      # National Record of Achievement (NRA).

1992   # Gateways to Learning.

      # All the former polytechnics and some other higher education establishments acquired university status.

      # Business Links launched by the DTI as 'One-Stop Shops' to support smaller businesses of 10–200 employees.

1993   # Learning for Work.

      # Training for Work (TfW) – replaced ET, EA and HTNT.

      # Community Action.

      # Business Start-Up.

      # TEC Challenge.

      # Workstart.

      # Jobplan Workshops.

      # Out-of-School Childcare Grant.

      # National Advisory Council for Education and Training Targets (NACETT). Targets set by this body supersede the CBI targets set in 1991.

1994   # Some TECs/LECs joined forces with the local Chambers of Commerce to
circa   become TEC Chambers, thus emphasising the employer-driven nature of the new partnership.

Appendix 5

Post-16 education opportunities

Primary phase:
Stage 1: up to 7, infants
Stage 2: 7–11, juniors

Secondary phase:
Stage 3: 11–14, pre-GCSE
Stage 4: 14–16, preparation for GCSE

Choice for 16-year-olds (broad comparison):

1	2	3
NVQ Prepares person for a particular job, usually studied within a work context. **Via college/work.**	**GNVQ** Prepares person for a range of jobs, usually studying within an educational context. (Vocational route to Higher Education.) **Via school/college/work.**	**HIGHER EDUCATION** Provides opportunity to study a wide range of subjects at General and Higher Education stages. **Via school/college.**
NVQ Level 1 Foundation	**GNVQ Foundation** (Usually one year)	**Four GCSEs from D to G**
NVQ Level 2 **Basic Craft**	**GNVQ 2 Intermediate** (Usually one year)	**Four GCSEs A to C**
NVQ Level 3 **Advanced Craft/Technician**	**GNVQ 3 Advanced** (Usually two years) #	**Two GCE A-level** (or equivalent AS levels)
NVQ Level 4 **Higher Technician/** **Management**	**GNVQ 4** ##	**Higher Education or** **Professional Training** **e.g. Degree**
NVQ Level 5 **Professional**	**GNVQ 5** ##	**Post-graduate Degree**

\# Students may need to gain a Merit or Distinction grade or complete additional subjects to get a place on some courses.
\#\# Decisions are yet to be made on developing GNVQs at higher levels.

Note: every 16- and 17-year-old leaving full-time education is encouraged to undertake vocational education or training by the offer of a Youth Credit enabling them to buy specific training from the establishment of their choice. See Appendix 6 for Youth Credits.

To continue in full-time education, either at school or college, a person may follow:

- A general education course: A-Level, AS-Level or GCSE.
- A vocational course: GNVQ, BTEC, City & Guilds, RSA, NVQ or other.
- A mixture of the above.

National Vocational Qualifications (NVQ)

- NVQs are mainly for people who are already in work or receiving work-based training.
- They are based on the skills, knowledge and understanding needed in jobs.
- They are assessed under working conditions.
- The qualification shows that a person can do the job.
- The qualification is made up of units which can be taken at a person's own pace.
- NVQs can be studied at work, in college or sometimes in school sixth forms.
- NVQs can provide entry to higher level full-time vocational courses.
- NVQs/SVQs are arranged in five levels, the highest being Level 5. See Appendix 1.

General National Vocational Qualifications (GNVQ) (The new vocational A-levels)

- Mainly for young people in full-time education, but some may be offered part-time.
- They can be graded pass, merit and distinction.
- The GNVQ can be gained unit by unit.
- The qualification is tested by coursework with some external examinations.
- Courses prepare people for a 'range of jobs', unlike NVQs, which show that a person can perform the job they have been trained for.
- GNVQs are gradually replacing some older style qualifications offered by BTEC, C&G, RSA, LCCI and PEI.

The Foundation GNVQ

- Broadly equal to at least four GCSEs at grades D to G.
- No previous qualifications are required to study Foundation GNVQs.
- Usually lasts one year.
- After Foundation or Intermediate a person can enter training, employment or continue with a full-time higher course.

The Intermediate GNVQ

- Is broadly equal to at least four GCSEs at grades A to C.
- Intermediate GNVQ students usually need one or two GCSEs at A to C, or a Foundation GNVQ.
- Usually lasts one year.

The Advanced GNVQ

- Is broadly equal to two GCE A-levels.
- Advanced GNVQ courses normally take two years.
- Students usually need five GCSEs at grades A to C or a GNVQ at Intermediate level before they can take an Advanced GNVQ.
- The Advanced GNVQ can lead to further education, higher education or directly into employment.

General Certificate of Secondary Education (GCSE)

- This became the UK's single system of examining at 16+ in 1988. There was an emphasis on knowledge and skill and not just memory.
- Pass grades are from A to G. Below this they are unclassified.
- The right GCSE grades will provide entry to Advanced (A) or Advanced Supplementary (AS) GCE courses.
- More GCSEs can be taken in a sixth form or a further education college.

The Advanced (A) and Advanced Supplementary (AS) General Certificate of Education (GCE)

- Advanced GCE courses take two years to complete.
- The AS is half the content of a GCE A-level at the same standard.
- Some students take AS courses to broaden their GCE A-level studies.
- A suitable number of A and AS GCE Certificates will provide entry to higher education.

Appendix 6

Youth credits

Under the Youth Training Programme there are two choices available to young people, the Standard Youth Credit Package and the Modern Apprenticeship.

A Youth Credit is a monetary reward that can be claimed when a young person leaves school at 16. It is claimed in the form of a Youth Credit Card and can be used to buy high quality training from an employer. To claim the Youth Credit Card a young person completes an Action Plan at school.

Standard Youth Credit Package

- The training will lead to a National Vocational Qualification (NVQ) Level 2.
- The training is bought from an employer and may include day release or block release to a local college or training organization.
- In addition to the money to buy training, a young person will also receive a weekly allowance during the training.
- On completion of the NVQ Level 2 it may be possible to join a Modern Apprenticeship Scheme and work towards NVQ Level 3.

Modern Apprenticeship

- A Modern Apprenticeship is another kind of training a young person (16–17) can buy with their Youth Credit Card.
- A Modern Apprenticeship involves higher level training with an employer which will lead to NVQ Level 3 or above. (The 'standard' Youth Credit package leads to Level 2.)
- The Modern Apprenticeship is not to be confused with the old style apprenticeships.
- They are being set up in a wide range of occupational sectors and are intended for all young people.
- There is no fixed time but in general, it will take about three years to attain Level 3.
- Most of the training will be provided by the employer, but off-job training may be provided by local colleges.
- Candidates will be selected by the prospective employers.
- There can be exceptions to the age range 16–17 (see the Careers Office).
- In addition to the knowledge of the chosen occupation, emphasis will be placed on 'core skills': literacy, numeracy, IT, problem solving and personal effectiveness.

Accelerated Modern Apprenticeships

- Accelerated Modern Apprenticeships will be available from September 1995 for 18- and 19-year-olds leaving school or college, and who are facing their first career choice. They offer the same opportunities as Modern Apprenticeships.
- All young people will be employed.
- Time taken to get the skills needed may be eighteen months rather than three years. This is because young people can build on previous qualifications and experience.

See also Appendix 5, Post-16 Education Opportunities.

Appendix 7

Types of objectives

DAVIES (1971) TYPE OBJECTIVE

Davies prepares objectives which can be used as both a pre-test and as a post-test.

Example: Running effective meetings

At the end of the workshop, the trainee will be able to:

Cognitive objectives

- Identify four core types of meetings.
- Prepare:
  - an effective meeting structure and
  - effective meeting objectives.
- Describe two elements of group behaviour at meetings in terms of:
  - task-orientated
  - group maintenance and
  - self-orientated behaviour.
- Identify three characteristics of an effective
  - chairperson
  - secretary
  - group member.
- List four effective questioning techniques.

Affective objectives

- Recognize the difference between an effective and an ineffective meeting.
- Respond appropriately to the feelings and non-verbal communications presented within the meeting.

MILLER (1962) TYPE OBJECTIVE

Miller tackles the problem of writing objectives from the point of view of skills analysis.

Example

1 Given a car with one flat tyre, a spare wheel with inflated tyre, car jack, torque wrench and wheel brace.

Told to replace the flat tyre with the spare inflated tyre, the trainee will:

2 Test that the spare tyre is correctly inflated to the standard pressure.
3 Locate and fit the car jack, as shown in the car manual.
4 Slacken wheel nuts using wheel brace.
5 Lift deflated car wheel clear of the ground, using car jack.
6 Remove wheel nuts using wheel brace, if required, and remove wheel.
7 Match spare wheel to locating studs, and if more height is required, lift car, using jack.
8 Locate spare wheel onto wheel studs and tighten nuts by hand.
9 Lower wheel to make contact with ground and tighten wheel nuts to the correct torque, using the calibrated torque wrench.
10 Unwind car jack and remove.
11 Replace wheel covers and tools.

REFERENCES AND FURTHER READING

The reader is reminded that an example of the Majer (1962) type objective is shown in Chapter 3.

Also see Appendix 8 for Areas For Learning Objectives.

Davies, I. K. (1971) *The Management of Learning*. Maidenhead, Berkshire: McGraw-Hill.

Majer, R. F. (1962) *Preparing Objectives for Programmed Instruction*. San Francisco, California: Fearon.

Miller, R. B. (1962) 'Task Description and Analysis' in R. M. Gagne (ed.) *Psychological Principles in Systems Development*. New York: Holt, Rinehart and Winston, 353–80.

Appendix 8

Areas for learning objectives

INTRODUCTION

The classification above is based on Pedlar's scheme (1978) which extended Bloom's (1956) and Krathwohl's (1964) well-known taxonomies. Referring to the range of learning objectives, indicated above, Gage (1979) said 'None of these kinds of behaviour is isolated from the other. While we are thinking, engaged in intellectual activity, we also experience emotions and display certain movements. When we are lost in feeling . . . we are nevertheless thinking and posturing, i.e. engaged simultaneously in certain cognitive and psychomotor behaviours.'

The following descriptions are indicative of the levels of learning that can be found within each of the five classifications or learning domains.

A COGNITIVE: KNOWLEDGE OBJECTIVES/VERBS

Cognitive objectives are concerned with knowledge, facts and their manipulation. From the lowest, 1, to the highest, 5, cognitive objectives can be categorized as:

1 Knowledge (Use memory to recall the facts)
Examples

Define	Write	Underline
State	Recall	Select
List	Recognize	Reproduce
Name	Label	Measure

2 Understanding (Grasp the ideas/techniques)
Examples

Identify	Illustrate	Explain
Justify	Represent	Judge
Select	Name	Contrast
Indicate	Formulate	Classify

3   Application (Apply knowledge and skill in standard situations correctly)

Examples

Predict	Choose	Construct
Select	Find	Compute
Assess	Show	Use
Explain	Demonstrate	Perform

4   Transfer (Transfer knowledge/skill to new and different situations)

Examples

Analyse	Synthesize	Evaluate
Identify	Combine	Judge
Select	Generalize	Relate
Criticize	Organize	Support
Compare	Discuss	Attack
Conclude	Summarize	Choose

B   AFFECTIVE: FEELING OBJECTIVES/VERBS

Affective objectives deal with feelings, emotions and values. From the lowest, 1, to the highest, 5, these can be categorized as:

1   Receiving – information

Listen	Accept	Be aware
Attend	Receive	Favour
Prefer	Perceive	Select

2   Responding – to information

State	Select	Record
Answer	List	Develop
Complete	Write	Derive

3   Valuing – information

Accept	Increase	Indicate
Recognize	Develop	Decide
Participate	Attain	Influence

4   Organizing – information

Organize	Find	Associate
Judge	Determine	Form
Relate	Correlate	Select

5   Characterizing – information

Revise	Accept	Demonstrate
Change	Judge	Identify
Face	Develop	Decide

C PSYCHOMOTOR LEARNING OBJECTIVES

Psychomotor skills are concerned with manipulation of materials or objects, or some activity which can be described as neuromuscular. It should be noted that to apply a skill some knowledge is also required. Thus Cognitive and Psychomotor objectives are often written side by side, i.e. the knowledge element and the corresponding skill element. Seymour (1966), identified six types of industrial skills shown below.

1 Handwork
2 Handwork with tools
3 Single-purpose machine work
4 Multi-purpose machine work
5 Group machine work
6 Non-repetitive work.

Beyond industrial skills, however, psychomotor skills are used as part of:

7 Interpersonal body language communication
8 Sports activities
9 Dance activities
10 Driving activities

and any activity which requires co-ordinating movement of the human body to carry out some task.

See also Simpson (1969) *Psychomotor Domain: A Tentative Clarification,* and Fleishman (1967) *Individual Differences and Motor Learning.*

D INTERPERSONAL LEARNING BEHAVIOUR

This refers to skills associated with face to face interactions. The skills are a blend of cognitive, affective and psychomotor skills. Interpersonal learning objectives can involve: seeking to express self clearly, developing trust, and developing understanding. To achieve this, trainees may need to practise using effective non-verbal communication, listening, observing, behaviour analysis and behaviour modification skills.

See also Argyle (1976) *Bodily Communication,* Argyle (1973) *Social Interaction,* Fisher (1983) *Getting To You* and Fisher (1989) *Getting Together.*

E SELF-KNOWLEDGE LEARNING OBJECTIVES

Self-knowledge focuses on objectives concerned with a better understanding of oneself. Self-knowledge objectives can embrace:

- being aware of strengths;
- being aware of weaknesses, bias and prejudices;
- identifying the things that 'must be' done (demands), the things that 'must not' be done (constraints) and the things that 'can be' done (choices);
- being sensitive to identifying opportunities to exploit strengths, strengthening weaknesses and increasing the range of choices;
- being aware of things, situations and people that can damage, threaten and unduly exploit oneself in some way (limitations);
- being aware of one's potential.

See also Boydell (1981) *Management Self Development,* Wood (1988) *Continuous Development: The Path to Improved Performance* and Lawrence and Yarlett (1995) 'Helping People Change Roles', *Organisations and People.*

F   ATTITUDE AND SKILLS

In the *Glossary of Training Terms* (1981) the well-known definition of training reads 'A planned process to modify attitude, knowledge and skill . . .' In terms of the learning domains described here, both Attitude and Skill are often a shorthand for an amalgam of Knowledge, Affective, Psychomotor, Interpersonal and Self-knowledge Skills.

Skills

It is only when we begin to analyse skills in terms of the learning domains (psychomotor, interactive etc.) that we can be specific.

Attitudes

Attitudes tend to be less easy to pin down, partly because they are inferred from behaviour, and thus are often described as a mixture of all the domains of learning. Another reason involves the fact that attitudes can embody deep-seated beliefs, may be associated with particular experiences, will have strong emotional ties and can be interwoven into a person's personality.

One difficulty is the human condition, in that, if a person is thinking, she/he is not feeling, and vice versa. Put another way, a person with an inappropriate attitude will not always be persuaded to change via appeals to his/her logic. To analyse this difficulty we can make use of the means (input/process) ends (results) model, Chapter 8. We can thus either try to understand what meanings the individual places on things (i.e. examine the means), or we can examine the ends (i.e. the consequences of the attitude in question), or we can attempt a dialogue between a person's logic and feelings.

To examine the 'means' (the person's psychological motivations), we could employ the use of counselling, coaching and with the aid of professional help employ an experienced psychotherapist. To examine the 'ends', the aim is to create a situation where undesirable attitudes can be compared against the effects of the attitude on the individual and others (i.e. the consequences that will follow). It is because emotion and logic can be separated, that the two can function independently and sometimes in conflict. Hence, 'I know it is wrong but I can't help myself doing it', is a common experience.

One way in which attitudes are observed to change is when a person has been subject to emotional and/or physical shock, such as can be experienced in a car accident. In this case, the shock can 'force' a dialogue between a person's emotion and logic, and thus cause that person to drive with more care. In another case it may take a confrontation of the consequences of the attitude (the ends) to create change. The following are 'hard' examples of helping learners focus on the consequences of attitudes.

Example 1

To change the negative attitude of workers to managers:

•   provide frequent opportunities for both to work very closely together.

Example 2

To persuade workers to wear safety goggles:

•   let them see and examine goggles that show dramatic examples of having protected people's eyesight;
•   give workers their own quality goggles;

- demonstrate dramatically (safely) the reasons for wearing goggles (e.g. drop an egg on a spike and ask for comments);
- let them meet people who have suffered from not wearing goggles;
- take them into hospital to witness the trauma, time, effort and resources that are necessary to deal with this situation.

Example 3

To persuade staff who fail to see the point of providing effective customer service:
- let them experience shopping and let them experience receiving poor customer service;
- let them meet customers who will explain why they are dissatisfied with the service provided;
- encourage the trainee to explain the consequences of not providing (and providing) an appropriate service (in terms of employment and repeat business).

Example 4

To change the attitudes of young people who are beginning to embrace breaking the law:
- allow them to compare their attitudes against the realities of those who are serving time in prison, and compare their attitudes against those held by the victims.

Example 5

To change the attitude of offenders to society:
- allow them to compare their attitudes with the consequences of their actions, e.g. the suffering of victims and the families involved.

DETERMINING OBJECTIVES

To help the trainer determine:
- the domain(s) of learning in use;
- the level(s) of learning required;
- particular skill(s);
- particular attitude(s).

Table A8.1 may help with analysis of training needs and formulation of training objectives.

REFERENCES AND FURTHER READING

Argyle, M. (1973) *Social Interaction*. London: Tavistock Publications.
Argyle, M. (1976) *Bodily Communication*. London: Methuen & Co. Ltd.
Bloom, B. S. (1956) *Taxonomy of Educational Objectives, Handbook 1: Cognitive Domain*. New York: McKay.
Boydell, T. H. and Pedlar, M. (eds) (1981) *Management Self Development*. Aldershot: Gower.
Fisher, R. and Brown, S. (1989) *Getting Together*. London: Business Books.
Fisher, R. and Ury, W. (1983) *Getting To Yes*. South Africa: Hutchinson.
Fleishman, E. A. (1967) 'Individual Differences and Motor Learning' in Gagne, R. M. (Ed.) *Learning and Individual Differences*. Columbus, Ohio: Charles E. Merrill.
Gage, N. L. and Borliner, C. (1979) *Educational Psychology*, 2nd edn. Chicago: Rand McNally.

TABLE A8.1 Areas and levels of learning
(Can be used by trainer to identify areas and levels of learning as part of the Training Needs Analysis)

Levels	Areas or domains of learning				
	COGNITIVE Knowledge Facts Concepts Procedures Rules	AFFECTIVE Emotions Feelings Values	PSYCHO- MOTOR Industrial* Interpersonal Body language Sport Dance	INTER- PERSONAL Responding Developing trust Developing understanding	SELF- KNOWLEDGE Strengths Weaknesses Choices Opportunities Potential Limitations **How to learn** Personal growth Own behaviour Likes and dislikes
Knowledge To recall facts					
Understanding To grasp the ideas					
Application To apply learning correctly					
Transfer To transfer learning to new situation					

Note on Attitude: For Binstead (1980) 'interpersonal attitude' may need to be examined in terms of Cognitive and Affective domains. For 'physical attitude', as in sport and dance, Affective and Psychomotor domains may need to be analysed. To examine attitude further may also require that Self-knowledge and interpersonal abilities be studied. *For Industrial learning categories, see Seymour (1966) and page 241.

Krathwohl, D. R., Bloom, B. S. and Masia, B. B. (1964) *Taxonomy of Educational Objectives, Handbook II: Affective Domain*. New York: McKay.

Lawrence, D. and Yarlett, P. (1995) 'Helping People Change Roles'. *Organisations and People 2, 1*, 18–21.

Pedlar, M. (1978) 'Negotiating Skills Training, Part 4: Learning To Negotiate'. *Journal of European Industrial Training 2, 1*, 20–25.

Seymour, W. D. (1966) *Industrial Skills*. London: Pitman.

Simpson, E. J. (1969) *Psychomotor Domain: A Tentative Clarification*. Urbana, Illinois: University of Illinois (unpublished paper).

Wood, S. (Ed.) (1988) *Continuous Development: The Path to Improved Performance*. London: Institute of Personnel Management.

Other related reading

Gronlund, N. E. (1971) *Measurement and Evaluation in Teaching*. New York: Macmillan.

Pedlar, M. (1974) 'Learning in Management Education'. *Journal of European Training 3, 3*, 182–194.

Seymour, W. D. (1968) *Skills Analysis Training*. London: Pitman.

Singer, E. J. and Ramsden J. (1969) *The Practical Approach to Skills Analysis*. London: McGraw-Hill.

Smith, R. G. (1964) *The Development of Training Objectives*. Washington, DC: The George Washington University, Human Resources Research Office.

Appendix 9

National targets for education and training 1995 to 2000

The National Advisory Council for Education and Training Targets (NACETT) was set up in 1993:

- to monitor progress towards the National Education and Training Targets and to advise government on performance and policies which influence progress towards the Targets; and
- to provide business leadership in raising skill levels and increasing employer commitment to the Targets.

AIM

To improve UK international competitiveness by raising standards and attainment levels in education and training to world class levels through ensuring that:

1 All employers invest in employee development to achieve business success.
2 All individuals have access to education and training opportunities, leading to recognized qualifications, which meet their needs and aspirations.
3 All education and training develops self-reliance, flexibility and breadth, in particular through fostering competence in core skills.

FOUNDATION LEARNING

1 By age 19, 85 per cent of young people to achieve five GCSEs at grade C or above, an Intermediate GNVQ or an NVQ level 2.
2 75 per cent of young people to achieve level 2 competence in communication, numeracy and IT by age 19; and 35 per cent to achieve level 3 competence in these core skills by age 21.
3 By age 21, 60 per cent of young people to achieve two GCE A-levels, an Advanced GNVQ or an NVQ level 3.

LIFETIME LEARNING

1 60 per cent of the workforce to be qualified to NVQ level 3, Advanced GNVQ or to GCE A-level standard.
2 30 per cent of the workforce to have a vocational, professional, management or academic qualification at NVQ level 4 or above.
3 70 per cent of all organizations employing 200 or more employees, and 35 per cent of those employing fifty or more, to be recognized as Investors in People.

(CBI) NATIONAL TARGETS FOR EDUCATION AND TRAINING 1991 to 1995

Below are the National Targets as launched by the CBI in 1991. The achievement of the Targets is also shown.

Foundation learning

1 By 1997, 80 per cent of young people to reach NVQ/SVQ 2 (or equivalent). 61 per cent of young people, up to and including age 19, have achieved either five GCSEs at grades A–C, an NVQ/SVQ 2 or vocational equivalent.
2 Training and education to NVQ/SVQ 3 (or equivalent) to be available to all young people who can benefit.
3 By 2000, 50 per cent of young people to reach NVQ/SVQ 3 (or equivalent). 37 per cent of young people, up to and including age 21, have achieved two A-levels, an NVQ/SVQ 3 or vocational equivalent.
4 Education and training provision to develop self-reliance, flexibility and breadth.

Lifetime learning

1 By 1996, all employees should take part in training or development activities.
2 By 1996, 50 per cent of the workforce aiming for NVQs/SVQs or units towards them.
3 By 2000, 50 per cent of the workforce qualified to at least NVQ/SVQ 3 (or equivalent). 38 per cent of the workforce possess either two A levels, an NVQ/SVQ 3, its vocational equivalent or higher level qualification.
4 By 1996, 50 per cent of medium to larger organisations to be 'Investors in People'. The first Investors in People were announced in October 1991. By the end of 1993, 198 organizations employing 200 or more employees, had achieved the Investors in People award. This represents about 2.5 per cent of all such organizations (and some 5 per cent of all employees working in medium and large organizations).

For comments on these Targets, see NACETT, *Review of the National Targets for Education and Training 1995,* and see the Employment Department report on *Labour Market & Skill Trends 1995/96.*

Appendix 10

Useful addresses and abbreviations

FOR ENQUIRY ABOUT: **CONTACT:**

Training

Management Training/   TECs/LECs
Development.   TAPs
Vocational Training.
Young People. Adult Training.
Employment Training. Disadvantaged
Groups.Information.

Small-business training and start-up information

Small-business training   TECs/LECs –Business Link
and start-up. Funding.   Local Enterprise Agencies (LEAs)
Loans. Information.   Chambers of Commerce
Advice. Business Development   DTI
Initiatives.   Job Centre/Employment Department
Europe.   European Information Centres (EICs).
                                                         Information: DTI/TECs/LECs
Trade.   Trade Associations and Small Firms
                                                             Organisations (Library)
Food. Farming. Leisure.   The Food, Farming, Land and Leisure
                                                             Consultancy (ADAS)
Rural.   The Rural Development Commission
For young people.   Livewire
For young people.   The Prince's Youth Business Trust

Qualifications/Education

Vocational qualifications   TECs/LECs
and training.   NCVQ
Adult education.   NIACE
                                                         Local colleges
Open and distance learning.   Open University
                                                         Open College
                                                         Henley Distance Learning

Careers

Careers. Information.   TECs/LECs
Career Development Loans.   Careers Offices
                                         CRAC
                                         NICEC (Research)

Schools/Colleges/Business links and project work

                                         TECs/LECs
                                         TCD
                                         SCIP
                                         Young Enterprise

IR/Equal opportunities/Racial equality

Industrial Relations   ACAS
Matters. Information.
Equal Opportunities.   EOC
Racial Equality.   CRE

ACAS   Advisory, Conciliation & Arbitration Service.
            Head Office: 27 Wilton Street, London SW1X 7AZ.
            Tel: 0171-210 3000. Fax: 0171-210 3708.

ADAS   The Food, Farming, Land and Leisure Consultancy.
            Tel: 0865 842742.

APL   Accreditation of Prior Learning.

AMED   Association for Management Education & Development.
            14-15 Belgrave Square, London SW1X 8PS.
            Tel: 0171-235 3505. Fax 0171-235 3565.

BTEC   Business & Technology Education Council (formerly Business & Tech-
            nical Education Council).
            Central House, Upper Woburn Place, London WC1H 0HH.
            Tel: 0171-388 3288. Cross-sector qualification NVQ Awarding Body.

BIM   British Institute of Management.
            Management House, Cottingham Road, Corby NN17 1TT.
            Tel: 01536 204222.

CBI   Confederation of British Industry.
            Centre Point, 103 New Oxford Street, London WC1A 1DU.
            Tel: 0171-379 7400.

CGLI   City & Guilds of London Institute.
            76 Portland Place, London W1 4AA.
            Tel: 0171-278 2468.

            Has been an independent examining body for over 100 years, setting
            national standards for operatives, craftpersons and technicians.
            Cross-sector qualification NVQ Awarding Body.

CPVE   Certificate of Pre-Vocational Education.

CRE   Commission for Racial Equality.
                Elliot House, Allington Street, London SW1E 5EH.
                Tel: 0171-828 7022.

CSE   Certificate of Secondary Education. No longer current.

CSV   Community Service Volunteers.
                237 Pentonville Road, London N1 9NJ.
                Tel: 0171-278 6601.

DFE   Department for Education. Previously Department of Education and
                Science (DES).
                Elizabeth House, York Road, London SE1 7PH.
                Tel: 0171-925 5000.

DTI   Department of Trade & Industry.
                Ashdown House, 123 Victoria Street, London SW1E 6RB.
                Tel: 0171-215 5000.
                For past National Economic Development Office (NEDO) information
                and papers, contact Business Round Table Ltd, 5th Floor, Landsdowne
                House, Berkeley Square, London W1X 6BP. Tel: 0171-636 6951.

ED   Employment Department Group.
                Moorfoot, Sheffield S1 4PQ. Tel: 0114 2753275.

Engineering   10 Maltravers Street, London WC2R 3ER.
Council   Tel: 0171-240 7891.

EEF   Engineering Employers Federation. East Midland Association.
                Tel: 01572 723711

EICs   European Information Centres. Contact for information:
                DTI/TECs/LECs.

EOC   Equal Opportunities Commission.
                Overseas House, Quay Street, Manchester M3 3HN.
                Tel: 0161-833 9244.

Henley   Greenlands, Henley on Thames, Oxon RG9 3AU.
Distance   Tel: 01491 571552.
Learning

EOSC   Employment Occupation Standards Council.
(TDLB)   Co-ordinating body for the Training Development Lead Body (TDLB),
(PSLB)   the Personnel Sector Lead Body (PSLB) and the Trade Union Sector
(TUSDB)   Development Body (TUSDB). 2 Savoy Court, Strand, London WC12R 0EZ.
                Tel: 0171-240 7474.

ET   Employment Training.

FE   Further Education.

FSB   Federation of Small Businesses.
              32 Orchard Road, Lytham St Anne's, Lancashire FY8 1NY.
              Tel: 01253 720911.

GCSE   General Certificate of Secondary Education.

GNVQ   General National Vocation Qualification. (Scotland: GSVQ.)

HE   Higher Education.

HSC   Health and Safety Commission. Set up in 1974 as a
HSE   result of the 1974 Health and Safety at Work Act. The work of enforcing
              the Act is carried out by Health and Safety Executive.
              1 Long Lane, London SE1 4PG.
              Tel: 0171-407 8911.

ILB   Industry Lead Body.

ILO   International Labour Organisation.
              CH-1211, Geneva, Switzerland.
              Tel: 010 4122 996111.

IPD   Institute of Personnel & Development.
              IPD House, Camp Road, London SW19 4UX.
              Tel: 0181-946 9100.
              The Institute of Training and Development (ITD), the Institute of Per-
              sonnel Management (IPM) and the British Association for Commercial
              & Industrial Education (BACIE) merged in July 1994.

The   Peter Runge House, 3 Carlton House Terrace, London SW1Y 5DG.
Industrial   Tel: 0171-839 4300.
Society

ITO   Industry Training Organisation. 120 set up in the UK.

LCCI   London Chamber of Commerce and Industry Examination Board.
              Marlowe House, Station Road, Sidcup, Kent DA15 7BJ.
              Tel: 0181-302 0261.
              Cross-sector qualification NVQ Awarding Body.

LEA   Local Education Authority.

LEAs   Local Enterprise Agencies. Over 400 in the UK.
              (See the National Federation of Enterprise Agencies (NFEA).)

LEC   Local Enterprise Company. Scottish equivalent of TEC.

LEN   Local Employer Network.

LIVEWIRE   Sponsored by Shell UK.
             Provides cash awards for young people 16-25.
             Livewire, Freepost, Newcastle upon Tyne NE1 1BR.
             Tel: 0191-261 5584.

NACETT   National Advisory Council for Education & Training Targets.
             7th Floor, 222 Grays Inn Road, London WC1X 8HL.
             Tel: 0171-211 5012. (Scotland: ASCETT.)

NCITO   National Council of Industry Training Organisation.
             10 Meadow Court, Amos Road, Sheffield SG1 BX.
             Tel: 0114-261 9926.

NETTs   National Education and Training Targets.

NC   National Curriculum.

NCVQ   National Council for Vocational Qualifications.
             222 Euston Road, London NW1 2BZ.
             Tel: 0171-387 9898.

NEBSM   National Examination Board in Supervisory Management.
             76 Portland Place, London W1 4AA.
             Tel: 0171-278 2468.

NFEA   National Federation of Enterprise Agencies.
             Lord Young of Graffham, c/o Cadbury Schweppes plc, Bournville
             B3E 2LU.
             Tel: 0121-458 2000. Ex. 3995.

NFMED   National Forum for Management Education & Development/
& MCI   The Management Charter Initiative.
             MCI, Russell Square House, 10-12 Russell Square, London WC1B 5BZ.
             Tel: 0171-872 9000.

NIACE   National Institute of Adult Continuing Education.
             19B De Montfort Street, Leicester LE1 7GE.
             Tel: 0116 2551451.

NRA   National Record of Achievement.
             Replaced National Record of Vocational Achievement NROVA.

NTA   National Training Awards.

NVQ   National Vocational Qualification.

OC   Open College.
             Freepost, PO Box 35, Abingdon OX14 3BR.

OST   Office of Science & Technology.
             Albany House, 84-86 Petty France, London SW1H 9ST.
             Tel: 0171-271 2000.

OU   Open University.
             Open Business School, Walton Hall, Milton Keynes MK7 6AA.
             Tel: 01908 274066.

PERA   Production Engineering Research Association.
             Nottingham Road, Melton Mowbray LE13 0PB.
             Tel: 01664 501501.

The Prince's PYBT, 5 Cleveland Place, London SW1 6JJ.
Youth   Tel: 0171-321 6500.
Business   Provides loans up to £5,000 and bursaries up to £1,500.
Trust   For young people 18-25 and 18-30 with disabilities.
             The Prince's Scottish Youth Business Trust.
             Tel: 0141-248 4999 .

RDC   Rural Development Commission.
             Tel: 01722 336255.

RSA   Royal Society for the Encouragement of Arts, Manufactures and
             Commerce.
             8 John Adam Street, London WC2N 6EZ.
             Tel: 0171-930 5115.

RSA (EB)   Royal Society of Arts Examination Board.
             Progress House, Westwood Way, Coventry CV4 8HS.
             Tel: 01203 470033. Cross-sector qualification NVQ Awarding Body.

SCOTVEC   Scottish Vocational Education Council.
             Hanover House, 24 Douglas Street, Glasgow G2 7NG.
             Tel: 0141-248 7900.

SVQ   Scottish Vocational Qualification.

TAP   Training Access Point.
             Available via public libraries, Careers Offices and TECs/LECs.
             A database of education and training opportunities.

TCD   Teaching Company Directorate. Tel: 01367 242822.
                     Creates partnerships between industry and higher education and
                     promotes effective, practical use of academic expertise.
                     Graduates spend two years in a company working on key projects.
                     70 per cent funding – Company under 250.
                     40 per cent funding – Company over 250.

TEC   Training and Enterprise Councils. See local telephone directory.

TEED   Training Enterprise & Education Directorate.
                     Moorfoot, Sheffield S1 4PQ.
                     Tel: 0114 2753275. Publications Tel: 0709 888688.

TfW   Training For Work.

TVEI   Technical & Vocational Education Initiative.
                     Kidbrooke School, Corelli Road, London SE3.
                     Tel: 0181-319 0610. Circa 1995 replaced by local schemes.

YC   Youth Credits.

YT   Youth Training.

Careers addresses

COIC   The Careers & Occupational Information Centre.
                     PO Box 348, Bristol BS99 7FE.
                     Tel: 0117 9777199.

CRAC   The Careers Research & Advisory Centre.

NICEC   National Institute of Careers Education & Counselling.
                     Sheraton House, Castle Park, Cambridge CB3 0AX.
                     Tel: 01223 460277.

CEDEFOP   Centre European Development Formation Profession.
                     Bundesalle 22, D-1000, Berlin 15, Germany.
                     Tel: 030 884120. Contact IPD in the UK.

SCIP   School Curriculum Industry Partnership.
                     Centre for Education & Industry, University of Warwick, Westwood,
                     Coventry CV4 7AL.
                     Tel: 01203 523951.

Young   Ewart Place, Summertown, Oxford OX2 7BZ.
Enterprise   Tel: 01865 311180.

Appendix 11

Training method classification with focus on usage

In Chapter 10 a classification of Training Methods was presented which listed training methods against the level of cognitive learning sought, namely: to acquire *knowledge*; to gain *understanding*; to *apply* skills correctly and to be able to *transfer* the skills to ever new situations (as shown in Appendix 8). An alternative version of the classification is to consider training methods against their intended use. Thus, is training aimed at:

*   the individual?
*   relationships?
*   the group?
*   inter-group processes/relationships?
*   the organization?

The result of comparing the focus (usage) of the training against the level of training sought is shown in the tabulated section which commences on the following page.

Both classifications (Chapter 10 and Appendix 11) are complementary and both are only indicative of the match between the level of cognitive learning and its intended usage.

The author notes, as a general observation, that when training is provided, too little preparation is done and follow-up support made available. With this in mind, when selecting training methods it is worth considering:

*   The amount of preparation, information and debriefing that will be required (Chapter 6).
*   What level of support may be necessary on-job to achieve the desired objectives? (e.g. coaching).
*   How each level of learning can be achieved?

Example 1

When using algorithms and flow charts. Having been briefed about the use of the algorithm (knowledge), do the staff need to understand its rational in every detail in order to (apply) it? Can there be a case for only dealing with Knowledge and Application levels with less emphasis on Understanding? Again see Appendix 8.

Example 2

When using Demonstration as a training method, the trainer needs to ask 'What level of learning needs to be achieved?' Is it to:

*   demonstrate Application only;
*   provide Knowledge + demonstrate Application;
*   provide Knowledge + Understanding + demonstrate Application?

If it is necessary to provide Knowledge + Understanding, it then begs the question 'How will this be done?' For example, will knowledge be provided verbally or in written form or both? And will understanding be checked verbally or through tests or both?

Example 3

When using Outward Bound training:

- Do we expect learners to Transfer their new found skills to the workplace, with or without in-house or external support?
- Do we expect learners to have fully acquired the Knowledge and Understanding to support their newly discovered skills?
- What will we do if a learner feels they have failed to make use of their skills in the Outward Bound situation?

By considering the level of learning sought and asking searching questions like these, the trainer can become clearer about how training objectives can be achieved, and become clearer about the level of preparation and support that is required.

TRAINING METHOD CLASSIFICATION WITH FOCUS ON USAGE

FOCUS	LEVEL OF LEARNING			
Individual Relationships Group Inter-group Organization	To gain KNOWLEDGE	To achieve UNDERSTANDING	To be able to APPLY the skills and knowledge correctly	To be able to TRANSFER the skills and know- ledge to ever new situations

INDIVIDUAL FOCUS

Handling information

	KNOWLEDGE	UNDERSTANDING	APPLY	TRANSFER
1 Lecture/Talk	●	➤	➤	
3 Reading	●	➤	➤	
4 Note-taking	●	➤	➤	
5 Quest/Answer	●	➤	➤	
6 Demonstration	●	➤	➤	
7 Case example	●	➤	➤	
8 Mnemonics	●	➤	➤	
9 Algorithms	●	➤	➤	
16 Symposium	●	●	➤	
17 Seminar	●	●	➤	
18 Syndicate	●	●	➤	
42 Traditional instruction	●	●	●	➤

Skill/Knowledge

	1	2	3	4
6 Demonstration	●	➤	➤	
20 Tutorial	●	●	➤	
23 Action maze	●	●	➤	
24 Test/Quiz	●	●		
27 In-tray	●	●	●	
33 Induction training	●	●	➤	
40 Exercise	●	●	●	
41 Drill	●	●	●	
42 Traditional instruction	●	●	●	➤
42 Discussion instruction	●	●	●	●

Educational

	1	2	3	4
20 Tutorial	●	●		
21 Traditional management education	●	●		

Feedback

	1	2	3	4
15 Panel Discussion	●	●		
31 Feedback meeting	●	●		
36 Follow-through meeting	●	●	➤	
37 Organizational mirroring	●	●	➤	

Individual development

	1	2	3	4
2 Programme learning	●	➤	➤	
41 Drill	●	●	●	
13 Technology-based learning	●	●	●	
23 Action maze	●	●	➤	
24 Test/Quiz	●	●		
29 Incident process case study	●	●	➤	
30 Critical incident	●	●	➤	
31 Self Diagnostic	●	●	●	
34 Field Visit	●	●	➤	
35 Project/Assignment	●	●	●	●
39 Role Set Analysis	●	●	●	
40 Exercise	●	●	●	
41 Drill	●	●	●	
42 Instruction Discovery	●	●	●	●
43 Language Laboratory	●	●	●	
52 Outward Bound	●	●	●	➤
53 Role Negotiation	●	●	●	

Method	1	2	3	4
54 Shadowing	●	●	➤	
55 Coaching	●	●	●	
56 Job Rotation	●	●	●	
56 Job Enlargement	●	●	●	
56 Job Enrichment	●	●	●	➤
57 Behaviour Modelling	●	●	●	
58 Behaviour Modification	●	●	●	
59 Management Style	●	●	●	➤
69 Action Learning	●	●	●	●
73 Management Development	●	●	●	●
*Self Development CH10	●	●	●	●
*Continuous Development CH10	●	●	●	●

Insight Development

Method	1	2	3	4
37 Organizational Mirroring	●	●	➤	
38 Scenario Training	●	●	➤	
48 Transactional Analysis	●	●	●	➤
49 Gestalt	●	●	●	➤
50 Encounter	●	●	●	➤
67 T-Group	●	●	●	➤

Experiential

Method	1	2	3
25 Games	●	●	➤
31 Diagnostic Instrument	●	●	●
40 Exercises	●	●	●

Simulation

Method	1	2	3
25 Game	●	●	➤
27 In-tray	●	●	●
44 Role Play	●	●	●
45 Role Reversal	●	●	●
54 Shadowing	●	●	●

RELATIONSHIP FOCUS

Method	1	2	3
39 Role Set Analysis	●	●	●
44 Role Play	●	●	●
45 Role Reversal	●	●	●
46 Intimacy Exercise	●	●	●
47 Meeting for Two	●	●	●
53 Role Negotiation	●	●	●

GROUP FOCUS

Generating Ideas

18 Syndicate	●	●	➤	
19 Buzz Group	●	●	➤	
26 Open Discussion	●	●	●	
51 Synetics	●	●	●	
*Brainstorming – CH8	●	●		

Group Development

14 Controlled/Leader Centred Discussion	●	●	➤	
26 Open/Group Centred Discussion	●	●	●	
28 Case Study	●	●	●	
29 Incident process case study	●	●	➤	
52 Outward Bound	●	●	●	➤
55 Semi-Autonomous Group	●	●	●	●
55 Autonomous Group	●	●	●	●
64 Group Development	●	●	●	●
65 Team Building	●	●	●	●
69 Action Learning	●	●	●	●
70 Process Consultancy	●	●	●	●
*Behaviour Analysis – CH9	●	●	➤	➤

Management Style

52 Outward Bound	●	●	●	➤
59 Action Centred Leadership	●	●	●	➤
60 Management Grid	●	●	●	➤
61 McGregor X/Y	●	●	●	➤
62 Reddin 3-D	●	●	●	➤
63 Likert	●	●	●	➤

Problem Solving/Change

25 Game	●	●		
26 Open Discussion	●	●		
28 Case Study	●	●		
29 Incident Process Case Study	●	●		
3̅ Project Method	●	●	●	●
̅le Play	●	●	●	➤
̅-group meeting method	●	●	●	●

68 Coverdale	●	●	●	●
69 Action Learn	●	●	●	●
71 Problem Solving	●	●	●	●
70 Process Consultancy	●	●	●	●
72 Kepner Tregoe	●	●	●	●

MOST METHODS

Chapter 8 Tools

*Where are we?	●	●	●	●
*Cause/Effect	●	●	●	●
*Demands/choices/constraints	●	●	●	●
*Post-it	●	●	●	●
*Force Field	●	●	●	●
*Brainstorming – CH8	●	●	●	●
*Input/process/result	●	●	●	●

INTER-GROUP FOCUS

66 Inter-group meeting method	●	●	●	●

ORGANIZATIONAL FOCUS

74 Organizational Development	●	●	●	●
75 Socio-technical programme	●	●	●	●

Chapter 3

*Re-Engineering	●	●	●	●
*Total quality management	●	●	●	●

key
● Indicates the level of cognitive learning that the training method is usually associated with.
➤ Indicates that further learning objectives can be achieved either via focused self-development, coaching, mentoring or some other learning mechanism.

Index